T0330044

Climate Change and Growth in Asia

Climate Change and Growth in Asia

Edited by

Moazzem Hossain

*Griffith Business School and Griffith Asia Institute,
Griffith University, Australia*

Eliyathamby Selvanathan

Griffith Business School, Griffith University, Australia

Edward Elgar

Cheltenham, UK • Northampton, MA, USA

Published by
Edward Elgar Publishing Limited
The Lypiatts
15 Lansdown Road
Cheltenham
Glos GL50 2JA
UK

Edward Elgar Publishing, Inc.
William Pratt House
9 Dewey Court
Northampton
Massachusetts 01060
USA

A catalogue record for this book
is available from the British Library

Library of Congress Control Number: 2010932047

ISBN 978 1 84844 245 0

Typeset by Servis Filmsetting Ltd, Stockport, Cheshire
Printed and bound by MPG Books Group, UK

Contents

PART III   CLIMATE CHANGE AND CHALLENGES

Abbreviations

ADB	Asian Development Bank
APCSE	Asia–Pacific Centre for Sustainable Enterprise
ARTS	accountability, responsibility, transparency and sustainability
AWG-KP	Ad Hoc Working Group Kyoto Protocol
AWG-LCA	Ad Hoc Working Group on Long-term Cooperative Action
BAU	business as usual
BCCSAP	Bangladesh Climate Change Strategy and Action Plan
BIMSTEC	Bay of Bengal Initiative for Multi-Sectoral Technical and Economic Cooperation
BRIC	Brazil, Russia, India and China
CANSA	Climate Action Network – South Asia
CCP	Chinese Communist Party
CDM	Clean Development Mechanism
CFCs	chloroflurocarbons
CO_2e	carbon dioxide equivalent
COP15	Conference of the Parties 15
CSO	Civil Society Organization
DFID	Department for International Development
DU	Dobson unit
EKC	Environmental Kuznets Curve
ESG	environmental, social and governance
EU	European Union
EWS	Early Warning Systems
FAO	Food and Agriculture Organization
FAOSTAT	Food and Agriculture Organization Statistics
FHFA	Federal Housing Finance Agency
GAI	Griffith Asia Institute
GBM	Ganges, Brahmaputra and Meghna
GBS	Griffith Business School
GCCA	Global Climate Change Alliance
GDP	gross domestic product
GFC	global financial crisis
GHG	greenhouse gas

GONGOs	Government-operated Non-governmental Organizations
HDR	Human Development Report
HYV	high yielding varieties
ICT	information and communication technology
IITM	Indian Institute of Tropical Meteorology
IPCC	Intergovernmental Panel on Climate Change
kgoe	kilograms of oil equivalent
km³	cubic kilometres
LDCs	least developed countries
LECZ	Low Elevation Coastal Zone
LUC	land-use change
LUCF	land-use change and forestry
MDGs	Millennium Development Goals
mmt	millions of metric tons
MRV	monitoring, reporting and verification
MVCs	most vulnerable countries
PAM	preparedness, adaption and mitigation
pm	per million
ppb	parts per billion
ppm	parts per million
PPP$	purchasing power parity dollar
PRC	People's Republic of China
PRSPs	poverty reduction strategy papers
R&D	research and development
REDD	Reducing Emissions from Deforestation and Forest Degradation
SAARC	South Asian Association of Regional Cooperation
SACEP	South Asian Cooperative Environment Programme
SAFTA	South Asian Free Trade Area
SAPTA	SAARC preferential trading arrangement
SBI	Subsidiary Body for Implementation
SBSTA	Subsidiary Body for Scientific and Technological Advice
SEE	sustainable enterprise economy
SLR	sea-level rise
SMRC	SAARC Meteorological Research Centre
TBD	to be determined
UN	United Nations
UNDESA	United Nations Department of Economic and Social Affairs
UNDP	United Nations Development Programme
UNEP	United Nations Environment Programme

UNFCCC	United Nations Framework Convention on Climate Change
UNICEF	United Nations Children's Fund
UN-REDD	United Nations Reducing Emissions from Deforestation and Forest Degradation in Developing Countries Programme
USAID	United States Agency for International Development
WB	World Bank
WHO	World Health Organization
wlucf	with land use change and forestry
wolucf	without land use change and forestry
WRI	World Resources Institute

Contributors

Dr Qazi Kholiquzzaman Ahmad is president of the Bangladesh Economic Association and one of the Intergovernmental Panel on Climate Change (IPCC) lead authors based in Dhaka, Bangladesh.

Mr A. Ahmed works at the International Training Networking Centre, Bangladesh University of Engineering and Technology, Dhaka, Bangladesh.

Mr A.H.M. Ali was High Commissioner for Bangladesh in the UK, and is presently a member of the Bangladesh Parliament.

Dr Moazzem Hossain is Senior Lecturer in the Department of International Business and Asian Studies, Griffith Business School and Griffith Asia Institute, Griffith University, Brisbane, Australia.

Dr Paul Howard is a lecturer at the Department of International Business and Asian Studies, Griffith Business School, Griffith University, Brisbane, Australia.

Dr Colin Hunt is a Consultant and Visiting Fellow of the Griffith Asia Institute, Griffith University, Brisbane, Australia.

Professor M. Adil Khan is an adjunct professor at the School of Social Sciences, University of Queensland, Brisbane, Australia and former Chief, Socio-economic Governance and Management Branch, United Nations Department of Economic and Social Affairs, New York, USA.

Professor Malcolm McIntosh FRSA is Professor of Sustainable Enterprise at Griffith University, Australia, and Director of the Asia Pacific Centre for Sustainable Enterprise. He also holds visiting professorships at the Department of Civil Engineering at the University of Bristol, the Centre for Peace and Reconciliation at Coventry University in the UK, and at the Sustainability Institute at the University of Stellenbosch in South Africa.

Dr Vikram Murthy is a consultant and an adjunct associate professor of the Business School, Auckland University of Technology, Auckland, New Zealand.

Professor M.A. Noor is Professor of Civil Engineering at Bangladesh University of Engineering and Technology, Dhaka, Bangladesh.

Professor M.H. Rahman is Professor of Civil Engineering and Pro Vice Chancellor of the Bangladesh University of Engineering and Technology, Dhaka, Bangladesh.

Professor Harun Rashid is Professor Emeritus, Department of Geography and Earth Science, University of Wisconsin – La Crosse, La Crosse, USA and Adjunct Professor, School of Resource and Environmental Management, Simon Fraser University, Burnaby, BC, Canada.

Dr Tapan Sarker is a researcher at the Asia Pacific Centre for Sustainable Enterprise of Griffith University, Brisbane, Australia.

Professor Eliyathamby Selvanathan is Professor of Statistics in the Department of International Business and Asian Studies, Griffith Business School, Griffith University, Brisbane, Australia.

Professor Clem Tisdell is Professor Emeritus, Department of Economics, University of Queensland, Brisbane, Australia.

Preface

Two interlinked and yet contrasting trends form the basis of the present volume: first, the information and communication technology (ICT) revolution and globalisation-induced trade expansions that have offered Asia unprecedented opportunities for growth, complemented by access to and effective management of knowledge and technology; second, as a counter trend, negative impacts of climate change that stand to significantly retard the growth opportunities in the region in the future. It is also widely recognised that as far as the coastal regions of Asia are concerned, climate change tends to threaten the coastal belt of the Bay of Bengal most, especially because the latter is characterised by high population density and pervasive poverty.

Thus, as far as Asia is concerned, the following issues are regarded as relevant for climate change: how and to what extent will climate change affect the growth of Asia, especially the coastal regions? Does climate change stand to take away the further growth opportunities of these countries? In the evolving scenario, what should be done, that is, within the context of perceived climate change risks, what preparedness, mitigation and adaptation plans should be adopted to ensure the sustainable growth of the region?

It has been well established that the Bay of Bengal region (southern India and Bangladesh) has enjoyed high to moderate growth over the last decade. The growth of India has been about 8–9 per cent and in Bangladesh it has been 5–6 per cent until the global financial crisis (GFC) hit in 2007. This region has also seen improved living standards during the final quarter of the twentieth century. What made this prosperity possible? It is now widely accepted that globalisation enhanced international trade and newly found trade allowed this region to prosper further.

While the region has been making strong progress in the early part of the twenty-first century, new challenges have also emerged. The most important among them is climate change and the devastating impact it brought to this region in recent years with the occurrence of frequent cyclones, floods and the rise in sea level over the last three decades. It has recently been noted by the media that the New Moore/South Talpatti Island on the Bay of Bengal has disappeared under a metre of water due to sea-level rise.

Like globalisation, the effect of climate change has no boundaries and, therefore, issues of climate change need to be debated globally, regionally and nationally. With this in mind, the editors organised an international workshop at Griffith University, Australia, on the subject of Climate Change and Growth in Asia in September 2009. Representing diverse institutions and experiences, this workshop brought together a panel of experts that included economists, social scientists, management specialists and political scientists from Bangladesh, New Zealand and Australia to brainstorm issues. Indeed, the task was challenging.

Griffith University's Vice Chancellor, Professor Ian O'Conner, made the opening remarks at the workshop and the Pro Vice Chancellor (Business), Professor Michael Powell, chaired the opening session and welcomed the international participants to Griffith. Their support for the workshop was crucial for organising the gathering at Griffith immediately before the UNFCCC Summit in Copenhagen (COP15). We sincerely acknowledge their cooperation.

This book was made possible by the financial assistance extended by the Griffith Asia Institute (GAI) and the Asia–Pacific Centre for Sustainable Enterprise (APCSE) of the Griffith Business School (GBS). We would like to acknowledge the support extended by the Directors of the GAI, Professor Haig Patapan, and the APCSE, Professor Malcolm McIntosh. Without their support, the project would have not been completed in time.

All of the chapters have undergone a rigorous review process by experts in the field. In this regard, the assistance by Dr Larry Crump, Dr Peter Ross, Dr Colin Hunt, Professor Clem Tisdell, Professor Ronald Keith, Professor Tom Nguyen and Professor Harun Rashid is highly appreciated. Adjunct Professor M. Adil Khan has supported the editors very closely from the beginning of this project and has helped to improve the presentation of this volume. We would like to take this opportunity to acknowledge his time and effort. Valuable logistical support was extended to us by Meegan Thorley, Natasha Vary and Kathy Bailey of the GAI. We appreciate their hard work and commitment towards the holding of the International Workshop on 8 September 2009 that provided the basis for this volume.

Robyn White of the Department of International Business and Asian Studies of the Griffith Business School applied her long-standing publishing skills to fine-tune the draft and format the manuscript for Edward Elgar Publishing Ltd. We are grateful to Robyn White for her unconditional commitment to this project.

Moazzem Hossain
Eliyathamby Selvanathan

Introduction

Moazzem Hossain

Since the awarding of the 2007 Nobel Peace Prize to the former US Vice President Al Gore and the United Nations (UN) Intergovernmental Panel on Climate Change (IPCC) for their work on climate change and global warming, both the developed and developing world have realised the urgency in fighting the menace of climate change. The IPCC prediction of global temperature rising by 4°C by 2100 appears to be credible and is acceptable to climate scientists. The chief cause of the warming is thought to be the burning of fossil fuels such as coal, oil and natural gas, which release carbon dioxide and other substances known as greenhouse gases into the atmosphere (see Chapter 1). What is the ultimate outcome? In simple words, as the atmosphere becomes richer in these gases, it becomes a better insulator, retaining more of the heat provided to the planet by the sun. Climate scientists use elaborate computer models of temperature circulation to study global warming. Based on these models, they have made several predictions about how global warming will affect weather, sea levels, coastlines, agriculture, wildlife and human health (Mia 2008). With this global environmental change on the horizon, several multilateral agencies have been carrying out various studies in recent years. These are summarised below.

RECENT CLIMATE CHANGE STUDIES AT MULTILATERAL LEVEL AND KEY FINDINGS

United Nations Development Program (UNDP)

The UNDP dedicated its 2007/2008 Human Development Report (HDR) to the issues of climate change globally (UNDP 2007). This study had four chapters which examined: first, the challenges of climate change in the twenty-first century; second, risk and vulnerability due to climate shocks in an unequal world; third, the possible strategies for mitigation of climate change dangers; and finally, adapting to climate change through national action and international cooperation.

The study has adequately stressed with proof that there is no 'if' or 'but' on the subject of climate change and that time has come for collective decision on tackling the challenges emanating from climate change. As climate change is economy neutral, mitigation measures must seriously consider how to bring both the developed and the developing world together in developing strategies that are mutually re-enforcing and environmentally sustainable. Global actions are needed to face the disaster locally.

The study has put forward five transmission ways by which climate change could affect livelihood and human development in the future. These are:

- Agricultural production and food security;
- Water stress and water insecurity;
- Rising sea levels and exposure to climate disasters;
- Ecosystems and biodiversity; and
- Human health.

Increases in global temperature of 3–4°C could result in 330 million people (5 per cent of the world's population) being permanently or temporarily displaced through flooding.

In order to avoid such a calamity in our lifetimes, unparalleled collective action and international cooperation is needed in the time ahead, since none of the above mechanisms will operate in isolation. Meaningful strategies should be devised for mitigation. Most importantly, carbon markets are a necessary condition for the transition to a low-carbon economy, however, these are not sufficient conditions. Why carbon markets? It is now established, without doubt, that a sustainable global carbon emissions strategy will be the major pathway of mitigation.

UN Intergovernmental Panel on Climate Change (IPCC)

The IPCC's sixth technical paper was released in June 2008 (Bates et al. 2008). This paper deals with the issue of freshwater. Sea-level rise has been dealt with only insofar as it can lead to impacts on freshwater in coastal areas and beyond. Freshwater is not only related to climate and biophysical systems, it is also interconnected with socioeconomic systems encompassing multi-country and multi-origin regional networks. Hence, the study makes clear that the relationship between climate change and freshwater resources is of primary concern to human society and also has implications for all living species.

The study found abundant evidence that freshwater resources are vulnerable and have the potential to be strongly impacted by climate change, with wide ranging consequences for human societies and ecosystems (p. 3). The following are the major conclusions of the study:

- Observing warming over several decades, it has been found that there is a link between warming and changes in large-scale hydrological cycles;
- By the middle of the twenty-first century, annual average river runoff and water availability are projected to increase as a result of climate change at high latitudes and in some wet tropical areas, and decrease over some dry regions at mid-latitudes and in the dry tropics;
- Increased precipitation intensity and variability are projected to increase the risks of flooding and drought in many areas;
- Water supply stored in glaciers and snow cover are projected to decline in the course of the century;
- Higher water temperatures and changes in extremes, including floods and droughts, are projected to affect water quality and exacerbate many forms of water pollution;
- Globally, the negative impacts of climate change on freshwater systems are expected to outweigh the benefits;
- Changes in water quantity and quality due to climate change are expected to affect food availability, stability, access and utilisation;
- Climate change affects the function and operation of existing water infrastructure – including hydropower, structural flood defences, drainage and irrigation systems – as well as water management practices;
- Current water management practices may not be robust enough to cope with the impacts of climate change;
- Climate change challenges the traditional assumption that past hydrological experience provides a good guide to future conditions;
- Adaptation options designed to ensure water supply during average and drought conditions require integrated demand-side as well as supply-side strategies; and
- Water resources management clearly impacts on many other policy areas.

Asian Development Bank (ADB)

The ADB has put in place several projects relating to climate change issues affecting the Asia–Pacific region. Most important among them are establishing climate change funds and reviewing the economics of climate change. The former concerns collaboration with member nations in Asia and the small island nations of the South Pacific in funding adaptation and mitigation projects on climate change impacts. The latter concerns the impact of climate change in Southeast Asian nations. The ADB is of the view that this region:

> is expected to suffer from many of climate change's most detrimental impacts. Coupled with recurring food, oil and financial crises, climate change will have very serious implications for the region's economic potentials and well-beings of its people. Climate change is now clearly recognized as a development issue, with significant impact on all our efforts for poverty alleviation in the Asia-Pacific in general, and Southeast Asia in particular. While climate change is by nature an environmental issue, it is of greatest concern to all of us and has much more far reaching adverse impacts on people's health, safety and livelihoods – with the poor being disproportionately affected. ADB believes that we can play an important role in this effort. Our recently approved *Strategy 2020*, ADB's long term strategic framework, provides a forward looking platform for us to focus on climate change responses as an integral element for sustainable growth and poverty reduction. (Schafer-Preuss 2008, pp. 2–3)

The regional review study of the ADB has three major objectives:

- Contribute to the regional debate on economic costs and benefits of unilateral and regional actions on mitigation and adaptation measures, for example, to promote consensus and cooperation among policy makers in the region on the steps needed to address climate change;
- Raise awareness of the urgency of climate change challenges and their potential socioeconomic impact in the Southeast Asian region to improve understanding of the economics of climate change; and
- Support government and the private sector to mitigate and adapt to climate change and also include other stakeholders such as civil society, academia and the media.

Under ADB's funding a few national consultations have been conducted in Indonesia, Philippines, Singapore, Thailand and Vietnam. The last consultation was held in Indonesia covering all participant nations in the region in November 2008 and this review is still in progress as of late 2009.

World Bank (WB)

The global financial crisis (GFC) and recessions since 2007, together with fuel and food price increases in 2008, have taken their toll on poverty alleviation in the South Asia region. Exacerbated by natural disasters and global economic turmoil, poverty in South Asia, once again, has taken an adverse turn. For example, Bangladesh's poverty in US$1 a day terms has increased from 35 per cent of the total population to 40 per cent in 2008. In India, it is feared that poverty has moved from 30 per cent to 36 per cent. A similar reverse trend can be witnessed in Pakistan and Sri Lanka (Hossain et al. 2010). With such a background the WB demonstrates how the South Asia region is coping with climate change challenges with respect to growth and poverty alleviation. On the impact of climate change on South Asia's poor, the Bank (World Bank 2008) concludes that there will be the following consequences:

- Decreased water availability and water quality in many arid and semi arid regions;
- An increased risk of floods and droughts in many regions;
- Reduction in water regulation in mountain habitats;
- Decreases in reliability of hydropower and biomass production;
- Increased incidence of waterborne diseases such as malaria, dengue and so on;
- Increased damages and death caused by extreme weather events;
- Decreased agricultural productivity;
- Adverse impacts on fisheries;
- Adverse effects on many ecological systems.

United Nations Framework Convention on Climate Change (UNFCCC) Summit in Copenhagen (COP15)

The 15th UN sponsored summit on climate change was held in Copenhagen between early and mid December 2009, 193 members participated, including hundreds of national and international NGOs. Throughout the conference, it was clear that there was a huge division in this UN sponsored summit. On one side, the wealthy and powerful developed North (US/EU led), and on the other, the weak and divisive South (G77, led by Sudan). In between, there were some least developed nations who played both as a part of the G77 or on some occasions on their own (Maldives and Bangladesh immediately come to mind). However, in the concluding two days, when the heads of governments began arriving in Copenhagen, it was no longer North versus South. It was more about big emitting nations: the mighty United States and emerging China–India backed by Brazil and South Africa. Out of this, it was recognizable that there had been a major difference between the leaders of the United States and China on the issue of transparent international monitoring of emission control and reaching a binding agreement. At the end, a 12 paragraph accord was presented to the summit by President Barak Obama from which both the monitoring and binding clauses had been removed. The full text of the accord is provided below:

[The participating UN member nations] have agreed on this Copenhagen Accord which is operational immediately.

1. We underline that climate change is one of the greatest challenges of our time. We emphasise our strong political will to urgently combat climate change in accordance with the principle of common but differentiated responsibilities and respective capabilities. To achieve the ultimate objective of the Convention to stabilize greenhouse gas concentration in the atmosphere at a level that would prevent dangerous anthropogenic interference with the climate system, we shall, recognizing the scientific view that the increase in global temperature should be below 2°C, on the basis of equity and in the context of sustainable development, enhance our long-term cooperative action to combat climate change. We recognize the critical impacts of climate change and the potential impacts of response measures on countries particularly vulnerable to its adverse effects and stress the need to establish a comprehensive adaptation programme including international support.

2. We agree that deep cuts in global emissions are required according to science, and as documented by the IPCC Fourth Assessment Report with a view to reduce global emissions so as to hold the increase in global temperature below 2°C, and take action to meet this objective consistent with science and on the basis of equity. We should cooperate in achieving the peaking of global and national emissions as soon as possible, recognizing that the time frame for peaking will be longer in developing countries and bearing in mind that social and economic development and poverty eradication are the first and overriding priorities of developing countries and that a low-emission development strategy is indispensable to sustainable development.

3. Adaptation to the adverse effects of climate change and the potential impacts of response measures is a challenge faced by all countries. Enhanced action and international cooperation on adaptation is urgently required to ensure the implementation of the Convention by enabling and supporting the implementation of adaptation actions aimed at reducing vulnerability and building resilience in developing countries, especially in those that are particularly vulnerable, especially least developed countries, small island developing States and Africa. We agree that developed countries shall provide adequate, predictable and sustainable financial resources, technology and capacity-building to support the implementation of adaptation action in developing countries.

4. Annex I Parties commit to implement individually or jointly the quantified economy wide emissions targets for 2020, to be submitted in the format given in Appendix I by Annex I Parties to the secretariat by 31 January 2010 for compilation in an INF document. Annex I Parties that are Party to the Kyoto Protocol will thereby further strengthen the emissions reductions initiated by the Kyoto Protocol. Delivery of reductions and financing by developed countries will be measured, reported and verified in accordance with existing and any further guidelines adopted by the

Conference of the Parties, and will ensure that accounting of such targets and finance is rigorous, robust and transparent.

5.   Non-Annex I Parties to the Convention will implement mitigation actions, including those to be submitted to the secretariat by non-Annex I Parties in the format given in Appendix II by 31 January 2010, for compilation in an INF document, consistent with Article 4.1 and Article 4.7 and in the context of sustainable development. Least developed countries and small island developing States may undertake actions voluntarily and on the basis of support. Mitigation actions subsequently taken and envisaged by Non-Annex I Parties, including national inventory reports, shall be communicated through national communications consistent with Article 12.1(b) every two years on the basis of guidelines to be adopted by the Conference of the Parties. Those mitigation actions in national communications or otherwise communicated to the Secretariat will be added to the list in appendix II. Mitigation actions taken by Non-Annex I Parties will be subject to their domestic measurement, reporting and verification the result of which will be reported through their national communications every two years. Non-Annex I Parties will communicate information on the implementation of their actions through National Communications, with provisions for international consultations and analysis under clearly defined guidelines that will ensure that national sovereignty is respected. Nationally appropriate mitigation actions seeking international support will be recorded in a registry along with relevant technology, finance and capacity building support. Those actions supported will be added to the list in appendix II. These supported nationally appropriate mitigation actions will be subject to international measurement, reporting and verification in accordance with guidelines adopted by the Conference of the Parties.

6.   We recognize the crucial role of reducing emission from deforestation and forest degradation and the need to enhance removals of greenhouse gas emission by forests and agree on the need to provide positive incentives to such actions through the immediate establishment of a mechanism including the United Nations Reducing Emissions from Deforestation and Forest Degradation in Developing Countries Programme (UN-REDD)-plus, to enable the mobilization of financial resources from developed countries.

7.   We decide to pursue various approaches, including opportunities to use markets, to enhance the cost-effectiveness of, and to promote mitigation actions. Developing countries, especially those with low emitting economies should be provided incentives to continue to develop on a low emission pathway.

8.   Scaled up, new and additional, predictable and adequate funding as well as improved access shall be provided to developing countries, in accordance with the relevant provisions of the Convention, to enable and support enhanced action on mitigation, including substantial finance to reduce emissions from deforestation and forest degradation (REDD)-plus, adaptation, technology development and transfer and capacity-building, for enhanced implementation of the Convention. The collective commitment by developed countries is to provide new and additional resources, including forestry and investments through international institutions,

approaching US$30 billion for the period 2010–2012 with balanced allocation between adaptation and mitigation. Funding for adaptation will be prioritized for the most vulnerable developing countries, such as the least developed countries, small island developing States and Africa. In the context of meaningful mitigation actions and transparency on implementation, developed countries commit to a goal of mobilizing jointly US$100 billion dollars a year by 2020 to address the needs of developing countries. This funding will come from a wide variety of sources, public and private, bilateral and multilateral, including alternative sources of finance. New multilateral funding for adaptation will be delivered through effective and efficient fund arrangements, with a governance structure providing for equal representation of developed and developing countries. A significant portion of such funding should flow through the Copenhagen Green Climate Fund.

9. To this end, a High Level Panel will be established under the guidance of and accountable to the Conference of the Parties to study the contribution of the potential sources of revenue, including alternative sources of finance, towards meeting this goal.

10. We decide that the Copenhagen Green Climate Fund shall be established as an operating entity of the financial mechanism of the Convention to support projects, programme, policies and other activities in developing countries related to mitigation including REDD-plus, adaptation, capacity building, technology development and transfer.

11. In order to enhance action on development and transfer of technology we decide to establish a Technology Mechanism to accelerate technology development and transfer in support of action on adaptation and mitigation that will be guided by a country-driven approach and be based on national circumstances and priorities.

12. We call for an assessment of the implementation of this Accord to be completed by 2015, including in light of the Convention's ultimate objective. This would include consideration of strengthening the long-term goal referencing various matters presented by the science, including in relation to temperature rises of 1.5 degrees Celsius.

The most important achievement of the COP15, however, is in support of the adaptation projects in least developed and vulnerable nations. Some commitments have been reached for the short to medium terms. As suggested by point 8, above, an adaptation fund of US$30 billion until 2012 has been promised by the developed members starting from 2010 with US$10 billion per year. Additionally, President Obama outlined a US$100 billion a year fund after 2020. In other words, the outcome of the summit in establishing an Adaptation Fund for nations vulnerable to climate change certainly generated interest for the long term.

The Accord's future support modalities have not been finalised yet, however, it emphasised that new funds will prioritise Africa, least developed vulnerable and small island nations. It was also agreed that a 'Copenhagen Green Fund' will be established for channelling some parts of this fund according to wish of the developing nations (*The Economist* 2 January 2010). The WB has been kept out of managing such a fund.

The next full summit (COP16) was held in Cancun in December 2010.

CLIMATE CHANGE AND GROWTH IN ASIA

Indeed, it is encouraging to watch the momentum in climate change debate in recent years both at multilateral and national levels. Most importantly, the bilateral assistance funds have started to flow through into the developing nations. For example, the Department for International Development (DFID) the development assistance arm of the British government allocated £250 million over the next five years to Bangladesh for climate change adaptation and the creation of a safety net for vulnerable people. Similar assistance projects have also been developed by the DFID for India.

The Bay of Bengal region (India and Bangladesh) has enjoyed high to moderate growth over the last decade. Table I.1 presents growth rate and Figure I.1 captures per capita income in purchasing power parity dollar (PPP$) terms for selected Asian economies.

While the region made strong progress in the early part of the twenty-first century, there also emerged new challenges. The most important among these is climate change and the devastating impact it has brought to this region in recent years with the occurrence of frequent cyclones, floods and the rise in sea level over the last three decades (see Chapter 4).

Table I.1   Growth rates for selected Asian nations, 1961–2007

Country	GDP growth				
	1961–70	1971–80	1981–91	1991–2000	2001–07
Bangladesh	4.1	1.6	3.9	4.8	5.6
India	3.9	3.1	5.9	5.3	7.0
Pakistan	7.3	4.6	4.3	5.2	5.5
Sri Lanka	4.6	4.3	4.4	5.2	4.3
China	3.7	5.4	9.3	10.2	9.4
Indonesia	4.2	7.9	6.3	4.4	5.9
Philippines	4.9	6.0	1.8	2.9	4.5
Thailand	8.2	6.9	7.9	4.6	5.1
Malaysia	6.5	7.9	6.1	7.2	4.8

Source: Dowling and Valenzuela (2010).

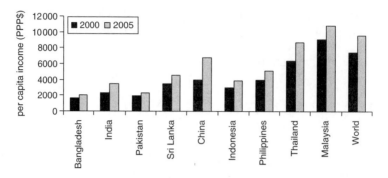

Source: Adapted from Dowling and Valenzuela (2010).

Figure I.1   Selected Asian nations per capita income (PPP$)

New Moore/South Talpatti Island on the Bay of Bengal has recently disappeared under a metre of water due to sea-level rise (see Figure I.2 and Appendix I.1).

As mentioned earlier, the present volume includes papers presented at an international workshop held in Brisbane, Australia in September 2009. In addition, three invited chapters on adaptation, climate security and climate justice have been included to cover more comprehensively the emerging issues and debates concerning climate change in Asia, more specifically, in South Asia. The volume is presented in three parts: climate change and growth issues; climate change and adaptation issues; and climate change and challenges. Presented below is a brief summary of all the chapters in each of these parts.

PART I: CLIMATE CHANGE AND GROWTH ISSUES

Part I deals with the core issues concerning climate change and growth in Asia. Four chapters are included in this part.

Hossain and Selvanathan present an account of recent population, poverty and carbon emissions in Asia. In his chapter, Tisdell demonstrates the issue of producing biofuels in Asia and the consequences for agricultural growth. Ahmad discusses the freshwater issues of Bangladesh and claims that freshwater is not only a problem of this nation due to global warming, but has implications all over Asia and, indeed, the world. Hossain, Ali and Selvanathan study livelihood issues in the Bay of Bengal delta.

Source: *The Age* (2010), 26 March, Melbourne.

Figure I.2   New Moore/South Talpatti, Bay of Bengal Delta

PART II: CLIMATE CHANGE AND ADAPTATION ISSUES

The second part of this volume addresses the issues surrounding adaptation and mitigation in the era of climate change.

In his chapter, Hunt maintains that China and Indonesia must assume major roles in Asia to reduce greenhouse gas emission alongside developed nations for future prosperity. The chapter by Rahman, Noor and Ahmed presents adaptation and related policies in Bangladesh, a highly vulnerable nation affected by climate change in Asia. Khan takes climate change and social parameters into consideration to demonstrate how Asian societies must seek increased partnerships at the regional level and adopt a more value-based approach to cope with the issues of climate risks. The chapter by Howard captures the challenges for China, a major contributor to greenhouse gas emission in Asia, from the viewpoint of future climate governance.

PART III: CLIMATE CHANGE AND CHALLENGES

In the final part of this volume, three chapters are presented with a view to addressing the challenges of climate change for Asia's big players in terms of security, politics and management in uncertain times.

Murthy's chapter demonstrates a new management model for growth at the time of global uncertainty in the era of climate change and GFC. The chapter by McIntosh and Sarker presents sustainable business enterprise and sustainable business issues in the era of climate change and global warming. The chapter by Rashid argues that climate justice must be taken seriously in vulnerable Asian nations and the global economic power-houses must take a leading role to bring climate justice to the forefront of the climate change debate in the future.

REFERENCES

The Age (2010), 26 March.
Bates, B., Z. Kundzewicz, S. Wu and J. Palutikof (eds) (2008), *Climate Change and Water*, Geneva: IPCC.
Copenhagen Accord 2009 (2009), *Copenhagen Accord 2009*, Copenhagen: UNFCCC.
Dowling, J.M. and M.R. Valenzuela (2010), *Economic Development in Asia*, 2nd edn, Singapore: CENGAGE Learning.
The Economist (2010), 2 January.
Hossain, M., R. Kathuria and I. Islam (2010), *South Asian Economic Development*, 2nd edn, London and New York: Routledge.
Mia, M.B. (2008), 'Effects of global warming', *The Daily Star*, 6 June, Dhaka, http://thedailystar.net.
Schafer-Preuss, U. (2008), 'A regional review of the economics of climate change in Southeast Asia', Welcome Remarks to the workshop on Knowledge Management and Sustainable Development on 20–21 November, Jakarta: Asian Development Bank, http://www.adb.org.
UNDP (2007), *Human Development Report 2007/2008*, Oxford: Oxford University Press.
World Bank (2008) 'The impact of climate change on South Asia's poor', www. worldbank.org, accessed on 23 January 2009.

APPENDIX I.1

A tiny island at the centre of a territorial dispute between India and Bangladesh has disappeared beneath the waves due to rising sea levels and erosion, scientists said. The uninhabited outcrop – called New Moore Island by India and South Talpatti by Bangladesh – was 3.5 km (approximately 2 miles) long and 3.0 km wide before it was swallowed up by the Bay of Bengal (see Table IA.1).

'There's no trace of the island anymore. After studying satellite images, I confirmed this from fishermen', said Sugata Hazra, a professor from the School of Oceanographic Studies at Jadavpur University in Kolkata.

Hazra said global warming and erosion were responsible for solving a point of contention in the sometimes fractious relations between India and Bangladesh, which both claimed the island. 'Climate change has obliterated the source of dispute', he said.

Hazra said temperatures in the region had been rising at an annual rate of 0.4°C (0.8°F). In 1981, the Indian navy planted its national flag on the island, but no permanent settlement was established.

The island, which is thought to have been created by a cyclone only about 40 years ago, sat in the Sundarbans mangrove delta in the mouth of the Hariabhanga River that divides India and Bangladesh. At its height, it was never more than 2 m (approximately 6 feet) above sea level.

Hazra said a larger island, called Lohachara, disappeared in the Bay of Bengal in 1996 after 4000 inhabitants had fled. At least five other islands in the region are also threatened, he said.

Bangladesh is one of the countries worst affected by climate change with some scientists predicting 20 million people will be displaced by 2050 because of rising sea levels.

Table IA.1   South Talpatti, Bay of Bengal

	Geography
Location	Bay of Bengal
Area	7 sq. km (2.7 sq. miles) to 14 sq. km (5.4 sq. miles)
Length	3.5 km (2.2 miles)
Width	3 km (1.9 miles)
Claimed by	Bangladesh and India
Demographics	
Population	0

Source: Agence France-Presse, news report, *The Age* (2010), 26 March.

PART I

Climate change and growth issues

1. Population, poverty and CO_2 emissions in Asia: an overview

Moazzem Hossain and Eliyathamby Selvanathan

1.1 POPULATION

A recent estimate of population growth suggests that all the populous nations of the southeast (Indonesia, the Philippines, Thailand, Vietnam); east (China); and south (India, Pakistan, Bangladesh, Nepal and Sri Lanka) of Asia comprise more than three billion people. More precisely, the figure was 3.40 billion in 2005 (Hossain et al. 2010). The Food and Agriculture Organization (FAO) recently estimated that one-sixth of the world's population (1.02 billion) is presently suffering from acute hunger, of which 642 million live in the Asia–Pacific region (FAO 2009). Demographically, therefore, Southeast, East and South Asia are the most critical regions of the world. By world standards, except for China (due to its single child policy), Asia is characterised by a very high rate of population growth, high density and high dependency. In order to investigate climate change and growth issues in Asia, it is important first to analyse clearly population and demographic issues. The reasons for analysing the demographic dynamics are to demonstrate and inform readers about the correlation between population growth and environment (Gaan 2000). Also, it shows how important population factors are in the debate surrounding climate change and economic growth.

An attempt is made, first, to outline the general demographic conditions in Asia. Table 1.1 shows that in 2005 the population of all the countries under study comprised almost half of the world's total. The average population growth rate for Southeast and East Asia over 1990–2005 was 1.21 per cent, whereas for China alone it was about 1 per cent. Among the Southeast Asian nations, the Philippines has the highest rate of growth (2.0 per cent) and Vietnam has the highest density per square kilometre (268). In South Asia, the highest rate of growth has been witnessed by Pakistan (2.4 per cent) and Bangladesh has the highest population density (1090 per sq. km) over 1990–2005.

Table 1.1   Demographic conditions

Country	Area (in '000 sq. km)	Population (million)			Population growth rate		Population ratio (rural/total)	
		1990	2005	2015*	1990–2005	2005–15*	1990	2005
East Asia**	12660	1495	1756	1882	1.38	0.98	68.3	58.0
China	9597	1135	1305	1378	0.9	0.5	70.6	59.6 (140)
Indonesia	1919	178	221	244	1.4	1.0	69.4	51.9 (122)
Philippines	300	61	83	99	2.0	1.7	51.2	37.2 (240)
Thailand	514	55	64	69	1.1	0.7	70.6	67.7 (126)
Vietnam	330	66	83	92	1.5	1.0	79.7	73.6 (268)
South Asia	4440	1098	1440	1661	1.84	1.46	79.6	76.1
India	3287	849.5	1095	1248.5	1.4	1.0	74.5	71.3 (368)
Pakistan	796	108	156	190.5	2.4	2.0	69.4	65.1 (202)
Bangladesh	144	104	142	168	2.1	1.7	80.2	74.9 (1090)
Nepal	147	19.1	27	32.7	2.3	1.9	91.1	84.2 (190)
Sri Lanka	66	17	20	21	1.0	0.7	82.8	84.9 (304)
Total (East & South)	17100	2593	3196	3543	1.61	1.22	74.0	67.0

Notes:
*   Projections by World Bank.
**   Both Southeast and East Asia are considered as East Asia in all tables.
Population density is in parentheses under the last column.

Source: World Bank (2004, 2007); http://www.infoplease.com/ipa/A0004379.html.

Table 1.2 provides further disaggregated estimates on population and land use in these regions. The populations of the Philippines and Vietnam have doubled between 1975 and 2005. Over the same period, the populations of China, Thailand and Indonesia have expanded more than one-and-a-half times (World Bank 2007). Population density in 2005 per square kilometre was very high in Vietnam (>250) and moderately high

Table 1.2   Population estimates and land use

Country	Population density (in per sq. km)		Land use			
	1995	2005	1990		2005	
			Arable land ha/100 people	Arable land (% of total)	Arable land ha/100 people	Arable land (% of total)
East Asia						
China	126	140	8.1	11.1	8.0	11.1
Indonesia	101	122	10.3	11.2	10.6	12.7
Philippines	230	240	7.4	18.4	7.1	19.1
Thailand	113	126	25.6	34.2	22.4	27.7
Vietnam	201	268	8.2	16.4	8.0	21.3
Averages	154	179	11.92	18.26	11.22	18.38
South Asia						
India	283	368	15.5	54.8	14.8	53.7
Bangladesh	833	1090	6.1	70.2	5.7	61.9
Nepal	149	190	9.4	16.0	8.9	16.5
Sri Lanka	273	304	4.7	13.5	4.8	14.2
Averages	340	431	10.18	36.2	9.66	34.78
Total averages	247	305	11.05	27.24	10.44	26.58

Source: UNDP (2004); World Bank (2004, 2007).

in China, Indonesia, Thailand and the Philippines. Land use in the arable category in 2005 was highest in Thailand (27.7 per cent) and lowest in China (11.1 per cent) out of the total land available to these nations. In South Asia, on the other hand, the population has doubled in almost all the nations under study, except Sri Lanka, over the last 30 years. Arable land use in 2005 was highest in Bangladesh (61.9 per cent) and lowest in Sri Lanka (14.2 per cent).

Distribution of population by age group and dependency ratio by country are presented in Table 1.3. In East Asia, in recent years (2005), children in the age group 0–14 years constitute the second largest proportion of the total population of each country. In 1996, this proportion was very high for all countries. In 2004, this ranged from less than 25 per cent in China and Thailand to above 29 per cent in Vietnam, Indonesia ynd the Philippines. The high proportion in Vietnam, Indonesia and the Philippines, in this respect, reduced the population in the working age

Climate change and growth in Asia

*Table 1.3   Distribution of population by age and dependency ratio,
1996–2005*

Country	Age group						Dependency ratio	
	1996			2005			1996	2005
	0–14	15–64	65+	0–14	15–64	65+		
East Asia								
China	27.2	66.5	6.3	21.4	71.0	7.6	500	400
Indonesia	32.2	64.0	3.8	28.3	66.2	5.5	560	500
Philippines	38.4	58.1	3.5	35.1	61.0	3.9	720	700
Thailand	26.2	68.2	5.6	23.8	69.1	7.1	470	400
Vietnam	36.0	58.5	5.5	29.5	65.0	5.4	710	600
Averages	32	63	5.0	27.6	66.5	6.0	592	520
South Asia								
India	42.3	60.2	4.0	32.1	62.7	5.3	662	600
Pakistan	45.5	51.1	3.4	368.3	57.9	3.8	966	800
Bangladesh	42.3	56.8	0.9	35.5	60.9	3.6	762	700
Nepal	–	–	–	39.0	57.3	3.7	–	800
Sri Lanka	31.7	64.2	4.1	24.1	68.6	7.3	545	500
Averages	40.5	58.0	3.1	33.8	61.48	4.74	734	680
Averages (East and South)	36.25	60.5	4.0	12.3	64	5.4	663	600

Source: US Census Bureau; Hossain et al. (1999).

group (15–64 years). The overall figures, however, suggest that the fertility rate in all these countries has declined over the last 10 years (Hossain et al. 2010). In the case of South Asia, the largest proportion of children below 14 years is in Pakistan (38.3 per cent) and the smallest is in Sri Lanka (24.1 per cent). Reduced fertility also helped to reduce population in South Asia over the same period.

In Table 1.3, the dependency ratio shows that children (aged 0–14 years) and older people (65 and above) constitute the dependency load for persons of primary working ages (15–64 years). The dependency ratios provided in Table 1.3 reveal that the Philippines had the highest ratio of dependency of 720 and 660 (per 1000), respectively, in 1996 and in 2005 among the countries in East Asia. However, dependency has declined for all the other nations. In South Asia, dependency declined in all nations between 1996 and 2005. The highest dependency is in Pakistan and Nepal (800 per 1000) in 2005, very high indeed.

$$\text{Dependency ratio} = \frac{\text{persons } 0-14 + 65 \text{ and above}}{\text{persons } 15-64} \times 1000$$

By 2005, East Asia's population reached more than 1.77 billion as against 1.5 billion in 1990. World Bank (2004) projections suggest that by 2015 the total population of the region will reach close to 2 billion. It is, however, a picture which is far less alarming than other parts of Asia, particularly, when one looks at population densities. In 2005, Vietnam's population density per square kilometre reached almost 300 persons while China had 140, Indonesia 122, the Philippines 240, and Thailand 126 persons. In contrast, by 2015, South Asia's population will reach 1.7 billion, almost the same as East Asia. In terms of population density in 2005, while Nepal (190 per sq. km), Pakistan (202), Sri Lanka (302) and India (368) have tolerable densities, Bangladesh is certainly in a very alarming position (1090).

Within South Asia, it appears that in recent years all nations have been experiencing difficulties as far as population control is concerned.

It must be emphasised that, particularly in Pakistan and Bangladesh, the population growth rate has been bouncing back in recent years after a significant slide in the final quarter of the twentieth century. The present increasing trend has been attributed to a lack of budget allocation and decline in support from the international community for direct population control measures. A recent report by the Population and Family Planning Department of the Government of Bangladesh identified several issues behind the collapse of the population programme implemented over the last two decades. These are: lack of a sustained field level workforce, corruption in procurement of relevant effective birth control devices and declining morale of the existing workforce due to the lack of initiatives by recent governments to keep the dedicated workforce working for the department. In particular, it has been reported that success in the past had been brought about by the field level workers who visited the households in rural areas regularly. For example, out of the total rural households in Bangladesh, almost 43 per cent were visited by population workers in 1993–94, this dropped to 35 per cent in 1997–98 and, in 1999–2000, this dropped even further to only 18 per cent. The major reason for such a drop in visits was the limited supply of condoms, contraceptive pills and other birth control devices. Moreover, out of more than 50 000 field workers almost 7500 positions are presently vacant (15 per cent of the total). This is no doubt contributing towards destroying the morale of the existing workforce and certainly results in the decline of services to rural people where a huge demand for birth control devices still exists (Hossain et al. 2010, cited from *The Daily Prathom Alo* 2009).

The last Indian census (2001) reported that the population of this nation rose by 21.34 per cent between the period 1981 and 2001. Hansen (2002) suggested that in the last few decades, fertility control policies in India have failed to promote a sustainable solution to the problem of population surge. What factors have caused these efforts to disintegrate? The following have been suggested:

> India reached one billion mark in August 1999 in a country one third the size of the United States [that] is certainly alarming. India's population has more than doubled between 1960 and 2000. In 1960 the population was less than half a billion (431 463 000).

It appears that the national sterilization scheme had not achieved the desirable outcome, and targeting female sterilization was a failure over the last few decades. In addition, the major challenge for India is the family's strong preference for sons. This makes the overall male and female ratio quite imbalanced in recent years (Begum 2007). The sex ratio in the 2001 census suggests that the number of females per 1000 males was 933, a marginal rise from 927 in the 1991 census (www.indiaeyewitness.com).

As mentioned earlier, Pakistan has the highest rate of population growth in the region. The population control policy has not been prioritised in Pakistan since 9/11. The US Agency for International Development (USAID) was the major donor agency in Pakistan and was the source of funds for the population and family planning department. There was a pause in the USAID assistance between 2001 and 2003, since the agency had closed its offices in Pakistan immediately after 9/11. USAID returned and extended US$60 million in 2008 to address population control issues. With the present Taliban insurgency and the threats from Mullahs, it is unlikely to put more resources into population control and the problem is going to worsen in the years to come (*The Nation* 2009).

Sri Lanka was a high achiever in controlling population in the 1970s and 1980s. When the nation went into a civil war in the early 1980s, it slipped from the radar of the demographic literature. However, it appears that most recently, the government policy is to satisfy the demand for various family planning methods, demand for which has been created by a well-developed and well-promoted fertility control programme during the past phases of policy implementation. Under this policy, greater emphasis is simultaneously being given to improving reproductive health (Dangalle 1998).

1.2 POVERTY

The UN Millennium Development Goals (MDGs) strategy has been in place in all developing nations since 2000 (see Chapter 7, Hossain 2007a,

Table 1.4   Eradication of extreme poverty

Region	Poverty (US$1 a day headcount ratio)		Share of consumption to poorest quintile (%)
	1998	2005	2005
East Asia			
China	16.6	9.9	4.7
Indonesia	7.5	7.5	8.4
Philippines	15.5	10.5	5.4
Thailand	< 2	< 2	6.3
Vietnam	–	–	9.0
South Asia			
Bangladesh	41.3	36.0	9.0
India	36.0	33.5	8.9
Nepal	41.8	24.1	6.0
Pakistan	28.6	17.0	9.3
Sri Lanka	15.0	5.6	8.3

Source: World Bank (2006, 2007).

2007b). All the multilateral agencies including the IMF and the World Bank are fully committed to implementing the MDGs' eight human development and poverty alleviation goals by 2015 (see poverty reduction strategy papers (PRSPs) by all developing Asian countries in www.imf.org; Hossain 2008). Given the conditions of population growth in East and South Asia illustrated above, an attempt has been made here to investigate how the countries under study have been coping with their commitments in achieving MDGs by 2015, under the given population and income growth. The investigation has been carried out by analysing the achievements between 2000 and 2005, the first five-year period of implementing the MDGs strategy. Since the global financial crisis (GFC) hit the nations from 2007, recent years have been assumed to be abnormal and kept out of this investigation.

In terms of eradicating extreme poverty MDG1, certainly East Asian nations are ahead of South Asia. The headcount ratio suggests that more than one-third of the population in Bangladesh and India live on less than US$1 a day per capita, although there was an improvement in the rest of the nations between 1998 and 2005 (Table 1.4). The improvement has been strong in all nations except Indonesia and Thailand (no change) and India (reduced by only 2.5 per cent). Certainly, these achievements have been encouraging although in South Asia a huge number of people remain in poverty in absolute terms.

Climate change and growth in Asia

Table 1.5   *Achieving universal primary education and promoting gender equality*

Region	Primary education completion (%)		Ratio of girls to boys in primary and secondary school (%)
	1991	2005	2005
East Asia			
China	103	98	99
Indonesia	91	100	98
Philippines	86	98	102
Thailand	–	82	98
Vietnam	–	98	103
South Asia			
Bangladesh	49	77	106
India	68	89	88
Nepal	51	76	90
Pakistan	–	63	98
Sri Lanka	97	–	102

Source: World Bank (2006, 2007).

Taking share of consumption by the poor into consideration, China, the Philippines and Thailand's poor have a relatively low consumption share compared to Indonesia and Vietnam among East Asian nations. In South Asia, Nepal is placed in this category.

It is disturbing to see that the populous nations of East and South Asia (China, Indonesia, the Philippines, Bangladesh and India), have been making slow progress in eradicating absolute poverty. In China and the Philippines one-tenth of the population lives in poverty and in Bangladesh and India this was about one-third in 2005.

The achievements in universal primary education and promoting gender equality as one of the targets of the MDGs are presented in Table 1.5. By 2005, the East Asian nations were ahead and have made strong progress since 1991. The progress in South Asia, however, is modest. This suggests that Thailand and Pakistan need further investment in the primary education sector to catch up with the rest of Asia.

Table 1.6 presents the child mortality rate and maternal mortality ratio of these regions. As far as child mortality is concerned, strong advances were made by all nations. However, in absolute terms, South Asia has been experiencing high mortality, except for Sri Lanka in 2005. This is also true in the case of maternal mortality until 2000.

Table 1.6   Reducing child mortality and improving maternal health

Region	Child mortality (under –5 mortality rate per 1000)		Maternal mortality ratio (per 100 000 live births)
	1990	2005	2000
East Asia			
China	49	27	31
Indonesia	91	36	230
Philippines	62	33	200
Thailand	37	21	44
Vietnam	53	19	130
South Asia			
Bangladesh	105	89	380
India	123	74	540
Nepal	145	74	740
Pakistan	130	99	160
Sri Lanka	32	14	92

Source: World Bank (2006, 2007).

1.3   IMPACT OF POPULATION ON POVERTY

1.3.1   A Generic View

Table 1.7 presents ratios of population growth between 1965 and 2005 and corresponding ratios of poverty for the same period for East and South Asia. The table suggests that in China, Indonesia, the Philippines and Thailand population grew by 59, 70, 93 and 81 per cent respectively as opposed to poverty which was reduced by 63 per cent in China and 81 per cent in the Philippines. In Indonesia and Thailand there were negligible poor in 1990 taking US$1 a day as the poverty line (post-1997 Asian currency crisis, however, reversed this achievement). It has been observed that, while in China and the Philippines population grew by 15 and 36 per cent, respectively, between 1990 and 2005, poverty declined by 40 and 32 per cent between 2000 and 2005. In other words, these two nations have reduced overall poverty to 10 and 15 per cent of the total populations, respectively, over the last 15 years, which meets the MDG's poverty target. Indonesia and Thailand have reduced poverty to 7.5 and below 2 per cent of their total populations, respectively, in 2005 (Table 1.4).

Table 1.7 further presents ratios of population growth between 1965

Table 1.7   *Population growth in individual countries and poverty alleviation taking the poverty line at US$1 a day per capita, 1965–2005*

Country	Population ratio 1965–90	Population ratio 1990–2005	Poverty ratio 1970–90	Poverty ratio 2000–05
China	1.59	1.15	0.37 (63)	0.60 (40)
Indonesia	1.70	1.24	neg. (0)	n.a.
Philippines	1.93	1.36	0.19 (81)	0.68 (32)
Thailand	1.81	1.16	neg. (0)	n.a.
Vietnam	n.a.	1.26	n.a.	n.a.
Bangladesh	1.88	1.37	0.46 (54)	0.87 (13)
India	1.74	1.29	0.24 (76)	0.93 (7)
Nepal	n.a.	1.41	0.74 (26)	0.58 (42)
Pakistan	2.05	1.44	0.23 (77)	0.68 (32)
Sri Lanka	1.48	1.18	0.07 (93)	0.37 (63)

Notes:
Figures in parentheses show percentage reduction.
Poverty ratio calculated taking poverty line at US$1 a day per capita.

Source: Dowling et al. (2004) and the present study.

and 1990 and corresponding ratios of poverty for the same period for Bangladesh, India, Nepal, Pakistan and Sri Lanka. Also, the same ratios are presented for 1990 and 2005. The table suggests that in Bangladesh, India, Nepal, Pakistan and Sri Lanka population grew by 88, 74, 105 and 48 per cent, respectively, between 1965 and 1990 (data for Nepal are not available) as opposed to poverty reduced, respectively, by 54, 76, 26, 77 and 93 per cent. It has been observed that, while in Bangladesh, India, Nepal, Pakistan and Sri Lanka the population grew by 37, 29, 41, 44 and 18 per cent, respectively, between 1990 and 2005, poverty has been reduced by only 13, 7, 42, 32 and 63 per cent, respectively, over the same period. In other words, these nations have brought down overall poverty to 41, 34, 24, 17 and 5.5 per cent, respectively, over the last 15 years, which does not satisfy the aims of the MDG's poverty target, except, of course, for Sri Lanka.

It has been argued in the literature of the World Bank and the IMF that the poverty line of US$1 a day should be expanded to US$2 a day for the period between 2005 and 2015 for poverty analysis due to the increases in per capita income and in food inflation witnessed between 1990 and 2005. Table 1.8 shows the figures for poverty for the ten countries in question under the new poverty benchmark (US$2 a day). These figures suggest

Table 1.8   Poverty alleviation taking poverty line at US$2 a day per capita, 1990–2005[a]

Region	Population below poverty line	
	US$1 a day	US$2 a day
East Asia		
China	9.9	34.9
Indonesia	7.5	52.5
Philippines	14.8	43.0
Thailand	< 2	25.2
Vietnam	28.9[b]	–
South Asia		
Bangladesh	41.3	84.0
India	34.3	80.4
Nepal	24.1	68.5
Pakistan	17.0	73.6
Sri Lanka	5.6	41.6

Notes:
[a]   Data refer to most recent years.
[b]   National poverty line for Vietnam.

Source: UNDP (2007).

that, given the experience over the last 15 years in poverty reduction in East Asian nations, it is likely to reduce poverty by half by 2015. However, this is unlikely to occur in South Asia. Taking the new benchmark into consideration, two-thirds of South Asia's population has been suffering from poverty, except in Sri Lanka. In Sri Lanka, more than 40 per cent of the people are living under poverty with US$2 a day per capita income. Thus, South Asia will remain behind in terms of poverty eradication (MDG1) for a long time to come.

1.3.2   A View Backed by Econometrics

This section presents an econometric analysis on the impact of population on poverty across ten countries in Asia. We employed a regression model with percentage of population below the poverty line (US$1 a day) as the dependent variable and population growth, percentage of rural population in the total population and population density per square kilometre as independent variables. A cross sectional data set consisting of ten countries at two time periods was used for estimation. Most of the data

Table 1.9   Results from an econometric model

Cross section observation	10 nations under study
Intercept	−26.2436 (−2.28)
Population Growth	11.3209 (3.24)
Per cent of Rural Population	0.3527 (2.3)
Population Density	0.0186 (2.27)
R-Square	0.65
Adjusted R	0.58

Note: Figures in parentheses are *t*-values which suggest all the variables are significant at 5% level of significance.

are from secondary sources, from government publications and Human Development Reports of the UNDP. It, however, must be emphasized that the dataset is limited, being taken from secondary sources of different origins, which means that one should apply some caution to the results. But the basic message is clear and consistent. That is, population matters significantly for the reduction of poverty in Asia.

Table 1.9 provides estimated results from the regression model. As can be seen, all the estimated coefficients are statistically significant at the 5 per cent level. The parameter estimates show that population growth has the right sign and is significantly associated with poverty. Rural population and population density also picked up a positive coefficient and are statistically significant.

The key results of this regression model estimation are:

- The coefficient on population growth is both positive and significant at the 5 per cent level of significance. The result suggests that, with a 1 per cent growth in population, poverty will increase by more than 11 per cent, quite a high impact.
- The positive and highly significant rural population estimates suggest that, with a 1 per cent increase in rural population, poverty will increase by more than one-third of a per cent.
- The coefficient on population density is both positive and significant and its estimated value is 0.0186. This implies that a 10 per cent increase in population density, on average, will result in only a 0.19 per cent increase in poverty. This certainly has a low impact.

In summary, the econometric analysis with cross sectional data confirms that population growth has a strong impact on poverty reduction, which is consistent with the generic view. The impact of rural population ratio on poverty was found to be moderate; however, once again, it was consistent with the generic view. The population density has a low impact on poverty, which suggests that perhaps population density is not yet remarkably high in some regions of Asia. In this regard, there seems to be room for improvement in populating those areas which are still seen to be less inhabited.

1.4 CARBON DIOXIDE (CO_2) EMISSIONS

Given the population and poverty menaces in Asia, let us discuss the third menace, carbon dioxide (CO_2) emissions and economic growth issues arising out of this human-made hazard in the regions under study. It has been established globally that CO_2 emissions must be checked and reduced to bring global warming under control before it turns into a major environmental catastrophe, not only for the populous or developing Asian nations, but also for the more developed nations, since the climate change menace has no boundaries (UNDP 2007).

In the literature, numerous studies show how economic growth and CO_2 emissions are related. Economists are divided into two camps in this regard: optimists and pessimists. Both these views have been formed based on the Environmental Kuznets Curves (EKC) (Selden and Song 1994; Tisdell 1997, 2001, 2003, 2005, 2009).

According to optimists, economic growth realised by adopting economic globalisation is a major force behind sustainable development (Sebastian and Alicbusan 1989; Hansen 1990). However, the pessimists warn that there are negative consequences of economic globalisation, in other words, economic growth on environment and sustainable development (Daly 1993; Lang and Hines 1993; Anderson 1998; Tisdell 1999).

Selden and Song (1994) established a first connection between the EKC and the Kuznets curve put forward by Simon Kuznets in 1955 (Kuznets 1955). In this seminal work, Kuznets hypothesised that there is a U-shaped relationship between income inequality and economic development. Following this line, Selden and Song (1994) hypothesised that environment–income might have an 'inverted-U' shaped relationship (see detailed analysis on EKC in Tisdell 2001). This means, 'raising income above the level at which the curve peaks will reduce pollution levels' (Tisdell 2001, p. 187).

Tisdell (2001) demonstrates the shape of the EKC and the EKC's behaviour under increased efficiency in pollution emissions as a result of globalisation. The simplest illustration of EKC is shown by the pollution intensity on the vertical axis and global growth on the horizontal axis (Figure 1.1). Applying EKC on the space of intensity of pollution emissions and global

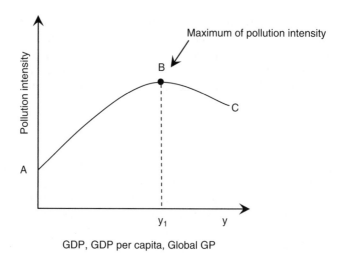

Source: Tisdell (2001, p. 187).

Figure 1.1   A 'normal' type of environmental Kuznets curve

growth, the curve shifts right in the post-globalisation era (Figure 1.2). The EKC shows in the post-globalisation era that, while it may decline because of increased efficiency due to globalisation, aggregate pollution levels may continue to rise as a result of economic growth (see Tables 1.10 and 1.11 for China).

Tisdell (2001, p. 194), comes to the conclusion that 'excessive conversion of natural resources into man-made capital may occur as a consequence of uncoordinated global economic growth stimulated by trade liberalization. The seriousness of these sustainability problems is likely to be exacerbated by the skew of economic growth in favour of major developing countries, such as China and India.'

With this theoretical illustration in mind, this section presents CO_2 emission accounts for the major Asian nations over time. CO_2, or for that matter greenhouse gas (GHG), emission has no borders. Thus, offenders in Asia have been blamed for contributing to this menace alongside other continents. Globally, it has been recognised that in 2004 the share of OECD's GHG emissions was almost one-half. The middle income and developing nations have contributed to the rest. Within the OECD, the USA contributes more than one-fifth of the total global emissions and, among the developing nations, China contributes close to one-fifth. In other words, both the USA and China contributed 40 per cent of the total global emissions in 2004 (UNDP 2007).

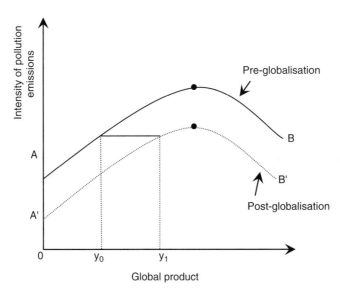

Source: Adapted from Tisdell (2001, p. 190).

Figure 1.2   EKC under globalisation

Table 1.10   Carbon dioxide emissions: selected Asian nations

Region	Total emissions (Mt CO_2)		Annual change (%)	Share of total (%)		Per capita (ton)	
	1990	2004	1990–2004	1990	2004	1990	2004
East Asia							
China	2398.9	500.7	7.8	10.6	17.3	2.1	3.8
Indonesia	213.8	378.0	5.5	0.9	1.3	1.2	1.7
Philippines	43.9	80.5	5.9	0.2	0.3	1.0	1.68
Thailand	95.7	267.9	12.9	0.4	0.9	1.7	4.2
Vietnam	21.4	98.6	25.8	0.1	0.3	0.3	1.2
South Asia							
Bangladesh	15.4	37.1	10.1	0.1	0.1	0.1	0.3
India	681.7	1342.1	6.9	3.0	4.6	0.8	1.2
Nepal	0.6	3.0	27.3	neg.	neg.	neg.	0.1
Pakistan	68.0	125.6	6.0	0.3	0.4	0.6	0.8
Sri Lanka	3.8	11.5	14.8	neg.	neg.	0.2	0.6

Source: UNDP (2007).

Table 1.11   Carbon intensity of growth

Region	Carbon intensity of growth CO_2 emissions per unit of GDP (kt of CO_2 per mill. 2000 PPP US$)		CO_2 emission change per unit of GDP	GDP in bill.	GDP in US$ in bill. PPP
	1990	2004	1990–2004	2005	2005
East Asia					
China	1.30	0.70	0.54	2234.3	8814.9
Indonesia	0.54	0.53	0.98	287.2	847.6
Philippines	0.19	0.22	1.16	99.0	426.7
Thailand	0.38	0.56	1.47	176.6	557.4
Vietnam	0.28	0.47	1.68	52.4	255.3
South Asia					
Bangladesh	0.12	0.15	1.25	60.0	291.2
India	0.48	0.44	0.92	805.7	3779.0
Nepal	0.03	0.08	2.67	7.4	42.1
Pakistan	0.39	0.41	1.05	110.7	369.2
Sri Lanka	0.09	0.15	1.67	23.5	90.2

Source: UNDP (2007).

At the current rate of GHG emission (upward-bound estimate), the temperature in the atmosphere will increase by up to 4°C by the end of this century (2100), which will mean a rise of sea level of 3 m. In order to arrest this upward-bound trend in temperature and sea-level rise, the concentration of CO_2 will have to be reduced from the current 389 ppm to below 350 ppm. If this can be achieved global temperatures will rise by only 2°C and sea level-rise will be reduced to below 1 m by 2100 (UNDP 2007, quoting IPCC).

The major sources of GHG emissions globally in 2000 have been identified as the burning of fossil fuels (more than 50 per cent) and power generation (25 per cent). It has been estimated that transport and energy supply have increased their GHG emissions by 120 and 145 per cent, respectively, in recent years. Land-use change and deforestation are also considered major sources of emissions. According to the IPCC, the share of emissions originating from deforestation ranges between 11 and 28 per cent of the total (UNDP 2007, p. 41).

National carbon footprints in Asia can be measured in terms of stock and flows. While emissions have been dominated by the developed nations in the last century, in Asia, China's emissions have been catching up with the developed nations over the last three decades. In Asia, in other words,

China dominates the overall emissions (Table 1.10). China's growth in emissions has reached almost 8 per cent per annum between 1990 and 2004. In per capita terms, the emissions were 3.8 tons in 2004 as opposed to 2.1 in 1990. The second largest emitter was Thailand. In per capita terms, this was 4.2 tons followed by Indonesia (1.7 tons) in 2004.

Turning from stocks to flows, like global accounts, Asian nations also suffer from concentration of emissions in a handful of nations. Out of the ten nations under study in 2004, the major offenders were China, India, Indonesia and Thailand (Malaysia's case has not been considered here; however, in per capita terms Malaysia was the top emitter in Asia, 7.5 tons per capita). Once again, like the global account, the differences in the size of carbon footprints are linked to industrial development. The newly industrialised nations of Asia are certainly the major emitters over the last three decades.

The UNDP (2007) estimates that, out of the top five emitters in the world, three are from Asia: China, India and Japan. The rest are the USA and Russian Federation. These nations account for more than half of the total emissions.

The carbon intensity of growth is an important indicator that shows how nations, individually or collectively, are responsible for emitting with GDP growth. In other words, it indicates per unit of GDP increase the corresponding increase in amount of CO$_2$ emissions. Table 1.11 shows that, in carbon intensity terms, among the Asian nations under study, Nepal is top in terms of emission change between 1990 and 2004. However, it must be remembered that Nepal's overall CO$_2$ emission has been very low and GDP in absolute value terms is also low. The large nations of East and South Asia have certainly brought major changes with respect to carbon intensity per unit of GDP between 1990 and 2004. For example, although China reduced emissions per unit of GDP by 85 per cent between 1990 and 2004, it remains the top emitter (see Table 1.10). However, it certainly shows an impressive improvement in 2004 over the 1990 figures, almost halving the rate of emissions over 15 years. In the case of India and Indonesia, the conditions are quite different in this respect. India shows a slight improvement (8 per cent), while Indonesia improved marginally (2 per cent) between 1990 and 2004.

It is well known that East Asia grew more strongly during the last four decades than any other regions of the world. Particularly, China's rate of growth has been exemplary. With such strong growth, the national poverty rates, however, have not fallen rapidly in East Asia. Two major reasons can be found for this unexpected outcome: per capita income still remains very low compared to the world average and the lowest quintile of the population still suffers from a very low consumption

Climate change and growth in Asia

*Table 1.12   Percentage below US$9237 income per capita (world
average), and consumption share by the poorest quintile, 2005*

Region	Income per capita below world average (%) and consumption (%)	
	Income per capita taking world average	Consumption share by bottom quintile
East Asia		
China	(–) 81.5	4.7
Indonesia	(–) 86.0	8.4
Philippines	(–) 87.0	5.4
Thailand	(–) 70.0	6.3
Vietnam	(–) 93.0	9.0
South Asia		
India	(–) 92.0	8.9
Pakistan	(–) 92.0	9.3
Bangladesh	(–) 95.5	9.0
Nepal	(–) 97.1	6.0
Sri Lanka	(–) 87.0	8.3

Source: Newsweek (21 November 2005); UNDP (2007).

share of the total. Table 1.12 shows that, despite rapid economic growth, East and South Asia remain far below the global average in per capita income terms. All the nations of these regions have fallen well below the world average income. This table also shows data on the consumption share by the poorest quintile. None in Asia crosses the minimum benchmark of more than 10 per cent of consumption by the poor in 2005. In these terms, Asia's catching up with middle income countries, let alone more developed nations, remains uncertain with the given GHG emission crisis and climate change's overall impacts both economically and socially. The chapters that follow will address this concern for Asia in more detail.

1.5   CONCLUSIONS

It is well known that East Asia grew more strongly during the last four decades than any other parts of the world. Particularly, China's rate of growth has been exemplary. Compared to China, although late by almost a decade, India, another populous nation of Asia, has been growing steadily over the last decade at a respectable rate. In this chapter, we have identified three major development menaces: population, poverty and GHG emissions, which have been acting as drivers behind arresting the growth momentum that Asia has enjoyed over the last two decades.

Population and its growth rates have been creating more major development crises for South Asia than any other parts of Asia. Moreover, population is working against the poverty eradication goal of the MDGs in Asia. An econometric analysis suggests that certainly the impact of population growth and the rural population ratio on poverty reductions are significant. Most importantly, it appears that GHG emissions, in CO_2 terms, are driving the economies of China and India on a collision course with more developed nations, since these two nations jointly emit a substantial amount and are among the top five emitters in the world. It is no secret anymore that the developed nations want binding commitments from China and India in reducing emissions and want a fruitful negotiation at the United Nations Framework Convention on Climate Change (UNFCCC)-led future summits (for example, COP16 in Mexico in November 2010 and COP17 in Durban in 2011).

While it is indeed a legitimate demand by the more developed nations, one may argue that if binding commitments have been at the expense of GDP growth, the Asian giants will certainly oppose such a move. Why? It has been argued that, if one looks at the overall position of Asia in global average income terms, it is right to say that most of the nations fall below 10 per cent of such an income, except China. For example, in 2005, China had 20 per cent and India had 8 per cent of the global per capita average income. Shedding growth in the future is something Asia can ill afford and by doing this would be unlikely to catch up with the rest of the world in average per capita income terms. Moreover, shedding growth drastically on CO_2 emission grounds will be a daunting move for Asia to eradicate poverty, when all nations are presently under stress in bringing the lowest quintile of their population under the fold of 10 per cent of consumption share. Conversely, according to more developed nations, they are not in any way opposing the growth trajectory of Asia, but they are arguing for a limit to GHG emissions by adopting renewable energy policies, technologies and framing adaptation which are friendly to growth at the same time as reducing pollution (Someshwar, 2008).

Indeed, the challenge for the climate change and growth fronts in Asia is paramount. In the following chapters of this volume the learned authors will address this challenge from global, regional and national (including local) perspectives. The next chapter is presented by Clem Tisdell, who addresses the contemporary issue of biofuels and their possible consequences for Asia's agricultural growth.

REFERENCES

Anderson, K. (1998), 'Agricultural trade reforms, research initiatives, and the environment', in L. Ernst (ed.), *Agriculture and the Environment: Perspectives on Sustainable Rural Development*, Washington DC: World Bank, pp. 71–82.

Begum, S.M. (2007), 'The economics behind son preference in South India', in *World Sustainable Development Outlook 2007*, A. Ahmad (ed.), Sheffield: Greenleaf Publishing, pp. 391–400.

Daly, H. (1997), 'Georgescu-Roegen versus Solow/Stiglitz', *Ecological Economics*, **22** (3): 261–6.

Dangalle, N. (1998), 'Controlling population growth in Sri Lanka: perceptions, polices and strategies', *Journal of Population Studies*, **1** (1): 1–24

Dowling, M.J. and R.M. Valenzuela (2004), *Economic Development in Asia*, Singapore: CENGAGE Learning.

FAO (2009), Global Financial Crisis and Poverty, Media Release, Rome.

FAOSTAT (Food and Agriculture Organization Statistics) (2009), Rome: Food and Agriculture Organization.

Gaan, N. (2000), *Environment and National Security: The Case of South Asia*, Dhaka: The University Press Limited, p. 264.

Hansen, S. (1990), 'Macroeconomic policies and sustainable development in the Third World', *Journal of International Development*, **2**: 533–57.

Hansen, S. (2002), *Population Control in India: A Review*, Concord, MA: Colby College.

Hossain, M. (2008), 'The millennium development goals (MDGs): what achievements in Asia?', in *World Association for Sustainable Development (WASD) Year Book 2008*, Sussex, UK: Science Policy Research Unit (SPRU), University of Sussex.

Hossain, M. (2007a), 'Post-crisis economic performance in East Asia: recovery or sustained decline?', *World Sustainable Development Outlook 2007*, Sheffield, UK: Greenleaf Publishing, pp. 296–303.

Hossain, M. (2007b), 'Human development and poverty alleviation in South East and East Asia: a post-crisis account', in C. Tisdell (ed.), *Poverty, Poverty Alleviation and Social Disadvantage*, New Delhi: Serials Publications, pp. 750–62.

Hossain, M., R. Kathuria and I. Islam (2010), *South Asian Economic Development*, 2nd edn, London and New York: Routledge, p. 272.

Kuznets, S. (1955), 'Economic growth and income inequality', *American Economic Review*, **45** (1): 1–28.

Lang, H. and C. Hines (1993), *The New Protectionism: Protecting the Future Against Free Trade*, London: Earthscan.

Prathom Alo (2009), 'Growth of population' by Shishir Kumar, *Bangla Daily*, Dhaka.

Sebastian, I. and A. Alicbusan (1989), 'Sustainable development: issues in adjustment lending policies', Environment Department Divisional Working Papers 1989–96, Washington DC: The World Bank.

Selden, T. and D. Song (1994), 'Environmental quality and development: is there a Kuznets curve for air pollution emissions?', *Journal of Environmental Economics and Management*, **27**: 147–62.

Someshwar, S. (2008), 'Adaptation as "Climate-Smart" development', *Development*, **51**: 366–74.

The Nation (2009), '$60 million population control programme launched', *English Daily*, Karachi.

Tisdell, C. (2009), *Resource and Environmental Economics*, Singapore and New York: Worldscientific, Chapter 7.

Tisdell, C. (2005), *Economics of Environmental Conservation*, 2nd edn, Cheltenham, UK: Edward Elgar Publishing, Chapter 12.

Tisdell, C. (2003), *Ecological and Environmental Economics*, Cheltenham, UK: Edward Elgar Publishing.

Tisdell, C. (2001), 'Globalisation and sustainability: environmental Kuznets curve and the WTO', *Ecological Economics*, **39**: 185–6.

Tisdell, C. (1999), *Biodiversity, Conservation and Sustainable Development*, Cheltenham, UK: Edward Elgar Publishing.

Tisdell, C. (1997), 'The environment and sustainable development in the Asia-Pacific: views and policies', *Asia-Pacific Economic Literature*, **11** (1): 39–55.

UNDP (2007), *Human Development Report 2007–08*, New York: United Nations Development Program.

UNDP (2004), *Human Development Report*, New York: United Nations Development Program.

US Census Bureau (undated), US Census Bureau, Washington DC, http://www.census.gov/cgi-bin/ipc/idbagg.

World Bank (2007), *World Development Indicators*, Washington DC.

World Bank (2004), *World Development Indicators*, Washington DC.

2. The production of biofuels: welfare and environmental consequences for Asia

Clem Tisdell

2.1 INTRODUCTION

The use of biofuels has been supported by many environmentalists (for example, the German Green Party) as a way to reduce global warming. This chapter expresses doubts about their potential to do this and focuses on the production of liquid biofuels (primarily ethanol and biodiesel) taking into account the implications of the rapid expansion in the global production of these fuels for Asian nations. Further substantial increases in the production of biofuels (stimulated by government subsidies and economic incentives) are expected in coming decades as available supplies of mineral oil begin to decline and the long-term real price of mineral oil rises.

Economic growth in Asia, particularly in China and India, has accelerated the demand of Asian nations for oil and this trend can be expected to continue as the number of motor vehicles in Asia escalates. Asia has insufficient oil to meet its demand and is heavily reliant on imports, and its oil deficit is expected to magnify. The oil deficit situation of Asian countries varies. Japan is completely dependent on imported oil, both China and India have a high degree of reliance on imports, and even Indonesia is now a net importer of oil. Given the pivotal role of oil in providing fuel for transport purposes in modern economies, the possibility of substituting biofuels for fuels derived from mineral oils seems *on the surface* to be an attractive option for Asian countries.

There are several reasons why Asian nations might want to produce biofuels. These include:

1. To increase their economic and defence security;
2. To reduce local air pollution;
3. To make some contribution towards reducing the intensity of their

greenhouse gas (GHG) emissions. However, Yan and Lin (2009, p. S4) suggest that this is not yet a high priority for most Asian nations;

4. Asian countries may also want to ensure that they have accumulated experience and knowledge in producing biofuels before the price of mineral oil rises substantially; and

5. Some Asian nations believe that the production of biofuel feedstock will boost agricultural incomes.

Nevertheless, as discussed below, Asian countries face several constraints in increasing their production of biofuels and, for most, substantial production of biofuel by them is not an attractive economic option.

Opportunity costs are involved in producing biofuels. These are discussed generally and then the pattern of global biofuel production is outlined along with economic measures that have been adopted by governments to support it. Subsequently, attention focuses on the production of biofuels by Asian countries for their own use, their exports and imports of biofuels and of biofuel feedstock, as well as associated foreign direct investment. Some of the economic consequences for Asian countries of higher income countries expanding their production of biofuels are also considered as well as their own decisions to increase their production of biofuels. Note that 'Asian countries' in this chapter refers only to those in east and south Asia.

2.2   THE OPPORTUNITY COSTS OF PRODUCING LIQUID BIOFUELS

Neoclassical economists placed considerable stress on the importance of the concept of 'opportunity cost'. They argued that, in general, because of resource scarcity, an increase in the production of one commodity can only be obtained by forgoing the availability of some other commodity or set of other commodities. Trade-off is required and the amount of the trade-off indicates the opportunity cost of increasing the supply of the focal commodity, which, in this case, could be a biofuel or a collection of biofuels.

However, economists also recognised that the need for trade-off could be avoided as a result of productivity enhancing technological progress, by reducing allocative inefficiency or X-inefficiency, or both, if they are present. Technological progress moves the production possibility frontier to the right and a reduction in the two types of inefficiencies mentioned moves production closer to an economy's production possibility frontier.

Neoclassical economists also envisaged capital accumulation as an additional means to bring about economic growth and push the production possibility frontier to the right. However, neo-Malthusian economists argue that the process may eventually result in unsustainable economic growth because capital accumulation tends to reduce the stock of natural capital (Tisdell 1997, 2005, Ch.11, 2010a, Ch. 7). Although the feedstock for biofuels is renewable, when the whole production cycle of biofuels is considered some non-renewable resources can be expected to be used up in the process and also a major expansion in biofuel production is liable to result in biodiversity loss both as a result of agricultural intensification and extension. This is clear in the case of production of first generation biofuels. These are being produced now using agricultural feedstock such as maize, wheat and so on.

The supply of feedstock for the production of first generation biofuels is likely to be at the expense of food production and, in some cases, natural fibre production such as cotton, rubber and other cultivated crops. Ethanol and biodiesel are the two main liquid biofuels produced today. Ethanol is produced from starch and sugar from several sources, for example, maize, sugarcane or sugar beet, wheat and, less frequently, sweet sorghum. Except for the latter, these are used for human consumption and also their grains are utilised to produce feed for livestock. Biodiesel is manufactured from natural oils. The main oils used for this purpose are canola (rapeseed), soy, palm and coconut. These are all edible oils and many have additional uses, for example, palm oil is used in manufacturing margarine and many soaps.

India has plans to extract oil from jatropha (*Jatropha curcus*) to produce biodiesel. Jatropha has a high (inedible) oil content and 'can grow in arid and semi-arid regions, tropical and subtropical areas and grow even on barren and wastelands, degraded soils having low fertility and moisture but cannot stand heavy frost' (Punia 2007). It fruits after 2 years and continues to do so for 30–40 years. Punia (2007) estimates that 40 million ha of wasteland could be developed in India to grow jatropha. However, it is unclear whether these so called 'wastelands' currently perform ecological functions of economic value or have some direct use, for instance, for light grazing by livestock. If so, the opportunity cost of using them to grow jatropha may not be zero. Secondly, there is no guarantee that the growing of jatropha will be confined to wastelands in India. Depending upon the profitability of growing it, it may displace existing crops in some areas or livestock production.

Second generation biofuels are being developed which rely on the use of cellulose and lignocellulose in plants. Conversion to ethanol or biodiesel is possible, but still remains very expensive. However, the costs involved are expected to fall as scientific research progresses. Several scientists agree that the opportunity cost involved in supplying feedstock for producing second generation biofuels is likely to be eventually much lower than for first generation biofuels. Fast growing grasses, unmerchantable forests and timber and cellulosic wastes from farms, timber mills and household garbage could, in theory, be converted to these biofuels. Their advocates argue that they will have a low degree of competition with existing crops for land use and that they may reduce pollution associated with the disposal of some cellulosic wastes.

Once again, however, there is no guarantee that this feedstock will not be grown in some areas used today to produce food, fibre and other agricultural products. Lack of substitution cannot be assumed. Furthermore, a greater and more extensive use of land to provide feedstock for second generation biofuels can be expected to bring about a further reduction in biodiversity and may actually increase GHG emissions.

Questions have also been raised about the contribution of biofuels to GHG reductions. In some instances, when the whole cycle of production is considered, they may even add to GHG emissions, as in the case of the production of ethanol from maize in the United States. This is probably also the case for biodiesel production from palm oil in cases where expansion occurs by the clearing of tropical forest. In addition, there is considerable loss of biodiversity. The same may be said of the expansion of soybean production in the Amazon to produce soya oil for the manufacture of biodiesel. While it is claimed that second generation biofuels will result in a greater reduction in GHG than first generation biofuels, their overall effectiveness in that regard has been questioned, for example, by Colin Hunt (2009, Ch. 6).

Yan and Lin (2009, p. S1) observe that:

> some biofuels, especially those linked to first generation biofuels, have received considerable criticism recently – most notably the biofuel potential to increase food prices; their relatively low greenhouse gas (GHG) abatement capacity yet high marginal carbon abatement costs; their continuing need for significant government support and subsidies; their direct and indirect impacts on land use change; and related greenhouse gas emissions.

Even in the case of second generation biofuels produced from forest resources, there is debate about their likely net impact on the stock of GHG in the atmosphere. While fuel from petroleum emits more CO_2e than biofuel obtained from wood, reduced stands of wood (and similar substances) reduce their capacity to sequester carbon. Therefore, even in this case, total CO_2e in the atmosphere may rise as a result of the production of these biofuels. In any case, if economic growth continues globally (and particularly in significant Asian countries), there may be little or no reduction in the total uses of petrol and diesel in the near future as a result of the increased supply of biofuels. In fact, total GHG emissions could actually increase because the combustion of biofuels still emits GHG gases, even if these are lower than for mineral fuels. Switching to biofuel is likely to be induced eventually by increasing scarcity of mineral oil and the long-term increase in its price rather than the reputed environmental advantages of biofuels. At least, this seems likely to be so for most Asian countries.

2.3 THE PATTERN OF GLOBAL BIOFUEL PRODUCTION AND OF ECONOMIC MEASURES TO SUPPORT IT

2.3.1 The Distribution of Global Biofuel Production

In 2006, 40 billion litres of ethanol and 8.5 billion litres of biodiesel were produced globally (World Bank 2007, p. 80). The same source indicates that the United States was the largest producer of ethanol (producing 45 per cent of the world's supply), followed by Brazil (42 per cent) and the European Union (EU) (4 per cent) with other countries accounting for 12 per cent of global production. The EU produced 75 per cent of the world's biodiesel in 2006, the US 13 per cent and the rest of the world 12 per cent. We can conclude that Asia (with the exception of China) is still a relatively small player in the production of biofuels. However, its production is expanding and is expected to grow quickly. China is reputed to be the third major producer of ethanol globally accounting for 9 per cent of global supply. As discussed below, Indonesia, Malaysia, Thailand, the Philippines and India have plans to increase their biofuel production, particularly their production of biodiesel.

Currently, Malaysia and Indonesia are producing biodiesel from palm oil and also exporting palm oil. One of its uses in the EU is for the production of biodiesel. The Philippines is producing biodiesel from coconut oil. The feedstock for ethanol production in Asia varies according to geographical region. In the south, sugarcane is mostly used for this purpose, but in the north, China has been utilising corn and wheat and in southern China cassava and tubers (Tian et al. 2009). These are all crops that are also utilised for food, including food for livestock.

Note that because of climatic differences, crops that may be utilised for producing biofuels differ and are likely to continue to differ in some Asian countries from those utilised in the United States and Europe. Furthermore, given the ambitious targets of the United States and the EU for increasing their production of biofuels, there are doubts about whether their domestic supplies of feedstock are going to be sufficient for this purpose. Therefore, it is likely that they will need to increase their imports of feedstock, some of which is likely to come from Asia. Already the EU imports palm oil for this purpose, thereby contributing to environmental degradation in Southeast Asia, according to some assessments (Swarna Nantha and Tisdell 2009).

2.3.2 Measures to Support the Production of Biofuels

The rapid growth in the production of biofuels has been mainly due to subsidies, government directives and measures to ensure trade protection for the biofuel industry, particularly in higher income countries. For example, imports of ethanol are restricted in the United States and large subsidies are paid for biofuel production and to farmers who produce feedstock for biofuel production. The situation is little different in the EU. For example, price supports are provided to farmers for production of rapeseed (canola) which is widely used to produce biodiesel. Many countries mandate the supply of mixtures of biofuels with fuels derived from mineral oil, and have programmes to increase the proportion of biofuels in the available fuel blends.

Table 2.1 summarises information about production of biofuels in selected countries for 2005 and provides some remarks on the policies of these countries.

Unfortunately, Table 2.1 does not provide information for Indonesia, Japan and Thailand. Table 2.2, in the next section, provides some further information. From Table 2.2, it can be seen that several Asian countries have adopted systems of mandates and economic incentives to boost their production of biofuels.

2.3.3 Economic Arguments and Government Support for the Production of Biofuels

In several circumstances, traditional economic analysis can be used to support the payment of subsidies to industrial production. For example, Pigou (1932) argued that if an industry generates a favourable environmental externality, subsidising its production could add to economic welfare assuming that the Kaldor-Hicks (or potential Paretian improvement) criterion is adopted. Therefore, if it can be shown that the production of biofuels has a positive environmental externality, that might be used as an economic reason for a subsidy.

It is not, however, clear that the production of all biofuels generates

Table 2.1   Biofuel profiles of selected countries, 2005

Country	Production (litres)		Leading feedstocks		Blend Mandates/ goals?
	Ethanol	Biodiesel	Ethanol	Biodiesel	
United States	15B	290M	Corn	Soybeans	Yes (28.35B litres by 2012)

National energy security is a large motivator for biofuel programmes; subsidy of US$0.50 per gallon of ethanol used in fuel and a US$0.50 or US$1 a gallon subsidy for biodiesel; many subsidies at state level as well.

EU	950M	2.3B (2004)	Cereals and sugar beets	Rapeseed	Yes (2% by 2005 (not met) and 5.75% by 2010)

Policy goals: mitigate climate change, secure energy supply, advance technology and diversify agriculture; land scarcity makes blending goals difficult without imports; tax concessions for bioenergy.

Brazil	16B	?	Sugarcane	Castorbean oil, soya oil	Yes (20–25% ethanol 2% biodiesel, 5% in 2013)

World's largest ethanol producer and exporter; produces ethanol at lowest cost; well developed biofuel transportation infrastructure; biodiesel 'H-Bio' recently developed and patented by Petrobras.

Guatemala	64M	?	Molasses	Jatropha	No

Excellent sugar cultivation; investigated by EU for dumping ethanol; Brazilian investors are investing in distillers and hope to create market for flexfuel cars.

China	3.6B	?	Maize, cassava, rice	Waste cooking oil, vegetable oils	Yes (in certain provinces)

Vehicle ownership increased 600 per cent in last decade driving fuel demand and the need for alternative fuels; China's policy on biofuels will largely determine the development of biofuels on a global scale; incentive programmes for ethanol.

The Philippines	83M	?	Sugar	Coco-methyl, ester, jatropha	Yes (1% biodiesel, 5% ethanol)

Table 2.1 (continued)

Country	Production (litres)		Leading feedstocks		Blend Mandates/ goals?
	Ethanol	Biodiesel	Ethanol	Biodiesel	

Government support to biofuel investment; biofuel production geared to social goals (job creation and related political stability); forthcoming Asian private investments for ethanol processing.

| India | 1.6B | ? | Molasses | Jatropha | Yes (5% ethanol in certain states, 20% biodiesel by 2012) |

World's second largest sugar producer; sweet sorghum and tropical sugar beet investigated as feedstock alternatives to sugar; sugar market heavily regulated; meeting future blending goals predicted to require imports.

| Thailand | 300M | ? | Sugarcane, molasses, cassava | Jatropha, palm oil | Yes (10% ethanol and biodiesel by 2012) |

Government-fixed ethanol price and revenue distribution; location, natural resources and government support create potential for ethanol exports, especially to China and Japan.

| South Africa | 390M | ? | Sugarcane, sweet sorghum, maize | Soya oil (jatropha use under debate) | Yes (since 2006 voluntary blending targets) |

Government in the process of finalising a national biofuels strategy; completing a lead phase-out programme in 2007 will expand market for ethanol; government and private sector investigating new energy crops; biofuel production geared to social goals (job creation in rural areas).

Source: Extracted from UNCTAD (2006, Table 1, pp. 20–21).

(or always generates) favourable environmental externalities. In estimating externalities the whole life cycle of biofuel production needs to be assessed. Very often estimates of reduction in GHG emissions compared to use of petrol and diesel fail to take account of the whole life cycle, such as changes in land use that may come about as a result of the production of biofuels (see Righelato and Spracklen 2007; Fargione et al. 2008;

Table 2.2   Biofuels policies in selected Asian countries

Country	Targets for first generation biofuels and plans for second generation biofuels	Blending mandate.
China	Take non-grain path to biofuel development.	Ethanol: trial period of 10% blending mandates in some regions.
India	No target identified. Promotion of jatropha.	Ethanol blending; 5% in gasoline in designated states in 2008, to increase to 20% by 2017.
Indonesia	Domestic biofuel utilisation; 2% of energy mix by 2010, 3% by 2015 and 5% by 2025. Seriously considering jatropha and cassava.	Diesel: blending is not mandatory but there is a plan to increase biodiesel blend to 10% in 2010.
Japan	Plan to replace 500M litres/year of transportation petrol with liquid biofuels by 2010.	No blending mandate. Upper limits for blending are 3% for ethanol and 5% for biodiesel.
Malaysia	No target identified. Promotion of jatropha, nipa, etc.	Diesel: blending of 5% palm oil in diesel.
Philippines	No target identified. Studies and pilot projects for jatropha.	Ethanol: 5% by 2008; 10% by 2010. Diesel: 1% coconut blend by 2009
Thailand	Plan to replace 20% of vehicle fuel consumption with biofuels and natural gas by 2012. Utilisation of cassava.	Ethanol 10–20% by 2008 (Gasohol 95). Diesel: 5% (B5) mix in 2007 and 10% (B10) by 2011.

Source: Extracted from Yan and Lin (2009, Table 1, p. S3).

Searchinger et al. 2008). Especially when forest is cleared to extend the area growing feedstocks for biofuels, GHG emissions can increase. There is also a loss of biodiversity and ecosystem services. These losses may also result from intensification of agricultural biomass production to supply extra quantities of feedstock. Figure 2.1 provides a primitive depiction of life-cycle considerations in assessing the environmental impacts of biofuels.

Furthermore, it is questionable whether biofuel production ought to be subsidised. Charging for GHG emissions (if these are the main environmental externalities of concern) is an alternative policy instrument. This could, in theory, be achieved by a cap-and-trade scheme (a system

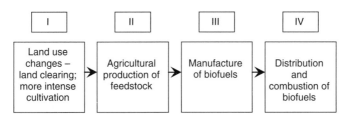

Figure 2.1   Life cycle of first generation biofuels

of tradable permits). This is a more direct approach to pollution control than Pigovian-type regulation but the practicality of such a scheme is a different matter.

On the other hand, it could be argued that biofuel production has the status of an infant industry and requires subsidies and trade protection to develop and reach a critical mass. However, infant industries often 'fail to grow up'. How much public financial support is required and for how long can be a contentious matter. The sympathy of some 'green groups' for biofuels (at least, initially) and their simple analysis of their environmental consequences, has opened the way for significant rent-seeking behaviour by those involved in the production of biofuels.

Income distribution, economic security and defence security arguments are also sometimes advanced in favour of the production of biofuels and used as reasons to provide economic support for their production. Yet as discussed later, biofuel production does not always have favourable income distribution consequences and the security arguments also need to be scrutinised carefully because they too can become a 'smoke screen' for the extraction of rents.

2.4   THE PRODUCTION OF BIOFUELS BY ASIAN NATIONS FOR THEIR OWN USE

2.4.1   Production Goals, Achievements and Incentives for Biofuel Production in Selected Asian Countries

As can be seen from Table 2.2, a significant number of Asian countries have started producing biofuels and plan to increase their production of these. Furthermore, some Asian countries, such as Vietnam, that are not as yet producing biofuels (except on an experimental basis) are expected to begin commercial production in the not too distant future (Malik et al. 2009). Except for Japan, all Asian nations producing biofuels have

Table 2.3   Economic supports for biofuel production in selected Asian countries

Country	Economic measures
China	Ethanol: incentives, subsidies and tax exemption for production. Diesel: tax exemption for biodiesel from animal fat or vegetable oil.
India	Ethanol: excise duty concession. Ethanol and diesel: set minimum support prices for purchase by marketing companies.
Indonesia	Diesel: subsidies (at the same level as fossil fuels).
Japan	Ethanol: subsidies for production and tax exemptions.
Malaysia	Diesel: plans to subsidise prices for blended diesel.
Philippines	Ethanol and diesel: tax exemptions and priority in financing.
Thailand	Ethanol: price incentives through tax exemptions

Source: Extracted from Yan and Lin (2009, Table 1, p. S3).

Table 2.4   Biofuel plants operated in China

Plant	Year built	Location	Capacity (t/year)	Feedstock
Huarun Ethanol Co. Ltd	1993	Heilongjiang	100 000	Corn
Jilin Fuel Ethanol Co. Ltd	2001	Jilin	400 000	Corn
Tianguan Fuel Ethanol Co. Ltd	2002	Henan	500 000	Wheat, tubers
Fengyuan Group	2002	Anhui	440 000	Corn
COFCO Bioenergy Co. Ltd	2005	Guangxi	200 000	Cassava

Source: Extracted from Tian et al. (2009, Table 2, p. S79).

mandated minimum targets for blending biofuels with other fuels and they either have subsidies or plan to introduce subsidies for biofuel production (see Table 2.3).

Let us consider the situation of these countries in turn as far as the production of biofuels is concerned. So far China has focussed mainly on the production of ethanol and has mostly used corn for this purpose. Some wheat and tubers (for example, sweet potato) and cassava are the basis of production in a few areas. China is the third largest producer of ethanol globally (Malik et al. 2009, p. S61). As can be seen from Table 2.4, the use of feedstock in China is influenced by the geographical region in which the production of biofuels occurs.

Currently, all the feedstock used by China for ethanol production

Table 2.5   Crops suggested to provide feedstock

Region	Suitable energy crops
North-east	Sweet sorghum
North China	Sweet sorghum, sweet potato
Loess plateau	Sweet sorghum
Inner Mongolia and Xingiang	Sugar beet, sweet sorghum
Middle and lower Yangtze	Sweet potato
South China	Cassava
South-west	Sweet potato

Source: Extracted from Tian et al. (2009, Table 4, p. S80).

consists of food items but possibly of inferior quality for eating. However, even inferior grains such as cassava can be used for feeding livestock. It is interesting that China intends, in the future, to discontinue its reliance on grains for producing biofuel. Presumably, this is intended to maintain its degree of self-sufficiency in grains. Alternative sources of feedstock that are under investigation are listed in Table 2.5, along with the regions suitable for their production (Tian et al. 2009). However, these are all agricultural crops and will compete for land use with other agricultural crops or livestock production, especially the latter. Tian et al. (2009) appear to assume that extra feedstocks for biofuel will be supplied by extending the area of cultivated land. The environmental impact of this needs investigation. Li (2007) points out that China is also considering non-food feedstock for its production of biofuels but is aware that this could involve opportunity.

India has been slower than China in developing the production of biofuels and has mainly relied on molasses (derived from sugarcane) to produce ethanol. This year (2010), however, it is short of sugar and is importing sugar. It appears to be placing its future hopes on the growing of jatropha as a feedstock for its biofuel.

Indonesia is producing ethanol from cassava and sugarcane and biodiesel from oil palm and jatropha (Kussuryani 2007). The Indonesian Government has, according to Kussuryani (2007), adopted a fast-track programme to create villages that are self sufficient in their supply of energy and promote the regional development of biofuel production. In addition, it is establishing special biofuel zones (areas of concentration in biofuel production) in which it provides the land and infrastructure for investors at no cost to them.

Little information is available for biofuel production in Japan, presumably because biofuel production in Japan is insignificant. However, it is reported to be considering the production of some biofuel from biomass (see Table 2.2). Japan is also reported to be investing in biofuel plants in Indonesia, possibly with an eye to importing some of this production to Japan.

Production of biofuels in Malaysia is focussed mainly on the supply of biodiesel using palm oil as feedstock. In 2007, four biodiesel plants were operating in Malaysia, another four were about to come on line and licenses for many more plants have been issued (Wahid et al. 2007). Until recently, all of Malaysia's biodiesel was exported to the EU and the United States, but now blending mandates have stimulated the use of biodiesel in Malaysia. Jatropha and nipa palm are also being promoted as feedstocks in Malaysia.

Thailand is producing biofuels from diverse feedstock. Feedstocks include sugarcane, molasses, cassava and oil palm. Thailand is a major producer of cassava.

The Philippines is using sugarcane, coconut oil and jatropha to produce biofuels and is providing economic incentives for investment in the refining of biofuels.

Of all the Asian countries, Thailand appears to have the most ambitious programme for making use of biofuels. Its target is to supply 20 per cent of its vehicle fuel from biofuels and natural gas by 2012 and to achieve a blend of 10–20 per cent ethanol in petrol. It also envisages the possibility of exporting biofuels, mainly to China and Japan.

2.4.2   An Assessment of Biofuel Production Possibilities in Asia

Asia faces several constraints in increasing the amount of its biofuel production and these constraints vary by country and by regions within each country. Furthermore, Asia spreads over a vast diverse geographical area. This implies, amongst other things, that the feedstocks likely to be used for producing biofuel in Asia are likely to be diverse and to vary by country and region.

Furthermore, the area of land available for expanding biofuel feedstock production in Asia without reducing food supplies, lowering output of natural fibres, decreasing production from trees and affecting livestock production is limited in many Asian countries such as China, India and Japan. Trade-offs are likely to be unavoidable.

Some scientists believe that wastelands can be utilised to grow biofuel feedstock. Wastelands may, however, have some use for livestock and/or provide environmental services. Unfortunately, use of the term 'wastelands' gives a biased perspective on their use. Similarly, the clearing of forests to grow biofuel feedstock can involve significant environmental costs and the cleared land may have opportunity costs in terms of lost timber and paper production or the growing of alternative crops. It is also argued by their proponents that second generation biofuels will be able to utilise biomass wastes from garbage and farms. Possibly, this could reduce some pollutants. However, organic farm waste may be better used by adding it to soils to create humus. Soil degradation may accelerate if increased amounts of organic matter are removed from agricultural land and the fertility of the soil could decline.

The production of some crops for supplying feedstock for biofuels requires significant water use, for example, in growing sugarcane and sugar beet. Production of ethanol is very water intensive. Malik et al. (2009) point out that up to 4 l of water are needed to produce 1 l of ethanol. Water is already in very short supply in parts of Asia. This will constrain possibilities for producing biofuels.

In order to make significant inroads into the use (and projected use) of petrol and diesel, Asian countries would need to allocate a very large area to the growing of feedstock for biofuels. In the absence of spectacular yield increases, this is likely to add to increasing food prices and disadvantage poor consumers. It is probably unrealistic to believe that Asia will be able to supply a large proportion of its liquid fuel by producing biofuels. It is possible that as the scarcity of mineral oil increases, Asian nations will become more reliant on natural gas as a source of energy for transport and other uses. This may explain why China and India have recently made agreements to purchase massive quantities of natural gas from Australia (Lewis 2009). Although this does not seem to be a high priority for most Asian nations, there is mounting scientific evidence that land conversion to provide feedstock for biofuels actually adds, in many cases, to GHG emissions when the whole life cycle of their production is taken into account (Righelato and Spracklen 2007; Fargione et al. 2008; Searchinger et al. 2008).

2.4.3 Exports and Imports of Biofuels and their Feedstock by Asian Countries and Foreign Investment in the Biofuel Industry

Given the emerging and dynamic nature of the development of biofuel production, only limited information is available on exports, imports and foreign investment in the biofuel industry. Malaysia is exporting biodiesel to the EU and the US and it exports palm oil to the EU, where one of its uses is to produce biodiesel. Indonesia is also an exporter of palm oil, some of which is used to produce biodiesel in Europe. There has also been foreign investment in oil palm plantations in Malaysia and Indonesia.

Thailand believes that it is likely to be able to export biofuel to China and Japan. I do not have information on the extent to which there has been foreign investment in the development of the Thai biofuel industry. Malik et al. (2009, p. S62) report that:

> The Thai government is looking at new oil palm plantings as well as growing other energy crops such as *jatropha* to increase supply of feedstock for biodiesel processing. The latter could be initially imported from neighbouring countries like Myanmar (their target is to plant close to 3 million ha of jatropha) and perhaps sourced from Lao PDR and/or Cambodia.

China, India and Japan are all potential importers of biofuels. However, their imports are likely to be influenced by the comparative prices of biofuels and their substitutes. Nevertheless, they may decide to import some biofuels as a diversification strategy and in order to increase their energy security.

There is a strong possibility that China may invest in biofuel production offshore, especially production of second generation biofuels. It already, for example, has large forest plantations in Brazil. This would reduce pressure on its own land areas and it may be able to use some biomass wastes from its Brazilian operations. Given China's large foreign reserves and its resource requirements, foreign investment to secure its resource needs is likely to be given high priority as it continues to develop. China's demand for imports of energy and natural resource impacts are expected to accelerate (Tisdell 2010a).

2.5   ECONOMIC CONSEQUENCES FOR ASIAN COUNTRIES OF INCREASED PRODUCTION OF BIOFUELS BY HIGH-INCOME COUNTRIES AND VICE VERSA

2.5.1   Impacts of Increased Biofuel Production by Higher Income Countries

Expansion of biofuel production in higher income countries has significant economic implications for most Asian countries. This is particularly so for expansion in production of ethanol (which has been largely based on corn) by the United States. Production of biodiesel based on soy oil also has economic impacts on Asia.

Asia is a significant export market for corn and soybeans much of which is used for livestock production, for example, in the rearing of pigs. A spike occurred in grain prices in 2008 prior to the deepening of the global recession. A significant proportion of this increased price has been attributed to US subsidies to support ethanol production using corn. The longer term consequences of this have been highlighted by Searchinger et al. (2008) and concerns have been expressed in publications such as *Lancet*

(Boddinger 2007) about the negative consequences of ethanol production for food supplies.

In practice, it is very difficult to determine exactly the impacts on food prices (for example, grain prices) of increased production of biofuel in higher income countries using agriculturally produced feedstock. This is because several factors can simultaneously influence changes in prices, and their separate impacts are difficult to disentangle empirically. For example, the spike in grain prices in early 2008 (including in Asia) was partly due to the significant expansion in US production of ethanol from corn, the high price of mineral oil and speculation about future food availability and oil prices. The situation was worsened because several food surplus nations restricted their food exports as a result of their growing concerns about food security. Furthermore, several food deficit countries began 'panic' buying of grains. Brahmbhatt and Christiaensen (2008, pp. 3–4) argue that the rise in international grain prices in the period 2004 to early 2008 can be attributed to 'global factors [which] include rising energy costs, the falling dollar and – most importantly – policies that have induced a sharp increase in biofuel demand for grains, although the impact on rice is more indirect'. They point out that World Bank studies covering the period 2004 to early 2008 indicate that rising energy and fertiliser prices contributed 35 per cent of the rise in world food prices *but* increased biofuel demand was the *largest* contributor to increased world grain prices. This was mainly because the United States diverted increasing amounts of its corn output to the production of ethanol. Brahmbhatt and Christiaensen (2008, p. 5) observe that:

> almost all the increase in global maize production from 2004 to 2007 (a period when grain prices rose sharply) went for bio-fuels production in the U.S. while existing stocks were depleted by an increase in global consumption for other uses. Land use changes due to increased use of maize and oilseeds for biofuels led to reduced plantings of wheat, the subsequent depletion of world wheat stocks to record lows, and a surge in wheat prices.

They then state that the rise in wheat prices was reflected in higher rice prices 'because wheat and rice are substitutes in consumption and imports'.

If this scenario is correct (as it appears to be), then consumers (especially those on lower incomes) were adversely affected by the expansion of biofuel production in the United States. Although with the onset of the global recession in 2008 and falling prices for mineral oil, grain prices have declined, the long-term consequence of increased production of liquid biofuels is likely to be to keep grain prices (and the prices of other commodities that are land-based) higher than they otherwise would be. Consequently, poorer consumers (including those in Asia) are likely to suffer reduced welfare if biofuel production expands rapidly.

The consensus within the World Bank appears to be that production of biofuels tends to push up food prices. The World Bank (2007, p. 70) reported:

> spurred by subsidies and the Renewable Fuel Standard issued in 2005, the US has diverted more maize to ethanol. Because it is the world's largest maize exporter, biofuel expansion in the US has contributed to a decline in grain stocks to a low level and has put upward pressure on world cereal prices. Largely because of biodiesel production, similar price increases have occurred for vegetable oils (palm, soybean and rapeseed).

While Sexton et al. (2009) do not deny that biofuel production in higher income countries has put upward pressure on food prices, they appear to be hoping for a 'technological fix' to the problem. They argue that 'biotechnology and transgenic crops can be powerful drivers of productivity growth, but it demands increased investment and reduced regulation. We argue that biotechnology is essential to reduce land-use changes associated with biofuel demand that not only reduce biodiversity but also release GHGs into the atmosphere' (Sexton et al. 2009, p. 130).

However, one should be wary of their argument. Certainly, advances in biotechnology do not guarantee a reduction in biodiversity loss or a reduction in GHG added to the atmosphere as a result of biofuel production.

Advances in genetic engineering could easily lead to intensification of the culture of feedstock for biofuels and the extension of the utilisation of land for providing feedstock thereby adding to biodiversity loss and increasing GHG emissions. Furthermore, the ecological fitness of many genetically modified organisms may not be sustained in the long term and consequently, sustainability issues can arise (Tisdell 2010b). In the long term, genetically modified organisms may reduce biodiversity. Although mankind has made tremendous scientific and technological progress, biodiversity continues to decline at an alarming rate, mainly due to human economic activity. Given this record, it is not apparent that further technological progress will prove to be a 'silver bullet'. Although technological progress often has the potential to alleviate environmental problems, demands for ever continuing economic growth tends to negate its environmental benefits.

2.5.2   Asian Economic Welfare Losses as Predicted by Neoclassical Microeconomic Theory

Traditional microeconomic theory indicates that Asian nations importing grain (or vegetable oil or oil seeds) are likely to suffer a net economic welfare loss as a result of the expansion of biofuel production in higher

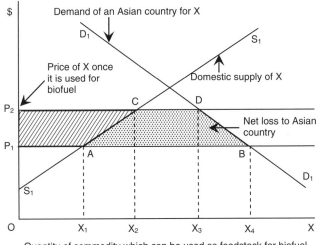

Figure 2.2   Net welfare loss from biofuel production

income countries. This is illustrated by Figure 2.2 for an Asian country
which is a net importer of feedstock used in higher income countries to
produce biofuel. Note that it is assumed in this analysis that Asian nations
are not concerned about any environmental changes that may come about
as a result of alterations in the structure of global markets for biofuels. For
example, they are supposed to disregard the environmental consequences
of changes in their land use (such as increased clearing of forests to grow
crops) that could occur as a result of increased demand for biofuels in
higher income countries. In addition, issues involving income distribution
are ignored in this traditional analysis which relies on the Kaldor-Hicks
(potential Paretian improvement) criterion as the basis of assessment of
changes in economic welfare.

In Figure 2.2, D_1D_1 represents the demand for the Asian country for a
commodity which it utilises for food but which is also used as feedstock
for biofuel in a developed country and S_1S_1 represents its domestic supply
of that commodity, X. In the absence of biofuel production in developed
countries, the import price of the commodity, X, is assumed to be P_1 but
once biofuel production takes off in higher income countries (such as the
United States), the export price of X rises to P_2. As a result, imports of X
by the Asian country fall from X_4–X_1 to X_3–X_2. Its domestic production
of X rises from X_1 to X_2 and its domestic consumption of X declines from
X_4 to X_3.

As a result of the rise in the price of commodity X due to its use in

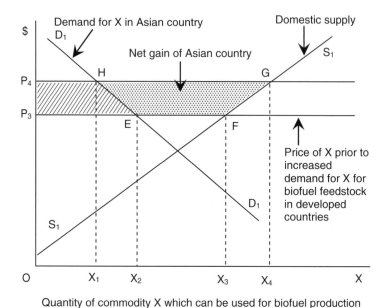

Figure 2.3   Net welfare gain from exports of raw materials to produce biofuel

developed nations to produce biofuel, the surplus of buyers of X in the Asian importing country falls by the area of the hatched quadrilateral plus the dotted quadrilateral. On the other hand, the surplus of domestic suppliers of X rises by the hatched area. Consequently, the net loss to the Asian economy is equivalent to the area of the dotted quadrilateral. Vietnam, for example, is an importer of maize from the United States and also imports soybean, much of which is used for its livestock production. Note also that farmers in the relevant Asian country may both intensify and extend their production of X once its import price rises thereby adding to GHG emissions and biodiversity loss.

On the other hand, Asian countries exporting commodities which are used for biofuel production are likely to experience a net economic welfare gain if demand for their feedstock increases in higher income countries. For example, an expansion in the demand for palm oil in higher income countries is likely to bring economic benefits for Malaysia and Indonesia. Using microeconomic analysis, the economic consequences for them is illustrated by Figure 2.3. The focal Asian nation is assumed to be an exporter of X which can be used as feedstock to produce biofuel. As before, the demand for X in the focal Asian commodity is indicated by line D_1D_1 and its domestic supply is shown by line S_1S_1. Prior to a hike in demand for X in higher income countries to produce biofuel, the Asian exporting country is assumed to obtain a price of P_3 for its exports of X, but after demand escalates due to increased foreign demand for X for biofuel production, the price of X rises to P_4. The Asian country's exports of X rise from X_3–X_2 to X_4–X_1, its consumption of X falls from X_2 to X_1 and its production of X rises from X_3 to X_4.

In the case illustrated in Figure 2.3, the Asian country has a net economic gain as a result of an increase in the export price of X. The surplus of its producers of X rises by the area of hatched quadrilateral plus the dotted one. The surplus of its domestic consumers of X falls by the area of the hatched quadrilateral. Therefore, the net economic benefit obtained by this Asian country increases by an amount equivalent to the dotted area shown in Figure 2.3, if the Kaldor-Hicks criterion is adopted. Despite this, its increase in production of X is likely to be obtained as a result of both intensification and extension of the area of land allocated to X. This could result in increased GHG emissions and greater biodiversity loss. This is an issue of concern in relation to increased palm oil production in countries such as Malaysia and Indonesia.

2.5.3   Impacts of Increased Biofuel Production by Asian Countries

If Asian countries mandate the increased consumption of biofuel and subsidise its production, this is likely to distort the allocation of their resources. If cropland is used for this purpose, the prices of crops can be expected to rise and if grazing land is used for this purpose the prices of some livestock products are likely to increase. In the short run, there is a misallocation of resources and reduced net economic welfare. Consumers have a reduced surplus but producers are likely to see their economic surplus increase. Traditional economic analysis indicates that the economic loss to consumers can be expected to outweigh the gain to producers. It is also likely that the environmental impacts of such a policy will be negative. However, if the biofuel industry proves to be an infant industry that will 'grow up' in a reasonable period of time, that could give some economic support to this policy. In the case of Thailand, expansion in its biofuel production may reduce its food exports. Currently, Thailand is a net exporter of food and animal feedstock (Malik et al. 2009, p. S62). This policy is likely to have negative economic consequences for countries that currently buy food and animal feedstocks from Thailand.

Once again, note that traditional microeconomic analysis relying on the Kaldor-Hicks principle (potential Paretian improvement principle) ignores the income distributional consequences of policies. Biofuel development could well be detrimental to the economic interests of the poor, even poor farmers. This needs further investigation.

2.6 FURTHER DISCUSSION AND CONCLUSION

There is little prospect of liquid biofuels replacing current levels of consumption of petrol and diesel (let alone projected levels of use of these substances) without causing severe economic distress. The amount of land that would be required for such substitution would be so large that it would greatly reduce food supplies and other economic uses of the land. For example, Rajagopal and Zilberman (2007) found that just offsetting 10 per cent of the oil imports of the United States and the EU by biofuels would require 30–70 per cent of their cropland to be allocated to the production of feedstock for biofuel. Hence, offsetting their total oil imports would require at least the use of 4 to 7 times the area of their present cropland to supply biofuels. Such an area is unlikely to be available.

Similarly, the World Bank (2007, p. 71) notes the projection that 30 per cent of the US maize harvest is likely to be used to produce ethanol by 2015, but that this will supply less than 5 per cent of United States gasoline consumption. This implies that if all maize production in the United States were allocated to the production of ethanol, it would only account for around 15 per cent of the gasoline requirements of the US in 2015.

From the above, it can be concluded that the economic cost in terms of food and other land-based commodities forgone, as well as the environmental costs of meeting a high proportion of the world's consumption of gasoline and diesel from biofuels, is likely to be very high, even prohibitive. There is also no reason to believe that the costs to Asian countries of substantially increasing their reliance on liquid biofuels will be low and expansion of production of feedstock for biofuels and biofuels themselves in many Asian countries (especially those in southeast Asia) is likely to be achieved at a high environmental cost in terms of lost biodiversity and increased GHG emissions.

It should also not be forgotten that even when the use of biofuels has lower intensity of GHG emissions compared to the use of fossil fuels, their use still adds GHG to the atmosphere. Many natural scientists seem to believe (naively) that if biofuels became available with lower intensity of GHG emissions than fossil fuels, this will lower aggregate GHG emissions. However, economic considerations indicate that this may not happen. It all depends on the rate at which biofuels will be substituted for fossil fuels. It is too simplistic to believe there will be one-for-one (perfect) substitution.

For example, suppose that the GHG emissions from use of a unit of biofuel are half those from a unit of fossil fuel and that both enable an equivalent performance. The latter is a generous assumption since the distance one can travel on a litre of ethanol is slightly lower than that for a litre of gasoline. It follows that if for every extra 2 l of biofuel used there is a reduction of 1 l in the use of fossil fuel, the level of GHG emissions remains constant. GHG emissions actually rise if the reduction in the use of fossil fuels is less than a litre for every extra unit of biofuel used. There are many circumstances in which the estimated reduction in GHG emissions for biofuels compared to the use of fossil fuels is less than 50 per cent. In such cases, a greater rate of substitution of biofuels for fossil fuels would be needed to lower GHG emissions.

Given the above, there is a possibility that the introduction of biofuels will add to GHG emissions rather than reduce these. Firstly, there may be insufficient substitution of biofuels for fossil fuels in cases where the latter has a lower GHG intensity resulting in a rise in aggregate GHG emissions. The new technology merely adds to total consumption of fuels. Secondly, natural scientists have shown that processes for producing several types of biofuels add to GHG accumulation in the atmosphere when the whole life cycle of their production is considered.

In addition, some less expensive options to the use of biofuels are likely to be available for Asian nations for many years to come, For example, Australia has extremely large natural gas reserves, especially if gas associated with underground coal seams is included. Furthermore, greater use of electric vehicles and hybrid vehicles can extend options. However, in the long run, as most neo-Malthusians believe, our best hope for coping with increased resource scarcity and growing environmental damages from economic production is to reduce excessive consumption by the richer members of society and limit population growth. China has done the latter, but few, if any, nations seem prepared to follow the former path.

REFERENCES

Boddinger, D. (2007), 'Boosting biofuel crops could threaten food security', *Lancet*, **370**: 923–4.
Brahmbhatt, M. and L. Christiaensen (2008), *Rising Food Prices in East Asia: Challenges and Policy Options*, Washington DC: World Bank.
Fargione, J., J. Hill, D. Tilman, S Polasky and P. Hawthorne (2008), 'Land clearing and the biofuel carbon debt', *Science*, **319**: 1235–8.
Hunt, C. (2009), *Carbon Sinks and Climate Change: Forests in the Fight Against Global Warming*, Cheltenham, UK and Northampton, MA, USA: Edward Elgar Publishing.

Kussuryani, Y. (2007), 'Biofuel development in Indonesia', paper presented at *USDA Global Conference on Agricultural Biofuels: Research and Economics*, http://www.ars.usda.gov/meetings/Biofuel2007/files/Intl%20Perspectives%20B-Revised.doc accessed 19 August, 2009.

Lewis, S. (2009), 'Chinese sign off on $50B gas deal', *The Courier Mail*, 19 August, p. 28.

Li, S.-Z (2007), 'Non-food feedstock and the road map of China's bioethanol industry', paper presented at *USDA Global Conference on Agricultural Biofuels: Research and Economics*, http://www.ars.usda.gov/meetings/Biofuel2007/files/Intl%20Perspectives%20B-Revised.doc, accessed 19 August 2009.

Malik, U.S., M. Ahmed, M.A. Sombillon and S.L. Cueno (2009), 'Biofuels production for smallholder producers in the Greater Mekong Sub-region', *Applied Energy*, **86**: S58–S68.

Pigou, A.C. (1932), *The Economics of Welfare*, 4th edn, London: Macmillan.

Punia, M.S. (2007), 'Current status of research and development on jatropha (Jatropha curcus)', paper presented at *USDA Global Conference on Agricultural Biofuels: Research and Economics*, http://www.ars.usda.gov/meetings/Biofuel2007/files/Intl%20Perspectives%20B-Revised.doc, accessed 19 August 2009.

Rajagopal, D. and D. Zilberman (2007), 'Review of environmental and policy aspects of biofuels', World Bank Policy Research Working Paper, No. 4341, Washington DC: World Bank.

Righelato, R., and D.V. Spracklen (2007), 'Carbon mitigation by biofuels or by saving and restoring forests?', *Science*, **317**: 902.

Searchinger, T., R. Heimlich, R.A. Houghton, F. Dong, A. Elobeid, J. Fabissa, S. Tokgoz, D. Hayes and T.-H. Yu (2008), 'Use of U.S. croplands for biofuels increases greenhouse gases through emissions from land-use change', *Science*, **319**: 1238–40.

Sexton, S., D. Zilberman, D. Rajagopal and G. Hochman (2009), 'The role of biotechnology in a sustainable biofuel future', *AgBioForum*, **12**: 130–40.

Swarna Nantha, H. and C. Tisdell (2009), 'The orangutan–oil palm conflict: economic constraints and opportunities for conservation', *Biodiversity Conservation*, **18**: 487–502.

Tian, Y., L. Zhao, H. Meng, L. Sun and J. Yan (2009), 'Estimation of un-used land potential for biofuels development in China', *Applied Energy*, **86**: S71–S85.

Tisdell, C. (1997), 'Capital/natural resource substitution: the debate of Georgescu-Roegen (through Daly) with Solow/Stiglitz', *Ecological Economics*, **22** (3): 289–91. Reprinted in C. Tisdell (2003), *Ecological and Environmental Issues*, Cheltenham, UK and Northampton, MA, USA: Edward Elgar Publishing.

Tisdell, C. (2005), *Economics of Environmental Conservation*, 2nd edn, Cheltenham, UK and Northampton, MA, USA: Edward Elgar Publishing.

Tisdell, C.A. (2010a), *Resource and Environmental Economics: Modern Issues and Applications*, Singapore: World Scientific.

Tisdell, C.A. (2010b), 'The precautionary principle revisited: its interpretations and their conservation consequences', *Singapore Economic Review*, **55** (02), 335–52.

UNCTAD (2006), 'The emerging biofuel market: regulating trade and development implications', UNCTAD/DITC/TED/2006/4, New York and Geneva: United Nations.

Wahid, M.B., Y.M. Chao and W.S. Lim (2007), 'Technological progress and commercialisation of biodiesel in Malaysia', paper presented at *USDA Global Conference on Agricultural Biofuels: Resource and Economics*, http://www.ars. usda.gov/meetings/Biofuel2007/files/Intl%20Perspectives%20B-Revised.doc, accessed 19 August, 2009.

World Bank. (2007), *World Development Report 2008: Agriculture for Development*, Washington DC: The World Bank.

Yan, J. and T. Lin (2009), 'Biofuels in Asia', *Applied Energy*, **86**: S1–S10.

3. Climate change and freshwater resources of Bangladesh

Qazi Kholiquzzaman Ahmad

3.1 INTRODUCTION

This chapter is concerned with freshwater resources of Bangladesh in the context of climate change. Water is so crucial for human life and living that slogans such as 'water for life', 'water for food' and 'water for ecosystem' have been coined. Even without climate change, the water sector is beset with problems as a result of ever increasing demand, constraints on the availability of quality water and complexities in water sharing and use within and across countries. In the wake of climate change, these problems are magnifying and other problems, such as shifting and changing patterns of rainfall and increasing rainfall deficits in dry areas, are emerging. In view of all these, water management and governance issues are crucially important.

3.2 CLIMATE CHANGE: IMPACT AND VULNERABILITY

3.2.1 Climate Change

Global warming caused by huge quantities of greenhouse gas (GHG) emissions, particularly over the past 150 years or so, has brought the global society face to face with an unprecedented threat in terms of intensifying global climate change. Natural climatic variability is usually small and one may not be much concerned about that. Anthropogenic climate change (that is, due to concentration of GHGs in the atmosphere emitted by human activities) is likely to be so devastating in the coming years and decades that it poses the greatest threat to the humankind as well as to planet Earth. The ramifications have already begun to be serious and will further worsen in future, in terms of, for example, ice melt, sea-level rise and erratic and shifting precipitation. Thus, extreme weather events are increasing both in frequency and intensity around the world, which include floods, river erosion, cyclones, storm surges, salinity ingress, hurricanes, tornadoes, prolonged and ever more serious drought in dry regions and moisture loss as a consequence of lower rainfall and increasing heat.

3.2.2 Responsibility and Vulnerability

It is now recognised that developed countries have been mainly responsible for GHG emissions over a long period of time leading to global warming and climate change. But developing countries are also now emitting increasing amounts of GHGs, particularly the larger and faster growing developing countries. At the same time, the developed countries continue with their old ways in relation to life styles and consumption, emitting increasing amounts of GHGs. Since developed countries have brought the world to where it is today in relation to climate change, they have the primary responsibility to act fast to reverse the process. Of course, developing countries should be mindful that they play their appropriate roles in combating the intensifying climate change.

It is also recognised that poor developing countries, particularly those countries whose geographical locations are climatically difficult suffer the most as a consequence of climate change. For example, Bangladesh is arguably one of the most vulnerable countries, given its geographical reality, socioeconomic conditions and the size of population. Other highly vulnerable countries include small island countries and countries with vulnerable long coastal belts and/or large drought-prone areas.

3.2.3 Climate Change Management

Broadly speaking, responses are two pronged: mitigation and adaptation. Both are crucial. Mitigation process must be started seriously without further loss of time by drastically reducing global GHG emissions, and the main responsibility here lies with developed countries. In the Copenhagen Summit in December 2009, it was agreed by the participating countries that drastic reduction in GHG emissions is absolutely necessary in order to combat climate change. If the required action is not taken soon, the situation may become irreversible in 40 or 60 years. By then, emission control may not be of much avail given the vastness of the quantity of GHGs already in the atmosphere; and even the cost may not be bearable. Now countries, both developed and developing, are making their own proposals in pursuance of the agreement reached in Copenhagen, which will form the basis of negotiations leading to the next COP (Conference of the Parties) meeting in Cancun, Mexico, scheduled for November 2010, where a binding agreement is expected and one would like to see that happen in the interest of the peoples of the world. The question would still remain of the implementation of the agreed responsibilities. But first, of course, a binding agreement must be reached by the countries concerned.

As to the least developed countries (LDCs), they emit small quantities of GHGs and they are not obliged to reduce emissions. For example, Bangladesh emits only about 0.30 t per capita per annum compared with about 2 t in India, 4 t in China, 6–12 t in European countries, about 20 t in the United States and over 20 t in Australia. However, the LDCs may voluntarily follow a low carbon path with support in terms of transfer of finances and technologies not only for mitigation but also for adaptation from the international community as provided for in the Copenhagen Accord. In so doing, they obviously need to keep their urgent need for economic growth and poverty reduction in perspective. Obviously, it is adaptation on which a least developing country needs to focus, while insisting that the developed countries quickly reduce their GHG emissions.

3.3   CLIMATE CHANGE AND BANGLADESH

As pointed out earlier, Bangladesh is at the forefront of adverse climate change impact. This is mainly because the country already suffers from multiple stresses which will be further accentuated by climate change impacts. These stresses include:

- Disadvantageous geographical location and climatic reality;
- A deltaic country with long coastal belt and low-lying areas inland, with mighty rivers criss-crossing the country and large-scale river bank erosion as a consequence of strong flooding;
- Very high density of population;
- High levels and widespread poverty;
- Policy and institutional weaknesses;
- Low human capability development: a high illiteracy level, quality deficit at all levels of education and poor healthcare systems;
- A lack of effective local governance;
- Shortages of resources; and
- A lack of technological advancement.

Superimposed on these major stresses faced by Bangladesh, climate change is a huge threat to the country's economy and society. As land, water and other natural resources will become scarcer as climate change intensifies and the population continues to grow, there may be social tensions and conflicts over access to natural resources. Although reliable estimates are not available, it can be stated with very high confidence that consequent upon rising sea level caused by global warming, huge areas of land in the coastal areas of the country will be permanently inundated, the extent depending on the level of global warming and sea level rise. Also, as sea level rises, salinity ingress, which is already a major problem, will push further and further inside the country posing a severe risk to both natural and human systems.

The country is already experiencing ever more extreme weather events more frequently, which are certainly related to climate change. For example, the precipitation regime has been exhibiting erratic and shifting patterns in recent years. In 2008, Bangladesh suffered from drastically reduced rainfall during the rainy season (June–August). Also, the country was devastated by two floods and a severe cyclone in 2007 and another devastating cyclone in 2009. During the major floods, water and vector-borne diseases (malaria, diarrhoea, skin diseases) broke out widely.

Biodiversity, which is already threatened, will become even more vulnerable as climate change intensifies. As a result, environmental risks will increase and crop, fishery, forestry and livestock production and productivity will face further risks in addition to those imposed by changing water conditions and water availability and quality. With loss of agricultural lands to the extent of about 1 per cent per annum due to other uses, the prospective permanent inundation of a substantial proportion of agricultural land as well as salinity ingress on one hand and declines in agricultural productivity due to changing weather, water and physical conditions caused by climate change while the population is increasing, imply that, in the coming decades, Bangladesh will face severe food insecurity unless appropriate and timely adaptive measures are taken effectively.

3.4   CLIMATIC AND NON-CLIMATIC DRIVERS OF FRESHWATER RESOURCES

It is now known that the impacts of climate change fall heavily on the water sector. Both quantity and quality of freshwater resources are adversely affected in a major way by climate change. The climatic drivers include precipitation, temperature and evaporatic demand. As a result of climate change, temperature is increasing, sea level is rising and glacier melt is increasing. Precipitation is also shifting and its pattern changing. Sea-level rise is causing salinisation of increasing areas, affecting both groundwater and estuaries, thereby causing decreases in freshwater availability. Semi-arid and arid areas are particularly exposed to impacts of climate change in relation to fresh water ecosystems, human health and water system reliability, which are adversely affected by various forms of water pollution exacerbated by higher temperatures, increased precipitation intensity and longer periods of low flows. The functions and operation of existing water infrastructures are also affected by climate change impacts (IPCC 2007).

However, it is recognised that there are uncertainties associated with these conclusions. But, the uncertainties relate to intensity and pattern, not to the direction. There are some beneficial impacts in terms of increased run-off in certain areas but, overall, the negative impacts far outweigh the possible positive benefits. There are also non-climatic drivers which influence the quantity and quality of water resources. These include population, economic activity, land use and land cover.

Water management is indeed a key factor in relation to both climatic and non-climatic drivers that affect freshwater resources. Issues in management include development and use of water, water pollution vis-à-vis water quality improvement, desalinisation, reservoir construction and dismantling, waste water treatment, irrigation, groundwater abstraction and flood and drought management. It may be noted that both natural and human systems are suffering from shifting and changing precipitation patterns due to climate change. In particular, agriculture (crops, fisheries, livestock, forestry) face major upheavals. Inland navigation also faces problems.

3.5   ASPECTS OF BANGLADESH'S WATER REGIME

On an annual basis, Bangladesh has an abundance of water on a per capita per annum basis, although it is declining as population is increasing. Still by 2025, the availability will still be 7670 million m^3 (see Table 3.1).

But, this conceals the fact that, water becomes very scarce in the lean season, particularly during March–April, assuming crisis proportions in a large part of the country. Due to large-scale groundwater abstractions and

Table 3.1   Population growth and annual per capita water availability

Year	Population (mill.)	Per capita water availability (annual) m^3
1991	111	12 162
2000	131	10 305
2010	150	9 000
2020	170	7 941
2025	176	7 670

Source: Ahmad et al. (2001, p. 50).

inadequate replenishment, irrigation and household water shortages pose serious problems in the Barind area and other dry parts of the country. Consequent upon arsenic contamination of groundwater accessed through tubewells, which was the principal source of household water supply across the country, access to clean water for household purposes, including for drinking, has emerged as a serious problem in different parts of the country. In urban centres, particularly in Dhaka, clean drinking water availability is a major challenge as a result of ever increasing population, declining groundwater availability and pollution of river water. Southwest Bangladesh faces severe freshwater shortages and increasing salinisation during lean season, given low flows through the Ganges and little or no diversion of water from the Ganges to southwest Bangladesh through the Gorai in the absence of an intervention (barrage) in the Ganges to facilitate flow of water to that region. The whole coastal belt is affected by salinity ingress through tidal flows from the Bay of Bengal.

The water regime of Bangladesh comprises tributaries and distributaries of three major river systems: the Ganges, the Brahmaputra and the Meghna; and numerous perennial and seasonal wetlands such as haors, baors and beels. In fact, Bangladesh is criss-crossed by 230 rivers, of which 57 are transboundary – 54 coming from India and 3 from Myanmar (Figure 3.1 shows the major rivers of Bangladesh and Figure 3.2 shows the transboundary rivers). The discharges peak in July–August and are the lowest in April–May in the three river systems. In fact, the average flow of the Brahmaputra reaches some 20 times and that of the Ganges up to 30 times the respective dry season flows. In the Meghna, the range is also high.

A serious complication arises because water is a transboundary resource, given common rivers and shared lakes and other water bodies. Water tends to be politicised by co-riparians. It is usually the case that upper riparians abstract unduly, having more water during the lean period, leaving the lower riparians with lower and lower flows, particularly the lowest riparian is most disadvantaged with extremely limited water flows. On the other hand, it has to drain most of the waters generated in the common river basins during the rainy reason. For example, Bangladesh drains 92 per cent of the total water generated in the Ganges–Brahmaputra–Meghna (GBM) basins annually. During the lean season (1 January–31 May), Bangladesh suffers from scarcity of water due to low flows through the transboundary rivers due to large upstream abstractions. So, Bangladesh's water regime is characterised by too much water during the rainy season and too little during the lean season.

A huge quantity of up to 1.8 billion metric tonnes of sedimentation is carried from upstream through the common rivers on to Bangladesh

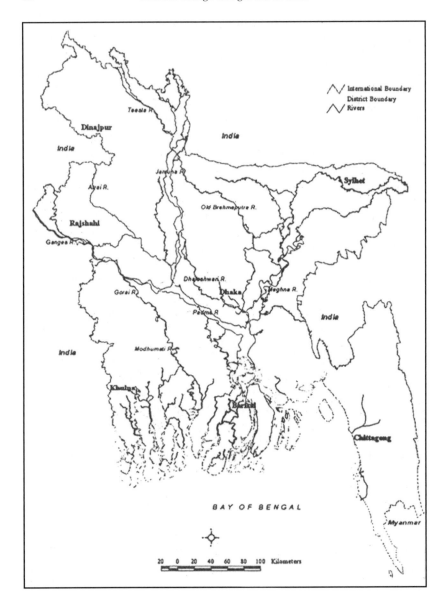

Source: Ahmed et al. (2001, p. 36).

Figure 3.1   Major rivers of Bangladesh

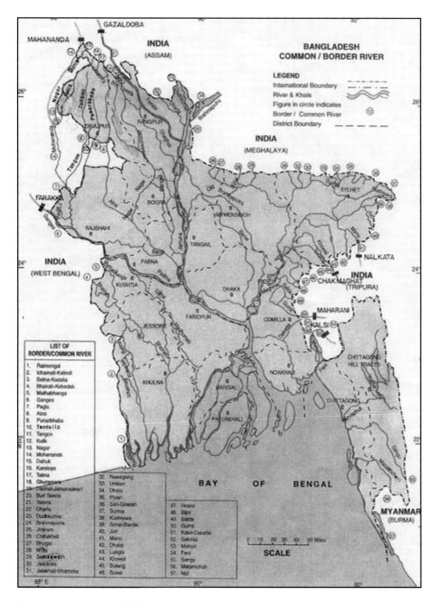

Source: Ahmed et al. (2001).

Figure 3.2 Transboundary rivers involving Bangladesh

annually. Part of it goes down to the Bay of Bengal, but part remains in the rivers and canals, raising the river and canal beds. As a result, floods occur at a level of water flow lower than it should otherwise be if the river beds were not silted up. Fisheries are affected as a result of habitat loss, partly because of sedimentation, but partly also because of low precipitation, encroachment on the river and river water pollution.

3.6 WATER GOVERNANCE

Proper and efficient water governance is required both nationally and regionally. Also, both supply and demand issues must be addressed.

A country's water governance needs to recognise spatially differing realities within the country due to differing precipitation patterns and access to rivers and other water bodies such as lakes and wetlands. The approach needs to be multi-layered because what happens in the local space depends on policies adopted and actions implemented by central governments directly or acting through other levels of governance, including local government. The actions include water development and distribution, flood management, drought management, information flows, resource mobilisation and timeliness and appropriateness of actions undertaken. The issue of water development and distribution has become contentious even within a country, given that demand for water is increasing as a result of population growth and expansion of economic activity. But useable water availability is declining as a result of increasing water pollution and not enough attention being given to water development.

Harvesting of rainwater in, for example, ponds in rural areas with measures in place for purifying the pond water and through rooftop facilities in urban areas, may substantially enhance availability of freshwater. Rainwater harvesting was, in fact, practised thousand of years ago in parts of the Middle East as well as of the Indo–Pak–Bangladesh subcontinent. It is now enjoying a resurgence in different parts of the world, including in India (Water Harvesting in India). Regarding management of demand for water, optimal utilisation and conservation of water and needs-based water distribution are crucial elements. Awareness building among the water users is crucially important in this regard. Joint water management by water institutions and water users within the framework of a policy of optimal utilisation of water, ensuring equitable access of all, has the potential of generating the best possible water-use pattern and structure. With climate change altering the water regime realities, functioning of the systems at all levels and in all contexts needs to be appropriately adjusted in relation to both policies and actions.

3.6.1 National

Bangladesh faces issues in water governance in relation to local realities which vary from one part of the country to another. With approaches to governance working through various levels of the government, appropriate vertical coordination between various levels of interventions and horizontal coordination between the agencies of the government and other actors are of paramount importance.

As the contexts are changing as a result of climate change, it is essential to undertake appropriate research activities to determine what needs to be done in which part of the country. The required funds need to be mobilised from own resources and from the international community and utilised properly. Given that developed countries are responsible for climate change, Bangladesh has the right to receive additional (to usual official development assistance) finances and technologies to address climate change impacts, including in the water sector. One particular issue may be elaborated in more detail, this is flood management. Floods occur every year in Bangladesh inundating 22–30 per cent of the country's land area, but people have learnt to live with these floods. Flash floods occur suddenly and cause substantial damages and losses. Rainwater flooding occurs in places where heavy in-country rainfall occurs. River flooding is caused largely by heavy rainfall upstream. When all three river systems (the Ganges, the Brahmaputra and the Meghna) rise together, the flood may cover up to two-thirds or more of the country, as was the case with the 1998 flood. Major floods also occur in response to a combination of two together or one system rising. Climate change threatens to accentuate floods of all types, both in terms of frequency and impacts. Effective flood management calls for regional cooperation in flood forecasting and learning from one another, national policies and activities and community approaches as the affected people themselves can do a lot better still, if their capacity is enhanced through information, training, and enabling them to work together (BUP 2004).

Bangladesh adopted a National Water Policy in 1999 (Ministry of Water Resources 1999), which covers all aspects of water management, except one major issue. There is no clause requiring attention to water management under climate change. The policy must be revised to recognise climate change as a crucial issue in water management. The policy has rightly provided for participatory water management implying that water users have an important role to play. To guide the process for both water management institutions and water users to play their appropriate roles, Guidelines for People's Participation in Water Development Projects were adopted in 1995. But, the implementation of the policy and the guidelines remain in large deficit. A broad-based National Water Management Plan was also adopted in 2004 (Ministry of Water Resources 2004) focussing on year round water management, social and environmental conservation, full participation of stakeholders, including water users, in the planning and implementation processes. But, the projects identified have not yet been prioritised.

The coastal belt of Bangladesh is 710 km long along the Bay of Bengal. It accounts for about a third of the country's geographical area and over one-quarter of the country's total population. Lives and livelihoods of the coastal people are affected by such natural hazards as soil erosion, water logging, soil and water salinity and various forms of pollution. The area is prone to cyclones, storm surges and floods, which are likely to be more frequent and devastating in future as a consequence of intensifying climate change. However, Bangladesh has adopted an integrated coastal zone management approach. A Coastal Zone Policy (Ministry of Water Resources 2005) and a Coastal Zone Strategy (Ministry of Water Resources 2006) have already been adopted by the government, based on an integrated socioeconomic–political–environmental approach. In respect of the water sector, it has several proposals including salinity control, enhancement of minor irrigation networks by constructing small reservoirs, appropriate water management with the polders, rainwater harvesting, water conservation, excavation of ponds and tanks for storage, local technologies for water treatment and sustainable use and management of groundwater. However, implementation has been neglected.

In July 2009, the Government of Bangladesh adopted the Bangladesh Climate Change Strategy and Action Plan (BCCSAP). The strategy focuses on adaptation and an integrated approach to socioeconomic development and climate change management. The BCCSAP considers water management, including drainage of rivers and river training. In order to manage the water sector and utilise the available financial resources for the sector as effectively as possible, it is essential to prioritise the identified actions and keep the implementation process under regular review as climate change introduces new dimensions and complications. Also, the implications of changes in non-climatic drivers of freshwater resources must be kept in view and addressed as appropriate.

Rainwater harvesting is yet to be adopted purposefully in Bangladesh. As it has been found to be a useful way of enhancing access to freshwater in different countries, including India, Bangladesh may initiate activities in collecting rainwater in ponds by promoting cooperative groups in rural areas and requiring that urban houses include rooftop rainwater harvesting facilities.

3.6.2   GBM Regional

Since Bangladesh's location is at the bottom of the three mighty river systems, namely, the Ganges, the Brahmaputra and the Meghna, the country is extremely vulnerable to both floods (during the rainy season) and scarcity of water (during the lean season). Regional issues of water management are, therefore, crucially important for Bangladesh.

The GBM river systems constitute the second largest hydraulic region in the world. Bangladesh and India share all three river systems, China shares the Brahmaputra and the Ganges, Nepal only the Ganges and Bhutan only the Brahmaputra. The total drainage area of the GBM basins is about 1.75 million sq. km across five countries: Bangladesh (7 per cent), Bhutan (3 per cent), China (18 per cent), India (64 per cent) and Nepal (8 per cent). This can be seen from Figure 3.3. It should also be noted that the three basins constitute only about 0.12 per cent of the world's total land mass, but are home to about 10 per cent of the world's population and over 40 per cent of the poor of the developing world (Ahmad et al. 1994).

The whole GBM region is characterised by too much water during the rainy reason and scarcity of water during the lean season. Bangladesh, being the lowest riparian, is the most badly affected on both counts. Moreover, the seasonal pattern of rainfall and, hence, water runoff is also changing due to climate change. Water management both within each country as well as in the regional context is becoming increasingly complex because of climate change impacts.

Many studies have pointed out that the overall abundance of water in the GBM region can, as a shared source, serve as the principal agent of development for people living in the co-riparians of the GBM basins (Ahmad et al. 2001 and 1994; Crow 1995). It will be a more effective way of addressing the complexities arising from climate change if the co-riparians work together, pooling resources and expertise, with a view to optimising mutual benefits. This can be best done within the context of total river basin management. It is now widely recognised that a transboundary river is best managed basin-wide for the best possible development of its water resources for equitable benefits of all co-riparians, each gaining more than is possible under narrow national approaches. If properly appreciated, the prospective net benefits of cooperation, that may be derived as suggested by different studies, being greater than the benefits under the ongoing non-cooperation mode, should be a powerful incentive for the regional countries to opt for cooperative management of transboundary rivers.

The benefits that can be derived from cooperative basin-wide management of transboundary rivers would include those: *from the river* (for example, increased food and energy production); *because of the river* (for

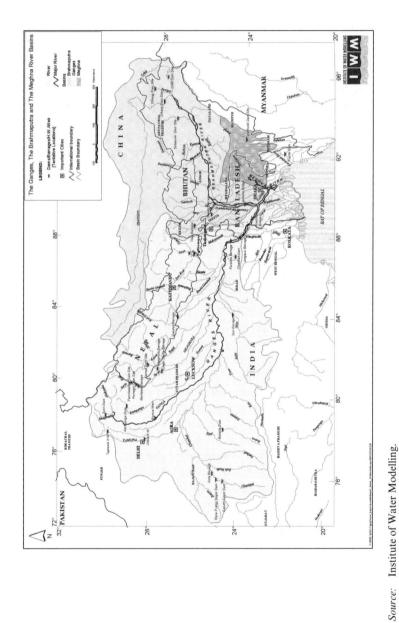

Source: Institute of Water Modelling.

Figure 3.3   The Ganges, the Brahmaputra and the Meghna River Basins

example, reduced geo-political tensions, enhanced flood management); *beyond the river* (for example, catalysing wider cooperation and economic integration); and *to the river* (for example, improved water quality, conserved biodiversity). While river waters are to be utilised for economic, social, transportation and household purposes, it is important that the river remains healthy so that it can be a perpetual source of benefits.

It is internationally recognised (that is, Helsinki Rules, UN Convention) in the case of a transboundary river that each riparian has the right to an equitable share of its waters. This is also recognised in the 1996 30-year Ganges Treaty between India and Bangladesh (Article 9 of the Treaty states: 'Guided by the principles of equity, fairness and no harm to either party, both the Governments agree to conclude water sharing Treaty/ Agreements with regard to other common rivers'). Yet, the development and utilisation of the GBM region's water and other natural resources have never been sought in an integrated manner by the GBM regional countries due to past differences, legacies of mistrust and goodwill deficits. But, the cost of non-cooperation is huge. The poor people of the region suffer the worst as a result. In the interest of the peoples of the region, the regional countries must, therefore, shun the old and persisting narrow mindset and join hands to come to terms with the geo-physical realities and embark upon a cooperative, integrated, holistic approach to the development of the region, beginning with water sources.

In relation to a forward move in forging GBM regional water-based cooperation, first of all, it is required that the GBM regional countries must agree to embark upon a path of flourishing cooperation in the water sector as well as in other potential areas. Once this agreement is reached, it will be necessary to work together to develop the most appropriate and equitable basin-wide management of the river systems to seek mutually beneficial goals, including:

- Improved management of floods;
- Optimal solutions to water scarcity and water quality problems;
- The best regional approaches to augment water flows in the Ganges system in the dry season;
- Improved irrigation opportunities for the riparians; and
- Hydroelectricity generation, particularly in Nepal and Bhutan, and its cross-border trading.

It is necessary to have a dedicated organization to take the decisions made by the governments of the co-riparians forward. Joint and expert committees have worked over the years, but, follow-through of the recommendations made has been lukewarm or absent. In order, therefore, to manage the forward move properly, a GBM Regional River Basin Authority should be created. But, a major thrust in regional water-based cooperation is unlikely to happen if bureaucrats and experts are left to their own devices. It calls for strong political will and a forward-looking decision at the highest political level by governments of the co-riparians on the basis of full appreciation of the compelling reasons in favour of cooperation, some of which, including mutual benefits to be derived, have been mentioned earlier in this chapter.

3.7   CONCLUDING REMARKS

Bangladesh faces the curse of climate change impacts, although this country has no responsibility in causing climate change. The impacts fall heavily on the water sector and through it to both natural and human systems. Special attention needs to be given to the management of the water sector under climate change. Given the geographical location of Bangladesh, the country is highly vulnerable in relation to both flooding (in the rainy season) and scarcity of water (in the lean season). Both are accentuated in the wake of climate change.

Bangladesh, therefore, has to streamline and implement water governance policies and strategies with respect to national issues, but regional cooperation in water management is also crucially important for the country, and, indeed, for other co-riparians as well. This chapter has highlighted aspects of the realities faced, policy directions and action plans in place, and how the way forward may be strengthened in addressing the prevailing and emerging issues.

REFERENCES

Ahmad, Q.K., A.K. Biswas, R. Rangachari and M.M. Sainju (2001), *Ganges–Brahmaputra–Meghna Region: A Framework for Sustainable Development,* Dhaka: The University Press Ltd.

Ahmad, Q.K., B.G. Verghese, Iyer R. Ramaswamy, B.B. Pradhan, and S.K. Malla (1994), *Converting Water into Wealth: Regional Cooperation in Harnessing the Eastern Himalayan Rivers,* Dhaka: Academic Publishers.

Bangladesh Unnayan Parishad (BUP), 'Synthesis of Manuals on Community Flood Management in Bangladesh, India, and Nepal', in *Asia Pacific Journal on Environment and Development* (APJED), Vol. 11, No. 1 and 2, Dhaka, June 2004.

Conference of the Parties (2009), 'Copenhagen Accord 2009', Fifteenth Session, Copenhagen, 7–18 December.

Crow, Ben (1995), *Sharing the Ganges,* The University Press Ltd, Dhaka.

IPCC (2007), 'Climate Change 2007: impacts, adaptation and vulnerability', *Forth Assessment Report*, Geneva: Working Group II, IPCC.
Ministry of Water Resources, Government of Bangladesh (1999), *National Water Policy 1999*, Dhaka.
Ministry of Water Resources, Government of Bangladesh (2004), *National Water Management Plan 2004*, Dhaka.
Ministry of Water Resources, Government of Bangladesh (2005), *Coastal Zone Policy 2005*, Dhaka: Water Resources Planning Organization (WARPO).
Ministry of Water Resources, Government of Bangladesh (2006), *Integrated Coastal Zone Management (ICZM) Strategy 2006*, Dhaka: Water Resources Planning Organization (WARPO).
'Water Harvesting in India' website: http://www.rain-barrel.net/rainwater-harvesting-india.html.

4. Analyses of livelihoods in the Bay of Bengal delta

Moazzem Hossain, A.H.M. Ali and Eliyathamby Selvanathan

4.1 INTRODUCTION

According to the World Bank, South Asia's poorest of the poor are most at risk due to the intensity of global warming in recent times. In particular, almost 30–40 million people of the coastal belt of the Bay of Bengal will suffer from inundation by 2030 (World Bank 2008). Stern (2007) is of the view that even a moderate rise in temperature could cause serious changes to the environment in South Asia. Stern led the 'Stern Report on the Economics of Climate Change' commissioned by the UK Treasury and released in October 2006. Moreover, according to Oxford University climatologist Mark New, over the past 30 years snow cover and ice cover may have been reduced by 30 per cent in the eastern Himalayas. There is now a real risk that these glaciers might disappear altogether in the coming decades. If this happens, Bangladesh's mighty rivers originating in the eastern parts of the Himalayas would be affected severely. Chapter 3 comprehensively analysed the freshwater issues of Bangladesh in the era of climate change.

The onslaught of global warming induced extreme weather conditions on the Bay of Bengal delta has been studied by various authors in the past. However, major studies had been conducted in this area with international participation based on Bangladesh-wide data. Among these, the following observations are of importance here: Bangladesh will receive heavier rainfall during the monsoon because the rate of evaporation is expected to increase by up to 12 per cent. Mean monthly rainfall may significantly change over current variability. Monsoon rainfall may increase by 11 per cent by 2030 and 27 per cent by 2070. Due to global warming, over the past 100 years temperature has increased by 0.5°C, but in the next 50 years, that is, by 2050, the temperature in Bangladesh is projected to rise by 1.5 to 2°C (Ahmed 2006; Islam and Neelim 2010).

A number of studies have found that high temperature would reduce the yields of high-yielding varieties (HYV) of rice over all seasons throughout Bangladesh. A recent study revealed that a 60 per cent moisture stress on top of other effects might cause as much as 32 per cent decline in Boro (winter) rice yield. A quarter of the country's landmass is currently flood prone in a normal hydrological year, which may increase to 39 per cent, and prolonged flooding can effectively reduce overall potential for HYV Aman (summer) rice production. Global warming would make tropical cyclones and tornadoes in Bangladesh more frequent. The frequency of recent cyclones, Sidr in November 2007, Aila in 2009 and Nargis in southern Myanmar in 2008 have drawn worldwide attention to the destruction they caused for lives and properties in recent years (SMRC 2007; Cline 2009).

It has been, thus, recognised by the multilateral donors of Bangladesh that out of its 150 million people more than 30 million are likely to be affected directly by global warming in the next 30 years (World Bank 2008). In this chapter, therefore, our major aim is to investigate the extreme weather conditions experienced in recent years and their impacts on the livelihoods of the millions of inhabitants of the Bay of Bengal delta. Before attempting this, let us review a few global and regional studies that have been carried out in recent years.

4.2 EARLIER STUDIES

It is now widely recognised that the coastal regions of both the developed and developing world would suffer heavily, both in economic and social terms, from frequent natural hazards due to the direct impact of extreme weather conditions and rising sea level. It has been noticed that in recent years sea-level rise, frequent storms and cyclones and erosion have taken a serious turn in coastal regions all over the world. The threats from rising sea level and other climatic hazards are now genuine whether the people live in the small island nations of the South Pacific or Bay of Bengal delta (IPCC 2007). It is important to investigate the impact of recent climatic hazards on the livelihoods of coastal people. Presently, there are three major methods available to measure socioeconomic vulnerability from climate change and from other catastrophes. These are: economic, environmental and institutional methods (see Jha et al. 2009 for economic method; Barnett et al. 2008 for environmental approach; and Sarker et al. 2009 for institutional method).

The Bay of Bengal delta is known to be one of the vulnerable regions of South Asia. This region is also identified as the most vulnerable region on earth due to climate change by the Copenhagen Accord, 2009. Bangladesh and West Bengal (India) are located at the confluence of the Ganges, Brahmaputra and Meghna (GBM) river systems which collect water from the Himalayas and north-eastern hills of India. The Ganges runs in a catchment area of 1 087 000 sq. km, Brahmaputra has 552 000 sq. km and Meghna 82 000 sq. km (Islam and Neelim 2010). Metcalfe (2003) states that, 'the Bangladesh landscape is a flat to gently undulating delta flood plain with a network of river systems. More than half of the delta plains are at elevation of less than 10 m' (p. 301). The southern coastal region forms part of the largest mangrove forest complex called *Shundorbon* (listed as a World Heritage Area). This mangrove forest is bordered by West Bengal in the west and Bangladesh in the east. Natural resources of this region include abundant summer freshwater, alluvial land, sweet water and sea fisheries, forests and wildlife. The huge and rapidly expanding population of this region places immense pressure on the natural resources and on the environment alike (see Chapter 1).

The sea level along the Bay of Bengal coastline is currently rising by 3 mm per year. Catastrophic rainy monsoons, which previously occurred in only every half a century, on average, are now occurring every 10 years or even more frequently (Palmer and Raisanen 2002). Increasing devastation from cyclones has also increased with rising sea level, which has impacted on the availability of coastal resources (World Bank 2000). Most recently back-to-back category 5/4 cyclones (Sidr 2007 and Aila 2009) brought a huge loss of lives and properties to this region (Rahman et al. 2009).

The Dhaka-based South Asian Association of Regional Cooperation (SAARC) Meteorological Research Centre (SMRC) has been working on extreme weather issues over the last few decades and investigates rainfall, temperature and sea-level rise along the Bay of Bengal coast. The rainfall data over 1961 and 1989 show, among the three threshold of precipitation days per year (heavy precipitation days, 10 mm, very heavy precipitation days, 20 mm and extremely heavy precipitation days, 50 mm), there is an increasing trend with the advancement of years for all three thresholds (SMRC 2008). Another SMRC study covering rainfall data until 1999 shows that in Bangladesh, monthly maximum 1-day precipitation has been declining, whereas 5-day precipitation has been increasing, which suggests there were more frequent wetter days in recent decades (SMRC 2009). Investigations on temperature suggest that the maximum daily maximum temperature did not increase between 1961 and 1989. However, a study found that there is a sign of warming in Bangladesh: the minimum temperature had been rising at a faster rate, even though the maximum temperature remained almost unchanged (SMRC 2008). Rising sea level in and around the coastal belt of the Bay of Bengal also remains a major threat to the livelihoods of millions of people of this delta. A study on Bangladesh suggests that the sea-level rise at the Bay of Bengal delta is likely to be in the range of 30 to 100 cm by 2100 (see more in Chapter 6).

4.3 EXTREME CLIMATIC CONDITIONS AND THE BAY OF BENGAL DELTA

While the SMRC and other studies in the past have made clear that the Bay of Bengal delta is certainly experiencing frequent extreme weather conditions, there was hardly any attempt made in the past to analyse the socioeconomic and political consequences. In the remaining parts of this chapter, these will be investigated by taking three major aspects of extreme climatic conditions: rainfall, temperature and cyclonic storms, including sea-level rise.

4.3.1 Rainfall

As mentioned earlier, the Bay of Bengal delta is not a stranger to extreme weather conditions, in terms of high precipitation, variable temperature and frequent sea water surges together with sea-level rise. The GBM combined rainfall catchment area is over 12 times larger than the size of Bangladesh and all the rain water flushes through the Bay of Bengal delta (Islam and Neelim 2010). Table 4.1 presents rainfall data for various coastal districts in recent years (over 2003, 2006 and 2008).

Four coastal weather stations have been chosen to investigate the climatic variations. Cox's Bazar is located on the south eastern point

Table 4.1   Rainfall in selected coastal regions in millimetres, 2003–08

Location	2003	2006			2008		
	Annual	Annual	Winter	Summer	Annual	Winter	Summer
Cox's Bazar	4113	3430	0	616	3543	7	775
Hatiya	3664	2519	25	703	3546	28	816
Bhola	1819	2142	0	345	1993	13	425
Khepupara	1758	3400	0	440	3010	25	603

Note: Winter months are December, January and February; summer months are June, July and August.

Source: Islam and Neelim (2010).

of the Bay. Hatiya is one of the island stations in the Bay. Bhoal is also an island station located almost 50 km north (close to mainland) of the coast. Khepupara is located right on the coast. Over the last 5 years (until 2008), the annual rainfall data show that, while two centres captured increased precipitation, this has declined in the rest. The summer season carries the bulk of the precipitation. The rainfall in the summer (June, July and August) was one-quarter of the total at Cox's Bazar and Hatiya. This was only one-fifth at Bhoal and Khepupara in 2008. The summer rain increased at all the weather stations between 2006 and 2008. This increase was 23 per cent for Cox's Bazar, 16 per cent for Hatiya, 23 per cent for Bhola and 37 per cent for Khepupara (estimated from Table 4.1).

These variations of rainfall in the coastal belt of the Bay of Bengal were not isolated cases, if one considers average annual rainfall all over Bangladesh. Historically, it is well established that since the nation is located north of the Bay of Bengal/Indian Ocean and south of the great Himalayan Mountains, geographically the nation is vulnerable to rainfall variations. According to Mirza (2002) about 80 per cent of the total rainfall occurs during the monsoon period, in the months of June, July, August and September. It has been estimated by the above author that the average annual rainfall of the country varies from 1200 mm in the west to 5000 mm in the east.

4.3.2   Temperature

Recently, Islam and Neelim (2010) comprehensively studied the temperature and warming issues in Bangladesh and examined their economy-wide consequences. While this study was comprehensive and covers the entire nation, the coastal temperature variations over time were also investigated with care. The study maintains that, over the last 60 years, the annual average temperature increased by almost 1°C. However, it is not the annual averages which matter most, it is the seasonal variation of temperature that is most important. In this respect, Islam and Neelim (2010) suggest that in the winter the minimum reading has been increasing at an alarming rate. There was a big jump in the minimum temperature over the last few decades compared to the maximum readings, which was experienced in almost all weather stations in the winter (Table 4.2).

While the nationwide readings showed that minimum temperature has been increasing and the gap between minimum and maximum has been shrinking over the last decade, it is clear that the number of hotter days over time will become more frequent. Let us look at this phenomenon from the data taken from the four weather stations on the Bay of Bengal delta.

Table 4.2   Nationwide annual mean temperature in Celsius, 1950–2008

Seasons	1950	1960	1970	1980	1990	2000	2005	2007	2008
Bangladesh									
Annual (Jan–Dec)	25.1	25.3	25.1	25.3	25.7	26.4	26.3	26.4	25.9
Winter (Nov–Feb)	20.0	21.0	21.0	21.5	21.8	22.6	21.6	22.3	21.3
Summer (Mar–May)	27.5	28.4	26.3	27.5	26.5	28.5	27.5	28.0	27.5
Monsoon (Jun–Oct)	28.1	28.3	28.0	27.9	28.3	28.4	28.3	28.9	28.5

Source: Islam and Neelim (2010).

Table 4.3   Average maximum and minimum temperature in Celsius, new readings

Bay of Bengal delta	Maximum		Minimum	
	Summer	Winter	Summer	Winter
Cox's Bazar	34.5 (31.15)	31.3 (26.7)	26.3 (24.5)	17.9 (13.4)
Hatiya	33.4 (28.15)	27.5 (26.0)	23.0 (21.4)	13.9 (12.4)
Bhola	34.3 (32.06)	27.0 (24.0)	20.5 (19.2)	16.0 (13.3)
Khepupara	33.3 (31.14)	27.2 (25.0)	26.0 (25.4)	14.5 (13.0)

Note: Figures in parentheses show base readings taken from the range of last 30–60 year averages.

Source: Islam and Neelim (2010).

Among these stations, summer maximum temperature has been recorded in Cox's Bazar at 34.5°C. Minimum high summer temperature was also recorded in Cox's Bazar (Table 4.3).A similar pattern has emerged for the winter for all other stations.

It appears that the variations between the maximum and the minimum summer temperature, taking the base year's temperature into consideration, has been increasing in the coastal region as well. This is also the case in the winter months. Thus, one can conclude, without reservation, that in the coastal region not only were there more and more warmer days in recent years, both in summer and winter, the days are becoming even hotter. These outcomes have major implications for agriculture, fisheries and tropical diseases (see Section 4.4).

In summary, on the one hand, in seasonal and annual mean temperature terms, a trend of 1°C rise between 1948 between 2007 has been established. On the other, over the time frame between 1980 and 2007, the annual temperature rise has more than doubled (2.14°C).

Table 4.4   Frequency of major cyclonic storms, 1960–2009

Years	Frequency	Range of wind speed (kph)	Nature of Storm
1960–1970	11	160–224	Cyclonic storm
1971–1980	1	163	Cyclonic storm
1981–1990	6	93–160	Cyclonic storm
1991–2000	9	60–278	Hurricane
2001–2009	7	65–223	Hurricane

Source: BBS (2008).

4.3.3   Cyclonic Storms and Sea-level Rise

The Bay of Bengal is known as the world's largest delta both in length and population size. The delta is more than 700 km long and more than 40 million people live within 100 km of the coast. The livelihood in this vast wet region has been based for centuries on agriculture, fisheries and small-scale tourism particularly in the south east corner (Cox's Bazar) and near Sundarbon in the south west. Although the environment and the climatic conditions have been very hostile in the region, the population density has been growing, compared to any other deltaic regions. Cyclonic storms, hurricanes and formation of depressions are regular occurrences in this part of the world.

Table 4.4 presents a picture of the occurrence of natural disasters between 1960 and 2009. On average, over the last 50 years, at least one cyclonic storm or a storm with hurricane intensity hit the coast of the Bay of Bengal every 1.5 years. Over the last five decades, the frequency of cyclonic storms has been very high, except between 1971 and 1980. The highest frequency was observed between 1960 and 1970 and the second highest was between 1991 and 2000. Due to the frequency and strength of storms and sea water surges more than half a million lives were lost between 1960 and 1970. In the 1980s, about 100 000 people perished due to the cyclonic storms. The damage was unprecedented both in terms of loss of lives and property in the 1960s and 1970s, since the disaster manage-ment capacity and the early warning devices then were almost absent. In the post-1990s, the nation has been establishing, with international assist-ance, cyclone shelters on the coast and early warning systems have been put in place making use of radio and TV networks and local volunteer corps. These have kept the loss of lives within tolerable limits; however, the damage to properties, businesses and crops have been greater in recent times, since the population has grown at an alarming rate, more than doubling during the last 30 years.

Most recently rare back-to-back cyclones hit the coastal belt in 2007 and 2009. Both were rated as category 5 cyclones, namely Sidr and Aila respectively. Sidr claimed more than 3000 lives, 9 million people were affected in 25 districts out of Bangladesh's 64, 750 000 acres of crops were destroyed and 175 000 acres were partially damaged. On top of these, livestock, fisheries and wildlife were the major casualties of simultaneous tidal surges (BBS 2008).

The debate on sea-level rise in recent years has been directed towards long-term prediction to 2100. The Intergovernmental Panel on Climate Change (IPCC) and Bangladesh-sponsored studies, in recent years, have found that the Bay of Bengal delta is too vulnerable to the sea-level rise due to ice melt in the Arctic and Antarctic, and melting of glaciers in Greenland and the Himalayas. For South Asia, SAARC Meteorological Research Centre (SMRC) began looking at this phenomenon in 2002 and the IPCC's Fourth Assessment paper examined this issue in 2007 (SMRC 2002; IPCC 2007). The SMRC (2002), concluded that the sea-level rise along the Indian coast in and around Visakhapatnam (south-west coast of the Bay of Bengal), has been increasing by 0.9 mm per year between 1937 and 1991. The variations in sea-level rise between seasons appear to be higher on the Bay of Bengal coast than any other coasts of South Asia. It appears that this region has been experiencing minimal rise in sea level in the post-monsoon period. According to the IPCC (2007), however, a 10 cm rise is expected by 2030. This would be sufficient to inundate 2500 sq. km which is about 2 per cent of the total land of Bangladesh along the 700 km long coastal belt. The IPCC's long term prediction on the sea-level rise along the Bay of Bengal coast suggests three scenarios: rising up to 1 m, up to 2 m and up to 5 m by 2100. With a minimum 1 m rise in mind, it is expected that all the districts located within 50–60 km of the coastal belt and most of the offshore islands on the Bay would be inundated, making 30–40 million people homeless by 2100.

The IPCC's prediction has been countered by a Bangladesh-based study and claims that the IPCC failed to consider the role of sedimentation in its prediction for sea-level rise (CEGIS 2010). This study concludes that even if sea levels rise by a maximum 1 m in line with the IPCC's 2007 predictions, most of Bangladesh's coastline will remain intact. This is due to the fact that the coastline of Bangladesh would rise with sediments originating and carried all the way from the Himalayas in the monsoon, which would ultimately raise the sea bed at least at a same rate of sea-level rise (CEGIS 2010). The sediment rise would mean that the relative sea level would be unchanged, particularly in the Bay of Bengal delta, the study claims. While the IPCC welcomes this observation it, however, warns that this body of scientific evidence was formed out of only a single study. Further studies are needed to make such a claim credible. In the future, the IPCC is expected to carry out further studies on the rate of sedimentation on the bed of the Bay of Bengal delta (Alam 2010).

4.4 LIVELIHOODS UNDER EXTREME WEATHER CONDITIONS

The global warming-induced extreme weather conditions discussed above would have major consequences for the livelihoods of the millions in the Bay of Bengal delta. While livelihood in the literature generally covers the economic issues, coastal populations endure adverse social and environmental conditions, which are also important. Thus, the rest of this chapter is concerned with the socioeconomic and political consequences of the extreme weather conditions along the Bangladesh part of the Bay of Bengal delta. Since the income of the inhabitants is predominantly based on agriculture and fisheries, let us investigate the food grain and fish production issues first.

4.4.1 Food Grain Production

Cropping contributes more than 80 per cent of value adding in agriculture in Bangladesh. Moreover, rice and wheat account for more than three-quarters of value adding in cropping. Therefore, the increase in food grains production is the major source of agricultural growth in Bangladesh (see trends for the last three decades in Figure 4.1). The southern parts of Bangladesh located on the mouth of the Bay of Bengal have contributed almost a quarter of this growth over the last three decades.

Figure 4.1 shows the food grain production in Bangladesh during the period 1980/81 to 2006/07. As can be seen, the production increases at a steady rate throughout the sample period, except for some variation during the mid 1990s. This indicates that the food grain production can be modelled using a linear trend model. The estimated linear model for the given data is:

Food grains production = 0.8907 Time + 14.419 $R^2 = 0.8438$

The high R^2 value indicates a good fit. This model can be used for forecasting food grain production.

The food grain production trends presented in Figure 4.1 certainly suggest that Bangladesh, as a whole, was successful in doubling production over the last quarter of a century keeping growth rate at, or even

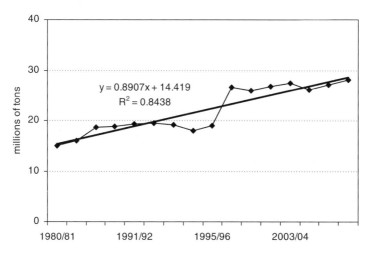

Figure 4.1   Food grain production Bangladesh, 1980/81–2006/07

exceeding, the rate of growth of population. This achievement was possible for at least three main reasons: adding additional land under irrigation, bringing additional land under cereal production and by increasing the rate of fertiliser use. For example, estimates of these factors of production between 1992 and 2003 suggest that irrigated land had increased by 20.5 per cent, land under cereal cultivation increased by 5 per cent and fertiliser use increased by 53 per cent (Hossain et al. 2010).

All these achievements are likely to be threatened by the extreme weather conditions in the years and decades to come. For example, a study by the SMRC (2007) examined the impact on rain-fed rice yield, locally known as *Aman* (summer) rice, due to the variation of temperature and rainfall in recent years. This study used Bangladesh-wide data for the period 1971–99. The study found that there was a significant negative correlation between monthly maximum temperature and rice yield during the months of September, October and November. The month of October was found to have the highest negative correlation with a correlation coefficient of –0.65. This means that the yield declined substantially with an increase in temperature. The rainfall data showed a negative (–0.48) correlation in August. This suggests that the excess rainfall in August caused yield reduction through physical crop damage due to flood and inundation over a prolonged period of time.

There were several studies conducted nationally and internationally over the last decade on the issue of sea-level rise along the Bay of Bengal delta (IPCC 2007; Rahman et al. 2009). A local study (Rahman and

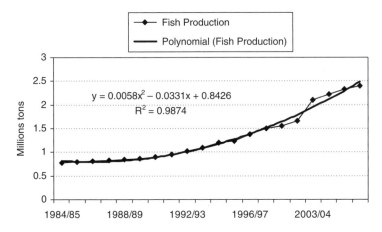

Figure 4.2   Fisheries production, Bangladesh, 1984/85–2006/07

Sarker 2007) with more than 10 years tidal data (1977–98) from three collection points (Hiron point, Char Changa and Cox's Bazar) found that
the mean tidal level had been increasing in all three points. The mean tidal
level at Hiron point showed an increasing trend of about 0.4 cm/year,
Char Changa (0.6 cm) and Cox's Bazar (0.78 cm). An estimate suggests
that salinity, water logging and acidification affect 3.05 million, 0.7 million
and 0.6 million hectares of crop land of the coastal belt, respectively.
Most importantly, the consequences of all of these, about 15–20 per cent
of arable land is expected to be inundated by saline water and this would
drop food grain production substantially by 2030. Salinity and inundation
of farm land would result in millions of farmers displaced from their land
and depriving them of their main sources of livelihood.

4.4.2   Fish Production

The fisheries sector contributes more than 5 per cent of the total exports
of Bangladesh. While this sector's growth has been extraordinarily high
over the last two decades, the sector has been facing major challenges due
to the climatic hazards that have frequently hit the nation, particularly
the southern part, the Bay of Bengal delta. Bangladesh, as illustrated in
Chapter 3, is a land of rivers, historically having abundant sweet water
fish (inland) together with vast marine fishery resources. Both of these
fisheries sub-sectors combined have been progressing well over the last
two decades (see trend in Figure 4.2). The southern parts of Bangladesh,
particularly those located on the coast of the Bay of Bengal, cater for huge
value adding to marine fisheries and have been the main source of exports.

Figure 4.2 shows fisheries production in Bangladesh between 1984/85 to 2006/07. As can be seen, fish production increased at a slower rate in the earlier period and continued to increase at a faster rate in the later period of the sample years. This indicates that fisheries production can be modelled using a polynomial model, rather than a linear model. When a linear model and polynomial model of order 2 were fitted for the data, it was found that a polynomial of order 2 fitted in terms of the model diagnostics. The estimated quadratic model for the given data is:

Fish production = 0.0058 Time^2 – 0.0331 Time + 0.8426 R^2 = 0.9874

The high R^2 value indicates a good fit. This model can be used to forecast fisheries production.

The fish production trend presented in Figure 4.2 certainly suggests that Bangladesh, as a whole, was successful in more than doubling production between 1984 and 2006. This high growth in the country was possible for at least three main reasons: strengthening the government's extension programme on natural fish cultivation in rural areas, encouraging more and more private investment in shrimp cultivation along the Bay of Bengal delta and increased export opportunities. Hossain et al. (2010) found that there has been considerable success in developing a sizeable export trade in frozen and otherwise processed fish products, of which shrimps have been the dominant export items. Exports hit more than US$500 million in 2007 (BBS 2009).

The achievements in the fisheries sector illustrated above are now under major threat from sea-level rise. Finan (2009) painted a very alarming picture for the development of shrimp aquaculture in the coastal belt of the Bay of Bengal due to sea-level rise. In recent decades, commercial shrimp production alone has been earning more than US$350 million each year from exports. According to Finan, sea-level rise will likely result in a much larger volume of saline water moving into the canals that feed the beels (shallow water lakes), contaminating water resources and eroding gher (commercial shrimp cultivation in earthen mini-polders) embankments, which are the major sources of commercial shrimp cultivation. Another likely result of sea-level rise is saltwater intrusion through groundwater flows. This would have major adverse consequences for the groundwater irrigation system of the delta.

4.4.3 Population Displacement

Sea-level rise and its consequences for the displacement of coastal populations all over the world have been predicted by the IPCC (2007) under various scenarios to 2100. As mentioned earlier, for the Bay of Bengal coast, the IPCC estimates the sea-level rise under three scenarios: low (up to 1 m), medium (up to 2 m) and high (up to 5 m). Taking the low scenario into consideration, it is expected that most of the Low Elevation Coastal Zone (LECZ) will be inundated. The LECZ is considered as those areas which are located within 10 m above average sea level. The inundation of low-lying lands would create an environment which would displace millions of coastal people and push them to higher grounds. It is estimated that almost a million people would be rendered homeless by 2030 under the medium scenario (Mandal and Rajan 2009). More on population displacement can be found in Chapter 6.

4.5 REGIONAL SECURITY ISSUES

In Bangladesh, after 2 years of military backed undemocratic civilian government over 2007 and 2008, a democratic government has been in place since January 2009. Sri Lanka's civil war of two decades has just ended but it has to go a long way to overcome the problems of depredation and restarting the development process. India's southern region has been relatively stable but has to catch up with the northern and western states in growth terms. A new threat is brewing in southern and eastern India from the so called Maoist arms movement, which have already made several attempts on the law enforcement agencies (police) and forcefully derailed passenger trains in recent times, killing hundreds of innocent bystanders. Myanmar, bordering Bangladesh along the Bay of Bengal coast, has not resolved its domestic crisis between civil politicians and military junta. The military has been in power for the last three decades forcing out the civil politicians (although something resembling an election was held in late 2010).

Global warming in such political conditions will exacerbate the existing developmental problems and may lead to both economic and political crises in respect of water sharing, searching for offshore gas and oil resources, fishing and so on (Figure 4.3). In fact, the Government of Bangladesh has already set in motion the process to start negotiations with India and Myanmar at UN level on the vexing maritime boundary question.

It is going to be a catastrophe for Bangladesh if a substantial area is flooded and 30 million people have to find shelter elsewhere in the subcontinent. As a matter of fact, the neighbouring countries are already worried about such a possibility. At the same time, countries of this region have also come together in promoting cooperation in trade, investment, people-to-people contact, energy, transport and communication both in the framework of SAARC (South Asian Association for Regional Cooperation) and

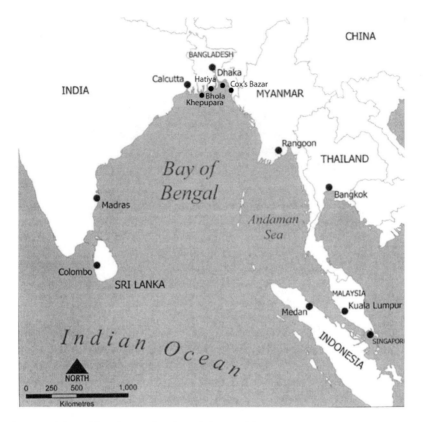

Source: Adapted from International Workshop on Climate Change and Growth in Asia (2009).

Figure 4.3 Bay of Bengal delta

in the context of BIMSTEC (Bay of Bengal Initiative for Multi-Sectoral Technical and Economic Cooperation – Bangladesh, India, Myanmar, Sri Lanka and Thailand with Bhutan and Nepal also joined later).

Under the SAARC framework, Bangladesh, Bhutan, India, Nepal, the Maldives, Pakistan and Sri Lanka joined together to formulate an agreement to establish a SAARC preferential trading arrangement (SAPTA). The agreement on SAPTA was signed on 11 April 1993 and entered into force on 7 December 1995. The basic principles underlying SAPTA are as follows: overall reciprocity and mutuality of advantages so as to benefit equitably all member states taking into account their respective levels of economic and industrial development, the pattern of their external trade and trade and tariff policy systems; negotiation of tariff reform step-by-step; recognition of the needs of the least developed member states and agreement on concrete preferential measures in their favour; and inclusion of all products, manufactured goods and commodities in their raw, semi-processed and processed forms. SAPTA was thus envisaged primarily as the first step towards a Customs Union, Common Market and, ultimately, maybe an Economic Union.

The agreement on a South Asian Free Trade Area (SAFTA) was signed on 6 January 2004 and was to enter into force on 1 January 2006. Under the trade liberalisation programme scheduled for completion by 2016, customs duties on products from the region will be progressively reduced. However, under an early harvest programme for the least developed member states, India, Pakistan and Sri Lanka are to bring down their customs duties to 0–5 per cent by 1 January 2009 for products from such member states. Under the BIMSTEC framework, the countries around the Bay of Bengal have since finalised the BIMSTEC Free Trade Agreement. This agreement enters into force on 1 January 2010. Member states have finalised the size of the negative list, fast track list, list of normal track reduction and list of normal track elimination.

Thus, despite the problems of underdevelopment, backwardness and poverty, the peoples of this region have shown the political will and courage to cooperate for social and economic development. Even outside of SAARC and BIMSTEC, Bangladesh had, some years ago, proposed a 'growth quadrangle' comprising Bangladesh, the north-eastern states of India, Nepal and Bhutan, either as a sub-region within SAARC or even by itself in such a scenario, the potential hydro-electricity production of 80 000 MW in Bhutan and Nepal or even half of that could be used to significantly to improve the quality of life of the people in the 'quadrangle'.

Another redeeming feature of Bangladesh's situation is as follows: while sea-level rise may affect Bangladesh, the coast is shallow due to sedimentation and many low-tide elevations have appeared over the years, a number of small islands have appeared out of the Bay. Thus, reclamation of land appears feasible if one can utilise the experience and expertise of countries like the Netherlands.

In spite of all the foregoing, the prognosis for the future looks good and even optimistic. Furthermore, with the return of democratic governance in Bangladesh, Pakistan and Nepal and the introduction of democracy in Bhutan and Afghanistan, the peoples of the SAARC and the BIMSTEC region are now well poised for strengthening cooperation for peace, security and ensuring mutual prosperity. It is here that they need the support of the developed countries in the West in that the negative impact of global warming will completely negate their struggle for development and a better livelihood.

As the then British Minister for International Development, Douglas Alexander, and Minister of Energy and Climate Change, Ed Milliband, said in Dhaka in late August 2009, 'the developed countries have the major responsibility for carbon emissions resulting in global warming. The developing countries, therefore, must act together as a region to claim additional resources.' In May 2010, the EU pledged almost 15 million Euro to Bangladesh, the Maldives and Cambodia out of the world's commitments in Copenhagen of a fund of US$30 billion for least developed nations for climate change adaptation until 2012 (*The Daily Star* 2 June 2010). This is a part of the EU assistance to these nations in order to strengthen their actions in the Global Climate Change Alliance (GCCA) formed by the developing countries in 2007. The GCCA members include all the least developed and small island nations of the Asia–Pacific region. The EU is supporting the GCCA nations in capacity building and in working jointly towards a legal binding agreement in the future at UN level.

4.6   CONCLUSIONS

The Bay of Bengal delta is one of the most vulnerable regions on earth due to the reality of global warming. Millions are under a genuine threat, not only from lost livelihoods, but they are also likely to face natural eviction from their land due to sea-level rise in the not too distant future. The coast of the Bay of Bengal is more than 700 km long and is the largest delta on earth. Historically, this region has been subject to climatic hazards, particularly from cyclonic storms and sea-water surges at least twice or three times in every 10 years. In recent decades, the frequency has increased to at least one cyclonic storm hitting the coast in every 1.5–2 years. In the literature, it has been recognised that due to geographical location, the Himalayas in the north and the Bay of Bengal/Indian Ocean in the south, make this delta even more vulnerable to the climatic hazards. According to a recent study, the funnel shape of the Bay of Bengal and the low elevation of the coastal region induce cyclones to hit intensely and frequently (Gani and Bari 2007). Due to the geographic position of the Bay of Bengal delta the extreme weather conditions faced in the past, however, were not isolated cases. It appears that these have become regular events due to climate change hazards. The investigation of climatic hazards in this study reinforces this argument, once again.

Due to the extreme weather conditions in terms of variations in rainfall, temperature and sea-level rise, this chapter reached the conclusion that for the people of the Bay of Bengal delta the outlook remains bleak for the years and decades to come. The extreme weather conditions will make life on the coast intolerable with the imminent threat of homelessness due to sea-level rise and inundation. It is now certain that within the next two to three decades, Bangladesh will face a major catastrophe in both economic and social terms, as it witnesses millions of people moving north to search for higher grounds as climate refugees. Whether the world likes it or not, in a few decades, climate refugees will become a reality, hitting the millions of the Bay of Bengal delta in the first instance.

REFERENCES

Ahmed, A.U. (2006), 'Bangladesh climate change impact and vulnerability: a synthesis', Dhaka: Department of Environment and Forestry, Government of Bangladesh.

Alam, S. (2010), 'Challenge to IPCC's Bangladesh predictions', AFP, 21 April, Dhaka.

Barnett J., S. Lambert and I. Fry (2008), 'The hazards of indicators: insights from the environmental vulnerability index (EVI)', *Annals of the Association of American Geographers*, **98** (1): 102–19.

BBS (2008), *Bangladesh Bureau of Statistics Yearbook*, Dhaka: Bangladesh Government Press.

CCC (2009), 'Generation of PRECIS scenarios for Bangladesh (Validation and Parameterization)', Dhaka: Climate Change Cell, DoE, MoEF.

CEGIS (2010), 'Report on Sedimentation', Dhaka: Centre for Environment and Geographic Information Services.

Cline, R.W. (2008), 'Global warming and agriculture', in *Finance and Development*, Washington DC: International Monetary Fund, March, pp. 23–7.

Finan, T.J. (2009), 'Storm warnings: the role of anthropology in adapting to sea-level rise in Southwestern Bangladesh', in H. Rahman et al. (eds), *Climate Change Impacts and Adaptation Strategies for Bangladesh,* University College London and British Council, UK: International Training Network, BUET, pp. 34–44.

Gani, A.K. and M.A. Bari (2007), 'Effect of environmental degradation on national security of Bangladesh', *Asia Pacific Journal on Environment and Development*, **14** (2): 35–54.

Hossain, M., R. Kathuria and I. Islam (2010), *South Asian Economic Development*, 2nd edn, London and New York: Routledge, p. 272.

International Workshop on Climate Change and Growth in Asia (2009), Griffith University, Brisbane, Australia, September 2009.

IPCC (2007), *Fourth Assessment Report of the Intergovernmental Panel on Climate Change,* Cambridge, UK: Cambridge University Press.

Islam, T. and A. Neelim (2010), *Climate Change in Bangladesh: A Closer Look into Temperature and Rainfall Data,* Dhaka: The University Press Limited, p. 80.

Jha, R., T. Dang and Y. Tashrifov (2009), 'Economic vulnerability and poverty in Tajikistan', *Economic Change Restructuring*, **43** (2): 95–112.

Mandal, M.K. and S.C. Rajan (2009), 'Climate migrants in Bangladesh: estimates and solutions', in H. Rahman et al. (eds), *Climate Change Impacts and Adaptation Strategies for Bangladesh*, University College London and British Council, UK: International Training Network, BUET, pp. 225–6.

Metcalfe, I. (2003), 'Long term environmental issues for Bangladesh', in M. Hossain et al. (eds), *Bangladesh's Development Agenda and Vision 2020: Rhetoric or Reality?*, Dhaka: The University Press Limited, pp. 309–18.

Mirza, M.Q. (2002), 'Global warming and changes in the probability of occurrence of floods in Bangladesh and implications', *Global Environmental Change*, **12**: 127–38.

Palmer, T.N. and J. Raisanen (2002), 'Quantifying the risk of extreme seasonal precipitation events in a changing climate', *Nature*, **415**: 512–4.

Rahman, M.H., M.A. Noor and A. Ahmed (2009), 'Climate change related policies and strategies: Bangladesh perspective', in H. Rahman et al. (eds), *Climate Change Impacts and Adaptation Strategies for Bangladesh,* University College London and British Council, UK: International Training Network, BUET, pp. 13–26.

Rahman, M. and M.A. Sarker (2007), 'Impact of sea level rise over Bangladesh', in *Proceedings of SAARC Seminar on Application of Weather and Climate Forecasts in the Socio-economic Development and Disaster Mitigation*, Dhaka: SMRC, pp. 71–8.

Sarker, T.K., D. Brereton and J. Permenter (2007), 'Pilot socio-economic impact assessment of mining on Groote Eylandt', *CSRM Research Report submitted to BHP Billiton*, p. 52.

SMRC (2002), 'Sea level variability along the Indian Coast', Dhaka: SAARC Meteorological Research Centre.

SMRC (2007), 'The impact of climate variability on the yield of rain-fed rice of Bangladesh', Dhaka: SAARC Meteorological Research Centre.

SMRC (2008), 'Understanding the rainfall climatology and detection of extreme weather events in the SAARC region. Part I: Bangladesh, Report 21', Dhaka: SAARC Meteorological Research Centre.

SMRC (2009), 'Understanding the rainfall climatology and detection of extreme weather events in the SAARC region. Part II: utilization of RCM data, Report 29', Dhaka: SAARC Meteorological Research Centre.

Stern, N.H. (2007), *The Economics of Climate Change: The Stern Review*, Cambridge, UK: Cambridge University Press.

The Daily Star (2010), 'LDCs should specify climate demands', *The Daily Star,* 2 June, Dhaka, Bangladesh.

World Bank (2000), *World Development Indicators 2000*, Washington DC: World Bank.

World Bank (2008), 'The impact of climate change on South Asia's poor', www.worldbank.org, accessed on 23 January 2009.

PART II

Climate change and adaptation issues

5. Greenhouse gas abatement in Asia: imperatives, incentives and equity

Colin Hunt

5.1 INTRODUCTION: EMISSIONS TRENDS IN DEVELOPING AND ASIAN COUNTRIES

5.1.1 Global Trends

Human-induced global warming is mainly a result of heat being trapped in the atmosphere by greenhouse gases (GHGs) that have accumulated due to the burning of fossil fuels since the beginning of the Industrial Revolution, together with the clearing of forests to make way for agriculture (see Figure 5.1). The concentration of the main greenhouse gas, carbon dioxide (CO_2), which is very long-lived in the atmosphere, is 35 per cent higher than it was in 1850.

The top ten emitting countries (with the inclusion of the European

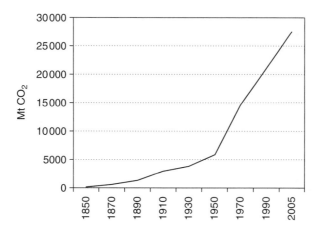

Source: WRI (2010a).

Figure 5.1 CO_2 emissions from fossil fuel combustion, annual, 1850–2005

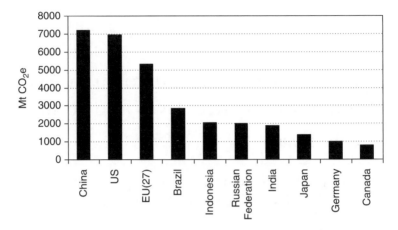

Note: LUC emissions are indicative only in many developing countries (see Appendix 5.1) but are included because they make up a large proportion of some of those countries' emissions, and because LUC is responsible for 12 per cent of total global emissions.

Source: WRI (2010a).

Figure 5.2   Top ten emitters of CO_2e, with land-use change, 2005

Union (EU)) were responsible for 70 per cent of global emissions of carbon dioxide equivalent (CO_2e) in 2005 (see Figure 5.2).[1] Five of the top ten are developing countries and four of these are in Asia, China being ranked first and Indonesia, India and Malaysia, fourth, seventh and ninth respectively.

The GHG emissions of developing countries increased by 57 per cent from 1990 to 2005 and those of Asian countries almost doubled due to their industrialisation and rapid economic growth. In contrast, emissions of developed countries remained static.[2] Developing countries now emit greater quantities of GHGs than developed countries and their contribution is forecast to increase to some 63 per cent of global emissions by 2020 (see Figure 5.3).

5.1.2   Trends in Asia

China, Indonesia and India are collectively responsible for over a quarter of contemporary CO_2e emissions. But while the emissions of China and India are overwhelmingly due to energy generation, Indonesia's are mainly due to land-use change; that is the release of carbon from biomass due to native forest harvesting and native forest replacement by agriculture. There are also large difference in emission per capita and trends in emission intensity between countries. The inter-country difference in

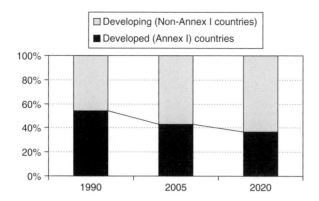

Source: Appendix Table A5.2.

Figure 5.3 GHG (CO_2e) emissions actual and projected

sources signals that approaches to mitigation of GHGs in Indonesia will be very different to approaches in China and India, the implications of which are further discussed below.

The correlation between the size of a country's economy and its level of GHG emissions is very high for Asian countries and higher than for the rest of the world.[3] Developed countries have been lowering their emission intensity by switching from coal to gas in electricity and heat generation. In contrast, in developing countries the share of coal in electricity and heat generation increased from 43 per cent in 1992 to 52 per cent in 2006 (IEA 2008a).

In China, the demand for electricity has been responsible for an exponential rise in GHG emissions in recent years. Rapid expansion of heavy industry to service large infrastructure investment has been accompanied by an increasing demand for Chinese products domestically and by overseas consumers. Electricity demand was stimulated to such an extent that new capacity was being added at the rate of two coal-fired power plants per week (China Electricity Council 2007, cited by IEA 2008a). As a consequence of the increasing share of coal in power generation, the Chinese economy, responsible for almost 20 per cent of global GHG emissions, became less – rather than more – emissions-efficient from 2002 to 2006. (See Figures 5.4 and 5.5.)

While inefficient coal-fired plants are being shut down and the use of natural gas is increasing, coal is forecast to maintain its market share for the foreseeable future and, therefore, its share of emissions from fuel combustion of 83 per cent (IEA 2008a, B165; IEA 2008b, p. 145).[4] Like China, India has experienced rapid economic growth, accompanied by an upward trend in emissions from the heat and electricity sector. As a consequence, India is now responsible for almost 5 per cent of global emissions from energy

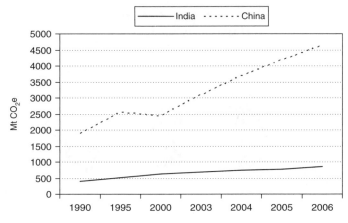

Source: IEA (2008a).

Figure 5.4   China and India: CO_2e emissions from coal, 1990–2006

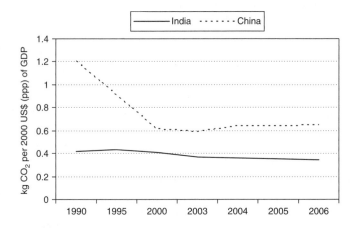

Note: ppp = purchasing power parity.
Source: IEA (2008a).

Figure 5.5   China and India: emissions intensity, 1990–2006

generation. However, while 68 per cent of India's electricity generation still comes from coal, the share of fossil fuels has declined steadily, as have emissions per unit of gross domestic product (GDP), as it expanded its renewable power capacity (IEA 2008a, p. xxix). Figures 5.4 and 5.5 contrast China and India for their level of emissions from coal, and emissions intensity.

In Indonesia considerable economic benefits flow from conversion of forest to crops, principally oil palm. Beneficiaries are loggers, farmers, oil processors, merchants and the Indonesian and regional governments (Hunt 2010). This conversion is a classical case of market failure in that the climate, environmental and biodiversity benefits of conserving the forest are non-market benefits and have no bearing on the commercial decisions to replace forest with agriculture. The increasing demand for palm oil seems inexorable, being driven by world population growth and higher disposable incomes.

5.2   COSTS AND BENEFITS OF MITIGATION IN ASIAN COUNTRIES

5.2.1   Climatic Impacts on Asia Under a Business As Usual (BAU) Scenario

The Intergovernmental Panel on Climate Change (IPCC) (2007) summarised the impacts of climate change on Asia as follows:

- By the 2050s, freshwater availability in Central, South, East and South-east Asia, particularly in large river basins, is projected to decrease.
- Coastal areas, especially heavily populated megadelta regions in South, East and South-east Asia, will be greatly at risk due to increased flooding from the sea and in some megadeltas flooding from rivers.
- The pressures on natural resources and the environment associated with rapid urbanisation, industrialisation and economic development will be compounded by climate change.
- Sickness and deaths due to diarrhoeal disease primarily associated with floods and drought, due to changes in hydrological cycles, are expected to rise in East, South and South-east Asia.

In the case of India, up to 85 per cent of dry season flows of the great rivers of the Northern Indian Plain are supplied by Himalayan glaciers and snowfields. The 30 per cent reduction in meltwater forecast over the next 50 years has major implications for irrigated agriculture in the region. Most of India's agricultural land is rainfed and therefore very vulnerable. Variations in rainfall and increases in seasonally averaged temperatures could reduce crop yield by up to 70 per cent by the end of the century. These impacts are against a background of a need to increase food

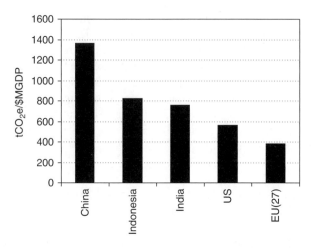

Source: WRI (2010a).

Figure 5.6   Emission intensity of economies in emission/GDP ratio, 2005

production by 5 million tonnes per year to keep pace with the predicted growth in population to about 1.5 billion by 2030 (Challinor et al. 2006; Roy 2006; Stern 2006).

As in India, the losses in China are mainly concentrated in the agricultural sector. Drought will impact most heavily on regions of north and north-west China and there will be an extension of arid regions and an exacerbation of water scarcity. Drought in the north and floods in the south have already increased in frequency causing heavy economic losses (Erda and Ji 2006; Stern 2006).

Indonesia, being a tropical archipelago, is vulnerable to an increasing likelihood of droughts and floods. Livelihoods and food security will likely be affected by impacts on agriculture, fisheries and forestry, and parts of the country will suffer inundation (PEACE 2007).

5.2.2   Emission Intensity of Asian Economies

The emission intensity of Asian economies, that is the emissions/GDP ratio, varies greatly. As would be expected, developed countries are more efficient given that they have switched to lower-polluting fuels, have shed heavy industry and have well-developed infrastructures. China is much more emission intense than Indonesia and India, given that its economy is characterised by a high proportion of heavy industry and ongoing infrastructure development, as well as a reliance on coal for heat and electricity generation (see Figure 5.6).

Given the relative emission intensities, it follows that a reduction in GHG emissions by all countries, contributing to a peaking of CO_2e emissions in 2020 and a stabilisation of 550 parts per million by 2050,[5] is estimated to have a relatively greater negative impact on developing countries and on China's economy in particular. Under this scenario China suffers a cumulative loss of 5 per cent of GDP between 2005 and 2050 and India 3 per cent, while for the United States and EU the loss is only 1 per cent (OECD 2008b, p. 114).

5.2.3 Benefits of Mitigation

There are two major sources of economic and social benefits to Asian developing countries from global action to limit GHG emissions. The first is the amelioration in the direct impacts of climate change and the second is the generation of indirect benefits, or 'co-benefits', such as improvement in urban air quality that comes about as a result of climate change mitigation (OECD 2008a).

The economic costs of climate change that can be reduced by mitigation are extremely difficult to quantify, for several reasons. The nexus between temperature rise and deleterious physical consequences is rather speculative and, therefore, so is their costing. A large uncertainty surrounds the incidence of very costly catastrophes. Moreover, present costs are very sensitive to the discount rate, given that the release of GHGs today incurs costs well into the future. Finally some impacts are reversible while others are not, again imposing difficulties when it comes to pricing them.

Regional assessments of GDP impacts of global warming are over a large range but do suggest that Africa and South Asia are most heavily impacted. Nordhaus and Boyer (2000, p. 91) estimate (the authors emphasise the speculative nature of such estimates) that the negative impacts on GDP of a 2.5°C global warming will be the greatest in India (–5 per cent), with the highest incidence and cost of catastrophic impacts and high agricultural and heath costs incurred during this century. A summary of three studies for a temperature rise of 2.0–2.5°C relative to pre-industrial levels has the cost for Africa falling in the range −1 to −9 per cent of GDP, and for south and south-east Asia between +1 and −9. The GDP costs for China, the summary suggests, are between +2 and –5 per cent (OECD 2008a).

The timing of the costs and benefits of mitigation actions are very different. The costs are immediate, while the uncertain benefits are in the future. Given the high future growth rates in Asian developing countries, those countries would be expected to apply a high discount rate to the long-run benefits of action. The reluctance of developing Asian countries to participate is reinforced by the cost savings of abstaining, on the grounds of differentiated responsibility, while enjoying the benefits of mitigation generated by participants. The conclusion of an international agreement that includes Asian developing countries and binds them to a specific strategy (that would preferably include specific targets in the medium term) would reduce the propensity to take the free rider option.

5.2.4 Distributional Implications

A more comprehensive assessment of the economic impacts of a mitigation policy is obtained if the distributional aspects of a mitigation policy within a country's population are analysed. A rise in the price of carbon resulting from a carbon tax or a cap and trade scheme has been found to be progressive in India and China (Brenner et al. 2005; Datta 2008). Car ownership is confined to high-income households, while poorer households use less fossil fuel for heating, relying on biofuels and kerosene for cooking. In contrast, a price on carbon is found to be regressive in most developing countries because low-income households spend relatively more on energy-related products (OECD 2006). The extension of electrification to rural areas is linked to health improvements, income generation opportunities and higher educational attainment (see, for example, Kangawa and Nakata 2006, 2008). Carbon price increases could slow the uptake of electricity and poverty alleviation, unless tax revenues are redistributed from rich to poor (see Brenner et al. 2005 for such a proposal for China).

5.3   ISSUES OF EQUITY

Equity has always been a guiding principle in international agreements designed to curb GHG emissions. The United Nations Framework Convention on Climate Change (UNFCCC) (United Nations 1992, Article 3) required 'That parties should protect the climate system . . . on the basis of equity and in accordance with their common but differentiated responsibilities and respective capabilities'. Only developed or Annex I countries were to commit to limit their emissions and protect and enhance carbon sinks (see Appendix 5.2 in this chapter for list of Annex I countries) (United Nations 1992, Article 4). The Kyoto Protocol, which put flesh on the bones of the Convention, required only these same countries (Annex B countries) to adopt specific limits on their 2008–12 emissions (United Nations 1998). The Bali Action Plan emphasised the application of the 'principle of common but differentiated responsibilities and respective capabilities, taking account of economic conditions and other relevant factors'; hence 'quantifiable emission limitation and reduction objectives' were agreed for developed countries, while only 'nationally appropriate actions', measurable and verifiable, were required of developing countries (UNFCCC 2007, p. 3).

The Group of 8, made up of countries with large economies, came to recognise that emission targets that would avoid dangerous climate change are not possible without quantifiable cuts by developing countries, but still maintained the principle of differentiated responsibilities. A G8 commitment to a reduction target of 80 per cent by 2050 was accompanied by a statement of the need for emerging economies to undertake quantifiable, but unspecified, actions to collectively reduce their emissions, so that an overall target of least a 50 per cent reduction in global emissions could be achieved by 2050 (G8 2009, Paragraph 65).

The differentiation is continued in the Copenhagen Accord and the Cancun Agreement in which the mitigation actions by Non-Annex I countries are to be voluntary.

The differentiation between developed and developing countries in the Convention facilitated its ratification by almost all countries. Now that it has become obvious that developing countries must adopt quantifiable limits if dangerous climate change is to be avoided (see Appendix 5.3) the debate on equity issues has tended to intensify.

Developing countries have mounted three main arguments for preferential treatment in international agreements to reduce global emissions. These are:

1. The developed countries are responsible for most of the accumulated CO_2 in the atmosphere; the onus for cutting atmospheric greenhouse gas concentrations is therefore on them.
2. The developing countries should be allowed to continue to increase their per capita emissions, which are lower than those of the developed countries.
3. The developing countries' per capita incomes are relatively low and their growth should not be inhibited by requirements to reduce emissions.

Table 5.1 shows that the incomes of Indonesia, China and India all lie in the lower quartile. The per capita emissions of China and India are also relatively low but Indonesia's are higher due to deforestation. Apart from a few countries, including the United States, there are few with both high emission indicators and high socioeconomic indicators. Thus no one indicator is able to embody the multiple principles enunciated

Table 5.1   Key country parameters, 2005

	GDP/Capita, US$, PPP[a]	CO_2/capita	% global CO_2e
US	42672	23.9	18.23
EU (27)	27642	10.9	13.76
China	4524	5.6	18.75
Indonesia[a]	3335	2.7	1.51
Indonesia[b]	3335	9.3	4.63
India	2416	1.7	4.84

Notes:
[a]   Indonesia without LUC;
[b]   Indonesia with LUC;
PPP = purchasing power parity in 2006 values at 2005 prices.

Source: WRI (2010a).

by the UNFCCC. The creation of indices that rank countries according to composite indicators that attempt to capture their disparate national circumstances, could guide agreements in the inter-country allocation of mitigation effort.

To this end, a range of scenarios using different combinations of indicators is presented by Karousakis et al. (2008). All countries are ranked by different combinations of total contemporary GHGs, historical GHGs, GHGs per capita, GDP per capita and GHG/GDP, the latter being the emission intensity of the economy.

The two combinations of parameters (with equal weight) that give credible rankings are total GHGs, with either GDP per capita or GHG per capita. These combinations generate high scores for the United States and China and give India an intermediate score.[6] When total historical GHG emissions are included, rather than total contemporary GHG emissions, or when total GHGs are excluded, China has a very low index; such rankings are unrealistic in that no mitigation architecture will stand up without the active participation of China, the world's greatest emitter of GHGs.

Jacoby et al. (2008) show that simple rules for allocation lead to disproportionate burdens among countries and are incapable of dealing with the highly varying circumstances of countries. While the development of indices does not solve the problem of how to allocate mitigation responsibilities between countries, it does nevertheless serve to inform the debate. A benefit of the inclusion of socioeconomic and emissions intensity parameters in the discussion is to indicate which countries should have priority in receiving financial and/or technological assistance in making emissions reductions.

5.4   ASIAN PERSPECTIVES ON MITIGATION

This section concentrates on official responses on mitigation by China, India and Indonesia. China views as urgent the adoption by developed countries of a mid-term emission reduction target: 'All developed parties to the Convention shall commit to reduce their GHG emissions by at least 40 per cent below 1990 levels by 2020' (UNFCCC 2009a, p. 1). This target is at the extreme of the range of cuts (−25 to −40 per cent) recognised by the Bali Action Plan as being necessary to limit greenhouse gas emissions to 450 ppm (the 2°C limit) (UNFCCC 2007, Box 13.7). But China's position is realistic in the sense that it recognises that such a deep cut will be necessary to achieve such a target (see Appendix 5.3). China justifies its call on the grounds of historical responsibility by developed countries and the need for developing country economies to grow. Mitigation actions by developing countries will be determined by each country individually taking into account national capacities and circumstances. Moreover, China (UNFCCC 2009a, p. 8) invokes Article 3 of the convention, which states that developing countries shall 'provide such financial resources including the transfer of technology needed by the developing countries to meet the full incremental costs of implementing measures' (United Nations 1992, Article 3), to be achieved by developed countries making contributions of 0.5 to 1.00 per cent of GDP, in addition to existing overseas development assistance.

India's position on the division of responsibilities in climate change mitigation is the same as China's: developed countries (Annex I), individually or jointly, shall reduce their emissions by at least 40 per cent below the 1990 baseline by 2020. Developing country mitigation to be on a voluntary basis, the agreed full incremental costs to be met by developed countries (Ministry of Environment and Forests 2009).

Preparedness by China and India to reduce emissions below what they would be without mitigation was signalled by the G5[7] countries in 2008 as follows:

> We, on our part are committed to undertaking nationally appropriate mitig-
> ation and adaptation actions which also support sustainable development. We
> would increase the depth and range of these actions supported and enabled by
> financing technology and capacity-building with a view to achieving a deviation
> from business-as-usual. (G5 2008, cited by VanBerkum et al. 2009, p. 16)

Indonesia has ratified the UNFCCC and the Kyoto Protocol, and as a non-Annex I country has been free of obligations to initiate mitigation measures. However, Indonesia acknowledges that as a major source of global GHGs from land clearing it needs technical and financial assistance in mitigation. To this end it has formalised an Indonesia–Australia Forest

Carbon Partnership (UNFCCC 2009b; Government of the Republic of Indonesia and Government of Australia 2008) and there is a major agreement with Norway (*ANTARA News*, 27 May 2010).

The United States will be influential in determining future international architectures for climate change post-Kyoto. It is therefore instructive to visit that country's draft protocol to the UNFCCC (2009c) in which it outlines a framework for mitigation actions by developed and developing countries. The United States continues to accept a differentiation of responsibility for mitigation between countries depending on their national circumstances. At the same time it does seek to commit developing countries; developing country Parties 'whose natural circumstances reflect greater responsibility or capability' would specify nationally appropriate mitigation actions from 2020 'that are quantified (for example, reductions from business-as-usual) and are consistent with the levels of ambition needed to contribute to meet the objectives of the Convention'. Each such party would formulate and submit a low carbon strategy for long-term emission reductions by 2050, consistent with the level of ambition needed to contribute to meeting the objective of the Convention (UNFCCC 2009c, p. 6).

The United States expects the private sector in both developed and developing countries to be the main source of funding rather than the public sector; that is, the carbon market would drive investment in mitigation. This is in contrast to the Chinese position that specifies that funds, as a proportion of GDP, be committed by developed country governments.

5.5   COMMITMENT BY COUNTRIES UNDER THE COPENHAGEN ACCORD AND THE CANCUN AGREEMENTS

The Copenhagen climate change conference in December 2009 failed to produce a new international treaty with binding commitments to reduce greenhouse gas emissions. A loose agreement reached, the Copenhagen Accord, has yet to be signed-off by countries. The Accord requires countries to report their intended voluntary mitigation actions by the end of January 2010 (UNFCCC 2009d).

China did not commit to an emissions target. Instead it

[W]ill endeavour to lower its CO_2 emissions per unit of GDP by 40–45 per cent by 2020 compared with 2005, increase the share of non-fossil fuels in primary energy consumption to around 15 per cent by 2020 and increase forest cover by 40 million ha and forest stock volume by 1.3 billion cubic metres by 2020 from the 2005 levels.

Likewise, India '[Will] endeavour to reduce emissions intensity of its GDP by 20–25 per cent by 2020 in comparison to the 2005 level'. In Indonesia's case the commitment is to achieve a 26 to 41 per cent CO_2e reduction by 2020 (UNFCCC 2010b). (See also the last paragraph under the section Policies of developing countries: the benefits of early action.)

China and India thus failed to meet the requirements of the United States for quantified reduction in emissions below BAU levels. Moreover, the bid by the United States to have reductions internationally monitored, reported and verified (MRV) also failed. The MRVs will be by the countries themselves, with international consultation and analysis of the reports. These failures did not add to the chances of the US Senate passing a bill to reduce US emissions by 17 per cent by 2020 on 2005 levels, which is its target submitted under the Accord (UNFCCC 2010a).

At the Cancun climate change conference in December 2010, the need for deep cuts in emissions to limit the increase in global temperature to 2°C was reiterated (UNFCCC 2010c, Clause 4). (Note that Figure 5A.1 suggests that to achieve this target, developing countries would need to cut BAU emissions by 29% even if developed countries were to cut by 40%.) However, there was no collective commitment to cuts by developed and developing countries that would achieve this, or a less ambitious, target.

5.6 ASIAN COUNTRY PARTICIPATION IN FUTURE CLIMATE CHANGE ARCHITECTURES

The Kyoto Protocol has been a remarkable achievement in that it adopts a range of market-based instruments, including international emissions trading, that lower the costs of achieving emission reductions. However, judged on the grounds of the extent of actual international participation in measures to curb GHG emissions, the Protocol has failed. On a country basis, the top four emitters, China, the United States, Indonesia and Brazil, together responsible for about 50 per cent of global GHG emissions, are free from quantitative emissions targets. Much of the potential gains from trade have been lost and the cost of mitigation has been higher than it would have been with broader participation. Moreover, carbon-intensive firms in countries with emission commitments may relocate to countries without commitments. This reduces the environmental benefits of the Protocol to participating countries and serves to create opposition to the adoption of climate change policy on competitiveness grounds (Aldy and Stavins 2008).

The analysis in this chapter supports the conclusion of other authors (Garnaut et al. 2008; Blandford et al. 2009) that developing countries and particularly the large fast-growing economies of Asia (Jotzo 2008) must take action to curb growth in GHGs if climate change is to be stabilised. A political perspective suggests that the United States will not join an international agreement because China has not signed up to a binding quantified target. In the future the key to participation of China and other developing countries will be the introduction of mechanisms that minimise economic costs and that continue to allow them to grow their economies. Such mechanisms are discussed in the next sections.

5.6.1   Minimising the Costs of Participation of Asian Developing Countries

The mitigation of global warming through the reduction of CO_2e emissions and the stabilisation of atmospheric CO_2e concentrations by the mid-twenty-first century will inevitably reduce global economic growth. The degree to which Asian countries will be impacted will depend on the depth of cuts in emissions that Asian countries take on, together with the energy and carbon intensity of their economies. Above, it was shown that the economies of China, India and Indonesia are emissions intensive and impacts on their economies of emissions reductions will inevitably be relatively greater than for developed economies. But even non-participating developing countries will be indirectly impacted as world growth slows. Non-participating countries could also face growth-restricting trade sanctions imposed by countries that have accepted binding commitments.[8]

Given the failure of the Copenhagen climate change conference to reach agreement on a new climate protocol, it is risky to predict the nature of the architecture that will emerge in the future. Nevertheless, factors that will decrease the effects of such an architecture on growth, for any given level of stabilisation adopted, include:

- Linkage of developing Asian countries to a market-based global architecture.
- Energy and emissions policies of developing countries.

5.6.2   Win–Win by Developing Country Participation

Two foundations of global architecture, both potentially very efficient in arriving at least-cost solutions in reducing carbon emissions, are 'cap and trade' and carbon taxes. Cap and trade schemes have the advantage of facilitating wealth transfer to participating low-cost countries (Olmstead 2008; Weiner 2008).

By developing countries accepting caps at or below a baseline of BAU,

Table 5.2   Win–win from developing country cap at BAU, or below, and trade

Gains from developing country participation	Economic gains	Environmental gains
Gains for developing countries	Price received for sold permits > cost of cutting emissions	Co-benefits e.g. air quality improvement
Gains for developed countries	Price paid for permits < cost of cutting emissions	Precludes leakage of emissions from non-members

Source: After Frankel (2008, Table 5.2.2).

and trading emission permits below BAU, all participating nations gain (see Table 5.2).[9] The extent of the abatement by developing countries below BAU depends on the payments to do so offered by foreign corporations or governments; the developed countries and their corporations make these offers of payment for permits because their costs of abatement are relatively great. One reason for this cost difference is that developed countries would need to scrap coal-fired plants to meet their caps, which is expensive, while growing developing countries can abate by installing new efficient systems (Frankel 2008).

If developing countries are to be fully compensated for their participation then the wealth transfer through emissions trading, to achieve a target of 50 per cent reduction in emissions by 2050, is very large. The importance of universal participation is twofold: costs are spread and the carbon leakage is reduced (carbon leakage to even a few free-riding nations could be substantial) (Jacoby et al. 2008).

Given the difficulty in forecasting GHG emissions there is a risk that fixed national caps could cause severe economic losses in rapidly growing developing countries.[10] Conversely, the sale of permits without any real reduction in emissions could occur where economic growth and hence emissions turn out to be well below BAU. An indexing approach that adjusts the cap for actual increases in GDP or GHG emissions above the projected values, and downwards for shortfalls, would lower the risks (Lutter 2000).

The Clean Development Mechanism (CDM) of the Kyoto Protocol has enabled investment and technology transfer to reduce emissions in India and China, in particular, the reductions being claimable against emission targets by Annex I countries. There is a strong consensus that the CDM will need to be improved or replaced to provide an adequate vehicle for developing country investment post-Kyoto.[11] A flaw in the CDM is that it provided a perverse incentive to ignore energy efficient investments by the host developing country; instead there have been rewards for avoiding such commitments (Wara 2007; Wara and Victor 2008). If developing countries take on emission targets, reductions in GHG emissions resulting from the adoption of new technology will be directly claimable by the developing country itself: the perverse incentive is replaced by a genuine incentive to invest.[12]

5.6.3   Policies in Developing Countries: The Benefits of Early Action

Even if the developed countries were to unilaterally and immediately reduce their emissions to zero, stabilising global emissions would still likely be impossible.[13] The level at which concentrations of GHGs are eventually stabilised depends overwhelmingly on the actions of developing countries. But while the developed countries are relatively impotent they, and particularly the United States, need to play a leadership role in international negotiations for a post-Kyoto international climate regime that involves full participation by developing countries. 'Without evidence of serious action by the US, there will be no meaningful international agreement, and certainly not one that includes the key, rapidly-growing developing countries. Policy developments in the US can and should move in parallel with international negotiations' (Stavins 2009, p. 1).

The heaviest burden of action will fall on the BRIC (Brazil, Russia, India and China) group of countries, given their higher energy expenditure, and the reliance on carbon-intensive fuels in the case of China and India. Given the long lead times to install improved energy infrastructure, near-future transfers of finance and technology are important to forestall energy-intensive growth. 'Without the technical means to reduce emissions while still enjoying the productive benefits of energy use, developing countries' decisions about whether to participate will be much more difficult, casting serious doubts on our ability to build an international coalition' (Blandford et al. 2009, p. 11).

Blandford et al. (2009) find that abatement costs are reduced massively for both developed and developing countries if key developing countries agree to the imposition of limits on their emissions at some future date, and follow up by taking account of such limits when making their long-lived capital investment decisions. Modelling by Bosetti at al. (2008, 2009) confirms this scenario; a delay by BRIC countries in responding to the need to make low carbon investment decisions is very costly for the world and developing countries alike, as the price of carbon would need to rise to very high levels to achieve stabilisation after delayed participation.

Bosetti et al. (2009) analyse China's actual and projected trends in green innovation and low-carbon technologies. China's policy is found to be anticipatory, its investment in nuclear power bringing in a large contribution by 2020. In addition total R&D spending is targeted at 2.5 per cent of GDP by 2020 compared with 1.5 per cent presently. The pattern of investment is compatible with the adoption of a mitigation policy by China by 2030 (Bosetti 2009, p. 7). It seems apparent, however, that limiting energy use and phasing out old power plants has not been motivated by China's climate change objectives but rather by concerns over energy security, energy costs and environmental factors such as air pollution (Downes 2004; Richerzhagen and Scholz 2008).

There is circumspection about China's efforts to reduce its carbon intensity rapidly between 2005 and 2020. Attempts to meet its 4 per cent annual reduction goal in energy intensity have met with limited success. In 2008, about an 8 per cent reduction in energy intensity had been achieved since the goal was launched in 2005. That leaves China only halfway to its 20 per cent target by 2010. Moreover much of the reduction was achieved in 2008 as a result of the global recession (Howes 2009, p. 420).[14] Thus the risk is exposed of accepting efficiency gains by China, rather than quantitative emission reductions, in a post-Kyoto architecture.

5.6.4 Prospects for Early Action in Indonesia

Emissions from deforestation amount to about 12 per cent (Le Quéré et al. 2009; Van der Werf et al. 2009) of global emissions and Indonesia's share of some 5 per cent of the global total, mostly due to deforestation, is an amount equal to more than a quarter of China's emissions.[15] An expeditious programme of reducing deforestation and forest degradation (REDD) has the potential to ease the overall burden of emission cuts on developing countries and thus on developing country growth.

A focus of the Bali climate change conference in December 2007 was on the development of measures to reduce deforestation and forest degradation (REDD). This was followed through in the Copenhagen Accord, which contains a collective agreement by developed countries to provide additional resources for climate change adaptation and mitigation in developing countries, including forestry, approaching US$30 billion for 2010–12, and rising to US$100 billion a year by 2020 (UNFCCC 2009d, Clause 8) (and reaffirmed at the Cancun climate change conference of December 2010 (UNFCCC 2010c, Clause 95)). At the same time, Australia, the United States, France, Japan, Norway and Britain pledged US$3.5 billion to support immediate steps to implement the Accord (Reuters 2009).

Effectively compensating for the loss of production and value adding will be no easy task, however. There are technical difficulties to be overcome in measuring carbon in tropical forests, in allowing for the possible impermanence of forest carbon sequestered, in estimating what would have been cleared in the absence of a scheme and in tracking leakage of deforestation to other sites or countries.

Even if an international market mechanism were established to compensate landowners, loggers, governments and industries for the loss of income involved, there is no guarantee that such a mechanism would be effective in reducing deforestation in Indonesia. The price of forestry carbon credits will depend heavily on the depth of cuts made by parties to a post-Kyoto agreement and the trading price of carbon in conserved forests will need to be sufficient to induce stakeholders to conserve, rather than convert, forests. Moreover, the price of forestry credits could well be discounted in the market because of the risks surrounding the permanence of such credits.[16] Given the relatively high income generated by palm oil in Indonesia, the price of carbon sequestered in forests in Brazil and Africa could well be cheaper than Indonesia's. Limits placed by parties committed to reductions in emissions on the level of use of forestry offsets in meeting those commitments could further curtail the effectiveness of an international market mechanism for sequestered carbon.[17]

The socioeconomic and political ramifications of reducing deforestation in Indonesia are also complex. By its very nature the exploitation of tropical forests invites corruption and illegal activities. Commentators have tended to minimise the difficulties of reducing deforestation, emphasising instead the low-cost availability of forestry offsets available from tropical countries (Garnaut 2008; Stern 2006). The author has illustrated the high costs of REDD in Indonesia (Hunt 2010), and had called for a reality check on REDD and a non-market approach to its introduction (Hunt 2009). Such an approach is now in place in the absence of a change in the CDM to include emissions reduction from REDD and the lack of mandated emissions cuts post-Kyoto.

Notwithstanding the manifest difficulties of securing sequestered carbon in standing forests in tropical developing countries, the Waxman-Markey Bill aimed at preventing international deforestation to achieve reductions equal to 10 per cent of US 2005 emissions by 2020. This equals 9 per cent of emissions from global deforestation and 26 per cent of emissions from Indonesian deforestation.

5.7 CONCLUSIONS

Large increases in temperature and potentially catastrophic climate change can only be avoided by developing countries committing to cuts in their GHG emissions. Asia is a very large emitter of GHGs and its contribution is rising rapidly. Therefore, Asian action is the key to climate change mitigation.

Most developed countries have already announced their intentions to cut their future emissions. The United States signalled that it wanted quantified cuts by developing countries that add up to achieving the objective of the Convention, which will be to stabilise greenhouse gas concentrations by the middle of the twenty-first century. However, following through on these intentions is contingent on complementary commitments by developing countries, and, in particular, Asian countries, and these so far have failed to materialise.

Rapidly growing Asian countries are naturally reluctant to forego present economic gains in exchange for benefits that are both uncertain and delayed for perhaps decades. A key to Asian country participation in the future is therefore an international climate agreement that minimises the impact on Asian growth. Enabling developing countries to sell reductions in emissions below their baseline has the potential to be a powerful incentive for developing country participation. As discussed, this arrangement can deliver wins for both developed and developing countries. Impacts of mitigation policies on the uptake of electricity and poverty alleviation in Asia would need to be tackled by internal policies that redistribute taxes.

Given the long lead time in achieving lower carbon economies, a second important element is the adoption of anticipatory investment policies by Asian countries. Technology and financial transfers to Asian developing countries will be most important for those not able to capture the benefits of trading, or that need assistance to bring deforestation under control.

Reduction in emissions from land-use change by just a few countries has the potential to ease the burden on all other countries. However, the complexity of the task has not been fully grasped by prominent commentators in developed countries. It will take time and considerable resources to tackle the technical, economic, political and social impediments to the prevention of the conversion of low value forests to high value agriculture.

The analysis in this chapter, together with other recent contributions, suggests that even a comprehensive international agreement to tackle climate change is unlikely to limit temperature increases to below 2°C by the end of the century. Ensuing climate change will have severe geophysical and socioeconomic impacts in South and South-east Asia. The importance of the development of adaption strategies for Asia is thus highlighted.

NOTES

1. CO_2e takes account of the warming potential of all the major GHGs. Unless otherwise stated, 'GHGs' and 'emissions' are all in terms of CO_2e.
2. Developed countries are defined as Annex I countries subject to caps on emissions under the UNFCCC (United Nations 1992) (see Appendix 5A.2 for a list of Annex I countries) and developing countries are defined as non-Annex I countries.
3. The correlation coefficient between 2005 CO_2e emissions per capita and 2005 GDP per capita for 190 countries is 0.85, while it is 0.93 for 18 countries of Asia (Bangladesh, Brunei, Darussalam, China, People's Republic, India, Indonesia, Korea North, Korea South, Malaysia, Mongolia, Myanmar, Nepal, Pakistan, Philippines, Singapore, Sri Lanka, Taiwan, Thailand and Vietnam), source of data WRI (2009).
4. China's eleventh 5-year plan, covering the period 2006–10, calls for the country to increase the share of natural gas and other cleaner technologies in the country's energy mix and close several smaller coal-fired plants that were less efficient and heavy polluters. The government plans to remove 31 GW of coal generation in the next 3 years. Coal consists of roughly three-quarters of the power generation feedstock and the EIA forecasts it will maintain this market share through 2030. Natural gas will see the greatest percentage rise in installed electricity generation capacity over the next decade, but coal is expected to show the largest increase in absolute terms. There are several examples of China's effort to bring new natural gas-fired power stations online, some in conjunction with LNG (liquid natural gas) terminals coming online, though the fuel will continue to play a marginal role in the power sector's fuel mix based on the higher cost of LNG and imported pipeline supplies versus coal (IEA 2009).
5. Which Appendix 5A.3 suggests would have a probability of 50 per cent of limiting a global temperature rise by the end of the century to 3°C.
6. It has already been demonstrated (note 3) that GDP per capita and GHGs per capita are highly correlated, so that a combination of these together in index creation is an unnecessary complication.
7. The G5 is made up of Brazil, China, India, Mexico and South Africa, presently responsible for 41 per cent of developing country (non-Annex I) CO_2e emissions, with land-use change.
8. For example the Waxman-Markey Bill HR 2454, which passed the US House of Representatives, includes a provision to impose border taxes on carbon-intensive goods from non-participating countries.
9. Bosetti et al. (2008) show that the substantial costs to developed countries in meeting targets are reduced if developing countries are allowed to trade from their BAU baseline. Weiner (2008) suggests that developing countries could accept targets less than BAU that reflect the climate protection and other co-benefits of joining the international cap and trade architecture. Bosetti et al. (2009) note that the choice of a BAU baseline is not an obvious one in that the fast growing developing countries with large investment possibilities might incorporate energy and carbon-efficient measures into their baselines.
10. Garnaut et al. (2008) illustrate the difficulty of accurate forecasting by reference to the forecasts of GDP by the World Bank and of CO_2e emissions from fossil fuels by the IEA.
11. See, for example, Keeler and Thompson (2008) and Victor (2008).
12. Another imitation of the CDM of the Kyoto Protocol, with relevance to Indonesia, is that it does not allow the purchase of offsets generated by the reduction in deforestation or forests degradation, being limited to offsets for afforestation and reforestation (see for example Hunt 2009).
13. Blandford et al. (2009) suggests stabilisation at 550 ppm CO_2e will be infeasible unless pessimistic economic growth follows the global financial crisis (GFC). This finding supports the conclusion derived in Appendix 5A.3 of this chapter on the feasibility of attaining stabilisation targets.
14. Even if China reduced its CO_2 intensity of GDP by about 50 per cent in 2020, compared with 2005, emissions in 2020 will still be about 40 per cent higher than in 2005 because of rapid economic growth (He et al. 2009).
15. The accuracy of all deforestation estimates is subject to the caveats of Appendix 5A.1.

16. The market price of CO_2e sequestered by afforestation/reforestation in the CDM is discounted heavily because they are temporary and must be replaced (Hunt 2009).
17. For example, the Waxman-Markey Bill puts limits on the use of international offsets by US firms.

REFERENCES

Aldy, J. and R. Stavins (2008), 'Climate policy architectures for the post-Kyoto world', *Environment*, **50** (3): 7–17.

Blandford, G., R. Richels and T. Rutherford (2009), 'Feasible climate targets: the roles of economic growth, coalition development and expectations', *Energy Economics*, doi:10.1016/j.eneco.2009.06.003.

Bosetti, V., C. Carraro, and M. Tavoni (2008), 'Delayed participation of developing countries to climate agreements: should action in the EU and US be postponed?', *Climate Change Modelling and Policy*, Fondazione Eni Enrico Mattei, Milan, http://ssrn.com/abstract=1265526.

Bosetti, V., C. Carraro and M. Tavoni (2009), 'Climate change mitigation strategies in fast-growing countries: the benefits of early action', *Energy Economics*, doi:10.1016/j.eneco.2009.06.011.

Brenner, M., M. Riddle and J. Boyce (2005), 'A Chinese sky trust: distributional aspects of carbon charges and revenue recycling in China', Working Paper Series, Political Economy Research Institute, University of Massachusetts at Amhurst, MA, available at http://www.peri.unmass.edu/fileadmin/pdf/working_papers/WP_Brenner_Riddle_Boyce.pdf.

Challinor, A., J. Slingo, A. Turner and T. Wheeler (2006), 'Indian monsoon: contribution to the Stern review', prepared for the Stern Review on the Economics of Climate Change, available at http://www.hm-treasury.gov.uk/stern_review_supporting_documents.htm

China Electricity Council (2007), 'China Electricity Council, Annual report of electricity sector statistics', Beijing: China Electricity Council.

Datta, A. (2008), 'The incidence of fuel taxation in India,' Discussion Paper 08–05, Delhi: Indian Statistical Institute, Delhi Planning Unit.

Den Elzen, M. and N. Höhne (2008), 'Reductions in greenhouse gas emissions in Annex I and non-Annex I countries for meeting concentration stabilisation targets', *Climatic Change*, **91**: 249–74.

Downes, E. (2004), 'The Chinese energy security debate', *The China Energy Quarterly*, **177**: 21–41.

Erda, L. and Z. Ji (2006), 'Climate change impacts and its economics in China', prepared for the Stern Review on the Economics of Climate Change, available at http://www.hm-treasury.gov.uk/stern_review_supporting_documents.htm.

Frankel, J. (2008), 'Formulas for quantitative emission targets', in J. Aldy and R. Stavins (eds), *Architectures for Agreement: Addressing Global Climate Change in the Post-Kyoto world*, New York: Cambridge University Press, pp. 31–56.

G5 (2008), Statement issued by Brazil, China, India, Mexico and South Africa on the occasion of the 2008 Hokkaido–Tokayo summit.

G8 (2009), 'Declaration of 2008 summit at La Maddalena L'Aquila', available at http://www.g8italia2009.it/G8/Home/G8-G8_Layout_locale-1199882116809_Atti.htm.

Garnaut, R. (2008), 'Interim report to the commonwealth, state and territory governments of Australia', *The Garnaut Climate Change Review*, Melbourne.

Garnaut, R., S. Howes, F. Jotzo and P. Sheehan (2008), 'Emissions in the platinum age: the implications of rapid development for climate change mitigation', *Oxford Review of Economic Policy*, **24** (2): 377–401.

Government of the Republic of Indonesia and Government of Australia (2008), 'Indonesia forest carbon partnership', April, available at http://www.climate-change.gov.au/international/publications/pubs/indonesia-australia.pdf.

He, J., J. Deng and M. Su (2009), 'CO_2 from China's energy sector and strategy for its control', *Energy*, doi:10.1016/j.energy.2009.04.009.

Houghton, R. (2003), 'Emissions (and sinks) of carbon from land-use change' (Estimates of national sources and sinks of carbon resulting from changes in land use, 1950 to 2000), Report to the World Resources Institute from the Woods Hole Research Center, available at http://cait.wri.org.

Houghton, R. (2005), 'Aboveground forest biomass and the global carbon balance', *Global Change Biology*, **11**: 945–58.

Howes, S. (2009), 'Can China rescue the global climate change negotiations?', available at http://epress.anu.edu.au/china_new_place/pdf/ch18.pdf.

Hunt, C. (2009), *Carbon Sinks and Climate Change: Forests in the Fight against Global Warming*, Cheltenham, UK: Edward Elgar Publishing.

Hunt, C. (2010), 'The costs of reducing deforestation in Indonesia', *Bulletin of Indonesian Economic Studies*, **46** (20): 187–92.

IEA (International Energy Agency) (2008a), *CO_2 Emissions from Fuel Combustion*, 2008 edn, Paris: IEA.

IEA (International Energy Agency) (2008b), *World Energy Outlook*, Paris: IEA.

IEA (International Energy Agency) (2009) 'Country analysis briefs', available at http://www.eia.doe.gov/emeu/cabs/China/Full.html.

IPCC (International Panel on Climate Change) (2007), *Climate Change 2007: Synthesis Report*, Cambridge, UK and New York, NY: Cambridge University Press.

Jacoby, H., M. Babiker, S. Paltsev and J. Reilly (2008), 'Sharing the burden of GHG reductions', Discussion paper 08–09, The Harvard Project on International Climate Agreements, Harvard Kennedy School.

Jotzo, F. (2008), 'Climate change economics and policy in the Asia Pacific', *Asian Pacific Economic Literature*, doi:10.111/j.1467-8411.2008.oo22.x.

Kanagawa, M. and T. Nakata (2006), 'Analysis of the energy access improvement and its socio-economic impacts in rural areas of developing countries', *Ecological Economics*, **62**: 319–29.

Kanagawa, M. and T. Nakata (2008), 'Assessment of access to electricity and the socio-economic impacts in rural areas of developing countries', *Energy Policy*, **36**: 2016–29.

Karousakis, K., B. Guay and C. Philbert (2008), *Differentiating Countries in Terms of Mitigation Commitments, Action and Support*, Paris: OECD.

Keeler A. and A. Thompson (2008), 'Industrialized-country mitigation policy and resource transfers to developing countries: improving and expanding greenhouse gas offsets', Discussion paper 08–05, The Harvard Project on International Climate Agreements, Harvard Kennedy School.

Le Quéré, C., M. Raupach, J. Candell and G. Marland (2009), 'Trends in the sources and sinks of carbon dioxide', *Nature Geoscience*, Focus, **2**: 831–6.

Lutter, R. (2000), 'Developing countries greenhouse emissions: uncertainty and implications for participation in the Kyoto Protocol', *The Energy Journal*, **21** (4): 93–120.

Meinshausen, M., N. Meinshausen, W. Hare, S. Raper, K. Frieler, R. Knutti,

D. Frame and M. Allen (2009), 'Greenhouse-gas emission targets for limiting global warming to 2°C', *Nature*, **4**, doi:10.1038/nature08017.

Ministry of Environment and Forests (2009), 'Climate change negotiations: India's submission to the United Nations Framework Convention on Climate Change', August, available at http://www.indiaenvironmentportal.org.in/files/UNFCCC_final.pdf.

Murdiyarso, D. and E. Adiningsih (2007), 'Climate anomalies, Indonesian vegetation fires and terrestrial carbon emissions', *Mitigation and Adaption Strategies for Global Change*, **12**: 101–12.

Nordhaus, W. and J. Boyer (2000), *Warming the World*, Cambridge, MA: MIT Press.

OECD (Organisation for Economic Cooperation and Development) (2006), *The Political Economy of Environmentally Related Taxes*, Paris: OECD.

OECD (Organisation for Economic Cooperation and Development) (2008a), *OECD Environmental Outlook to 2030*, Paris: OECD.

OECD (Organisation for Economic Cooperation and Development) (2008b), 'The economics of climate change mitigation: policies and options for the future,' Economics Department Working Paper No. 658, Paris: OECD.

Olmstead, S. (2008), 'The whole and the sum of the parts', in J. Aldy and R. Stavins (eds), *Architectures for Agreement: Addressing Global Climate Change in the Post-Kyoto World*, New York: Cambridge University Press, pp. 173–84.

PEACE (Pelangi Energi Abadi Citra Enviro) (2007), 'Indonesia and climate change: current status and policies', World Bank and DIFID, available at http://siteresources.worldbank.org/INTINDONESIA/Resources/Environment/ClimateChange_Full_EN.pdf.

Reuters (2009), 'US joins 3.5 billion scheme to fight deforestation', cited by Ecoseed, available at http://www.ecoseed.org/en/general-green-news/copenhagen-conference-2009/copenhagen-leading-stories/5618-U-S-joins-$-3-5-billion-scheme-to-fight-deforestation.

Richerzhagen C. and I. Scholz (2008), 'China's capacity for mitigating climate change', *World Development*, **36** (2): 308–24.

Rogelj, J., B. Hare, J. Nabel, K. Macey, M. Schaeffer, K. Markmann, and M. Meinshausen (2009), 'Halfway to Copenhagen, no way to 2°C', Commentary, *Nature*, online 11 June, doi:10:1038/climate.2009.57.

Roy, J. (2006), 'The economics of climate change: a review of studies in the context of South Asia with a special focus on India', prepared for the Stern Review on the Economics of Climate Change, available at http://www.hm-treasury.gov.uk/stern_review_supporting_documents.htm.

Stavins, R. (2009), 'Worried about international competitiveness? Another look at the Waxman-Markey Cap-and-Trade Proposal', available at http://belfercenter.ksg.harvard.edu/analysis/stavins/?p=117.

Stern, N. (2006), *The Economics of Climate Change*, Cambridge, UK: Cambridge University Press.

UNFCCC (United Nations Framework Convention on Climate Change) (2007), 'Bali Action Plan, Decision 1/CP.13', available at http://unfccc.int/resource/docs/2007/cop13/eng/06a01.pdf#page=3.

UNFCCC (United Nations Framework Convention on Climate Change) (2009a), 'China's submission on elements to be included in the draft negotiating text of AWG-LCA' (Ad Hoc Working Group on Long-term Cooperative Action under the Convention), April, available at http://unfccc.int/files/kyoto_protocol/application/pdf/china240409b.pdf.

UNFCCC (United Nations Framework Convention on Climate Change) (2009b),

'Reducing emissions from deforestation and forest degradation in developing countries: joint submission to the AWG-LCA and SBSTA', available at http://unfccc.int/files/meetings/ad_hoc_working_groups/lca/application/pdf/indonesia australia070809.pdf.

UNFCCC (United Nations Framework Convention on Climate Change) (2009c), 'Draft implementing agreement under the Convention prepared by the Government of the United States of America for adoption at the fifteenth session of the Conference of the Parties', available at http://unfccc.int/resource/docs/2009/cop15/eng/07.pdf.

UNFCCC (United Nations Framework Convention on Climate Change) (2009d), 'Decision CP.15, Copenhagen Accord', available at http://unfccc.int/files/meetings/cop_15/application/pdf/cop15_cph_auv.pdf.

UNFCCC (United Nations Framework Convention on Climate Change) (2010a), 'Appendix I – Nationally appropriate mitigation actions of developed country parties', available at http://unfccc.int/home/items/5264.php.

UNFCCC (United Nations Framework Convention on Climate Change) (2010b), 'Appendix II – Nationally appropriate mitigation actions of developing country parties', available at http://unfccc.int/home/items/5265.php.

UNFCCC (United Nations Framework Convention on Climate Change) (2010c), 'Draft decision-/CP.16, Outcome of the work of the Ad Hoc Working Group on the long-term cooperative action under the Convention', available at http://unfccc.int/files/meetings/cop_16/application/pdf/cop16_lca.pdf

United Nations (1992), *United Nations Framework Convention on Climate Change*, New York: United Nations, full text of the convention, available at http://unfccc.int/essential_background/convention/background/items/1349txt.php.

United Nations (1998), *Kyoto Protocol to the United Nations Framework Convention on Climate Change*, New York: United Nations.

VanBurke, C., S. Yun and E. Fitzgerald (2008), 'Hokkaido-Toyako G5 Summit Interim Compliance Report', Munk Centre for International Studies, University of Toronto, Toronto, available at http://www.g7.utoronto.ca/evaluations/2008compliance-interim/2008-interim-o5.pdf.

Van der Werf, G., R. Morton, J. de Fries, J. Olivier, R. Kasibhatla, R. Jackson, G. Collatz and J. Randerson (2009), 'CO_2 emissions from forest loss', *Nature Geoscience*, Commentary, **2**: 737–9.

Victor, D. (2008), 'Climate accession deals; new strategies for taming growth of greenhouse gases in developing countries', Discussion paper 08–18, The Harvard Project on International Climate Agreements, Harvard Kennedy School.

Wara, M. (2007), 'Is the global carbon market working?', *Nature*, **445**: 595–6.

Wara, M. and D. Victor (2008), 'A realistic policy on international carbon offsets', Working Paper 74, Program on Energy and Sustainable Development, Stanford University, Stanford, CA.

Weiner, J. (2008), 'Incentives and meta-architecture', in J. Aldy and R. Stavins (eds), *Architectures for Agreement: Addressing Global Climate Change in the Post-Kyoto World*, New York: Cambridge University Press, pp. 67–80.

WRI (World Resources Institute) (2009), *Climate Analysis Indicators Tool (CAIT) Version 6.0*, Washington DC: WRI.

WRI (World Resources Institute) (2010a), *Climate Analysis Indicators Tool (CAIT) Version 7.0*, Washington DC: WRI.

WRI (World Resources Institute) (2010b), 'A note on CO_2 emissions form land use change and forestry', available at http://cait.wri.org/cait.php?page=background &from=yearly&mode=view.

APPENDIX 5A.1 EMISSIONS FROM LAND-USE CHANGE AND FORESTRY

There is a great deal of uncertainty in the estimation of GHG emissions from land-use change and forestry (LUCF) caused by deforestation in tropical Asia (principally Indonesia) and South America (principally Brazil), in a particular year (WRI 2009). The likely errors stem from the estimation of biomass lost per hectare through land conversion as well as from errors in estimation of forest hectares converted (Houghton 2005).

The variability in emissions from land-use change is underlined in the case of Indonesia where Murdiyarso and Adiningsih (2007) estimate CO_2 emissions from forest fires were 5300 Mt in 1997, compared with 2560 Mt for 2003 estimated by Houghton (2003). Moreover, the WRI (2010a) estimates for LUC are much lower than for WRI (2009).[1] The author adopts OECD (2008b) LUCF estimates for 2005 and 2020 (12 per cent of total emissions) for the modelling of world emissions and the emissions cuts required by non-Annex I countries in 2020, the results of which are presented in Figures 5A.1 and 5A.2 and Appendix Table 5A.3.

Note

1. See also WRI (2010b). A note on CO_2 emissions from land use change and forestry, at http://cait.wri.org/cait.php?page =background&from=yearly&mode=view.

APPENDIX 5A.2 ANNEX I COUNTRIES

Table 5A.1   Annex I countries

Australia	Austria	Belarus*
Belgium	Bulgaria*	Canada
Czechoslovakia*	Denmark	European Economic Community
Estonia*	Finland	France
Germany	Greece	Hungary*
Iceland	Ireland	Italy
Japan	Latvia*	Lithuania*
Luxembourg	Netherlands	New Zealand
Norway	Poland*	Portugal
Romania*	Russian Federation*	Spain
Sweden	Switzerland	Turkey
Ukraine*	United Kingdom of Great Britain and Northern Ireland	United States of America

Note:
* Countries that are undergoing the process of transition to a market economy.
Annex B, subject to emissions limitations under the Kyoto Protocol, is made up of Annex I countries plus Liechtenstein, Monaco, Slovakia and Slovenia (United Nations 1998).

Source: United Nations (1992).

APPENDIX 5A.3   GLOBAL MITIGATION IMPERATIVES AND REALITIES

Impacts of increased GHG concentrations in the atmosphere are slow to become apparent. Even after their stabilisation, warming and sea-level rise will continue for centuries. Large reductions from current levels of emissions are required to stabilise the climate. The lower the level of stabilisation, the sooner cuts in emissions need to begin, and the deeper the long-term emission reduction needed. Delays in making cuts may lead to overshooting in targets for GHG concentrations, with deleterious social and environmental consequences from irreversible change.

The Bali Action Plan (UNFCCC 2008, p. 3) in responding to the IPCC's Fourth Assessment Report (IPCC 2007) acknowledged that 'deep cuts in global emissions will be required to achieve the ultimate objective of the Convention . . . and that delay in reducing emissions significantly constrains opportunities to achieve lower stabilisation levels and increases the risk of more severe climate change impacts.'

The IPCC's Fourth Assessment report, Working Group III, summarised the literature (IPCC 2007, Box 13.7) on the required emissions reduction ranges in Annex I and non-Annex I countries to achieve GHG concentration stabilisation levels. The summary indicates that Annex I countries as a group would need to reduce their emissions to below 1990 levels in 2020 by 25 per cent to 40 per cent for stabilisation at 450 ppm, and 10 to 30 per cent for 550 ppm, even while emissions from non-Annex I countries deviate substantially from their baseline in the case of the 450 ppm target.

5A.3.1   Cuts Required to Stabilise GHG Concentrations

The authors of Box 13.7 in IPCC (2007) (den Elzen and Höhne 2008, p. 250) have since conceded that: 'The current slow pace in climate policy and the steady increase in global emissions make it almost impossible to reach a relatively low global emissions levels in 2020 needed to meet the 450 ppm CO_2e'. An analysis of actual mitigation commitments as at mid-2009 made by 100 developed and developing countries leads Rojelg et al. (2009, p. 2) to conclude that 'unless there is a major improvement in national commitments to reducing GHGs we see no chance of staying below 2°C or 1.5°C.'

This section supports this conclusion of den Elzen and Höhne (2008) and Rogelj et al. (2009), and goes further in suggesting that the feasibility of achieving cuts to stabilise CO_2e concentrations to 550 ppm is also in doubt.

The results of modelling the cuts needed to limit CO_2e concentrations to 450 ppm, which would likely lead to temperature increases less than 2°C in the twenty-first century and to 550 ppm, which would likely lead to temperature increases greater than 2°C in the twenty-first century, are shown in Figures 5A.1 and 5A.2. These figures show the reduction required by non-Annex I (developing) countries for a given reduction by Annex I (developed) countries to achieve a 450 ppm emissions trajectory and a 550 ppm trajectory respectively. In Figure 5A.2, even large percentage cuts on 1990 CO_2e emissions by Annex I countries (Table 5A.1), which are highly unlikely, require significant reductions in 2020 BAU emissions by non-Annex I countries. Figure 5A.2 suggests that relaxing the target to 550 ppm still requires a large cut on non-Annex BAU by 2020 if Annex I countries adopted a lesser average cut of 20 per cent.

5A.3.2 Mitigation Commitments by Developed Countries and Implications for GHG Stabilisation

Even if Annex I countries reduced their emissions collectively by 20 per cent, non-Annex I countries would need to reduce emissions by 25 per cent on BAU by 2020 to achieve stabilisation at 550 ppm (see Figure 5A.2). A

Table 5A.2 World CO_2e emissions actual (1990–2005) and projected (2020) under BAU

	1990	1995	2000	2005	2020	Average annual rate of change average annual 2005–20
World wolucf	34392	35345	39051	43476	53600	1.55
Annex I	18582	18216	18091	18624	19764	0.41
Non-Annex I	15810	17129	20960	24852	33836	2.41
LUCF	4000	3900	5400	5700	5000	–0.82
Non-Annex I wlucf	19810	21029	26360	30552	38836	1.81
World wlucf	38392	39245	44451	49176	58600	1.28

Notes:
LUCF = land-use change and forestry;
wolucf = without land-use change and forestry;
wlucf = with land-use change and forestry.

Sources: Years 1990–2005 World, Annex I and Non-Annex I: IEA (2008a); Year 2020 World: OECD (2008b); Year 2020 Annex I and Non-Annex I distribution: author's estimates based on IEA (2008b); Years 1990–2020 LUCF: OECD (2008b).

Table 5A.3   Estimate of cuts required in CO_2e emissions to achieve 2020 stabilisation targets

		450 ppm CO_2e^a	550 ppm CO_2e^b
1.	Annex I countries 1990 Mt (from Table 5A.2)	18 582	
2.	Non-Annex I countries 2005 Mt (from Table 5A.2)	30 552	
3.	Non-Annex I countries 2020 projection wlucf Mt (from Table 5A.2)	38 836	
4.	World 2020 projection wlucf Mt (from Table 5A.2)	58 600	
5.	World 2020 targets Mt	40 000	45 000
6.	Cut required by 2020 Mt (5–4)	–18 600	–13 600
7.	Cut of 30% on 1990 levels by Annex I countries by 2020 Mt	–5 575	–5 575
8.	Cut required by non-Annex I countries by 2020 Mt (6–7)	–13 025	–8 025
9.	Non-Annex I after cuts in 2020 Mt (3+8)	25 811	30 811
10.	Change on non-Annex I countries BAU by 2020 % (8/3*100)	–34	–21

Notes:
[a]   Limiting the atmospheric concentration of CO_2e to 450 ppm, achieved by a world target of 40 000 Mt CO_2e in 2020, gives a probability of exceeding a 2°C rise in temperature throughout the twenty-first century of 19–56%, i.e. the probability of staying within 2°C is 'more likely than not' (Meinshausen et al. 2009, Figure S1c).
[b]   Limiting the atmospheric concentration of CO_2e to 550 ppm, achieved by a world target of 45 000 Mt CO_2e in 2020, gives a probability of exceeding a 2°C rise in temperature throughout the twenty-first century of 30–70%, i.e. the probability of staying within 2°C is 'less likely than not' (Meinshausen et al. 2009, Figure S1c).
wlucf = with land-use change and forestry.

result of modelling that reinforces the importance of developing country participation in meeting stabilisation targets is that even if developed countries reduced their collective emissions to zero in 2020, in the absence of a contribution by developing countries, the 450 stabilisation target would just be complied with. In Table 5A.3 (row 6) the cut required to achieve stabilisation at 450 ppm is 18 600 Mt CO_2e, which is about equal to the total Annex I country emissions in 1990 (row 1). Indeed, as Blandford at al. (2009) confirm, the level of stabilisation that can be achieved depends entirely on the actions of non-Annex I countries.

Another way of assessing the emissions curbs required by non-Annex I countries is to consider growth in emissions to 2020 compared with 2005.

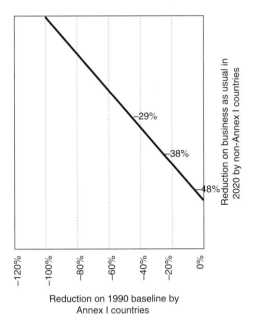

Source: Author's modelling. For probability of temperature rise for stabilisation targets, see Meinshausen et al. (2009).

Figure 5A.1   *Reduction in CO$_2$e emissions by Annex I and non-Annex I countries to achieve a 450 ppm trajectory*

Under BAU, their collective emissions are projected to grow by 43 per cent over this period (see Table 5A.2, p. 125); but achieving the 550 ppm target (given a cut of 20 per cent on 1990 level by Annex I countries) implies that non-Annex I countries will cut emissions by 5 per cent by 2020 compared with 2005.

Garnaut et al. (2008), in a sophisticated analysis, reach the conclusion that, if Annex I countries cut by 30 per cent on 1990 levels by 2020, a deep (26 per cent) cut will be required by non-Annex I countries to their BAU emissions in 2020 to achieve stabilisation at 550 ppm. The analysis in this chapter suggests a similar result; for a 30 per cent cut by developed countries, non-Annex I countries would need to reduce their BAU emissions by 21 per cent. (See Table 5A.3 for the detail of a 30 per cent cut by Annex I countries.) This BAU cut by non-Annex I countries in 2020 translates to a mere 1 per cent increase in emissions in 2020 compared with 2005.

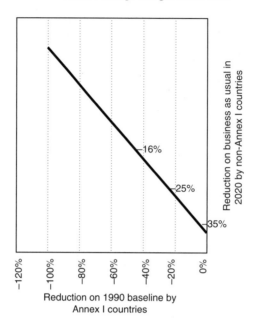

Source: Author's modelling. For probability of temperature rise for stabilisation targets, see Meinshausen et al. (2009).

Figure 5A.2   Reduction in CO₂e emissions by Annex I and non-Annex I
              countries to achieve a 550 ppm trajectory

6. Climate change impacts and adaptation strategies for Bangladesh

M.H. Rahman, M.A. Noor and A. Ahmed

6.1 IMPACTS OF CLIMATE CHANGE

The principal agents of climate change in Bangladesh are sea-level rise, temperature rise, increased evaporation, changes in precipitation and changes in cross-boundary river flows. These agents have an impact on several main natural system processes, such as, inundation, storm surges, low river flows, saltwater intrusion and river and coastal morphology. Moreover, the climate change-induced impacts may trigger a chain of consequences due to non-climatic activities and their outcomes. A subjective ranking of key climate change impacts and vulnerabilities for Bangladesh identifies water and coastal resources as being of the highest priority in terms of certainty, urgency and severity of impact, as well as the importance of the resources being affected. Impacts of climate change can be divided initially into two major parts: temperature and precipitation.

6.1.1 Temperature and Precipitation

The US Country Study Program (Manabe et al. 1991) for Bangladesh projected that temperature would rise 1.3°C by 2030 (over mid-twentieth century levels) and 2.6°C by 2070. Whether precipitation will increase or decrease under climate change is a critical factor in estimating how climate change will affect Bangladesh, given the country's extreme vulnerability to water-related disasters. During the period 1973–87, about 2.18 million tonnes of rice was damaged due to drought and 2.38 million tonnes due to flood. Drought affects annually about 2.32 million hectares and 1.2 million hectares of cropped land during the Kharif (summer) (November to June) and Rabi (winter) (July to October) seasons, respectively. The US Country Study also reports warming in the winter would be greater than the warming in summer. The study estimated little change in winter precipitation and an increase in precipitation during the monsoon (Ahmed and Alam 1999). The key issue is what ultimately happens during the monsoon season. More than 80 per cent of the 2300 mm of annual precipitation takes place during the monsoon period (Smith et al. 1998). Most of the climate models estimate that precipitation will increase during the summer monsoon because they estimate that air over land will warm more than air over oceans in the summer.

6.1.2   Sea-Level Rise

Bangladeshi scientists believe that due to sea-level rise coastal Bangladesh has already experienced the worst impacts, especially in terms of coastal inundation and erosion, saline intrusion, deforestation, loss of biodiversity and agriculture and large-scale migration. However, there is no specific regional scenario for net sea-level rises, in part because the Ganges–Brahmaputra delta is still active and the morphology highly dynamic. While literature suggests that the coastal lands are receiving additional sediments due to tidal influence, there are parts where land is subsiding due to tectonic activities (Huq et al. 1996). Since the landform is constituted by sediment decomposition, compaction of sediment may also play a role in defining net change in sea level along the coastal zone. A review of the literature and of expert opinion suggests that sediment loading may cancel out the effect of compaction and subsidence, so that net sea-level rise may be assumed. The US Country Study put the range at 30–100 cm by 2100, while the Intergovernmental Panel on Climate Change (IPCC) Third Assessment gives a global average range with lower values at 9 to 88 cm. In any event, the increases in mean sea-level rise need to be viewed in conjunction with the discussion on cyclones. Higher mean sea levels are likely to compound the enhanced storm surges expected to result from cyclones with higher intensity. Even in non-cyclone situations, higher mean sea levels are going to increase problems of coastal inundation and salinisation in the low lying deltaic coast.

Substantial amounts of arable land are affected by varying degrees of soil salinity. Soil salinity, waterlogging and acidification affect 3.05 million hectares, 0.7 million hectares and 0.6 million hectares of crop land, respectively. The temperature and rainfall projections for Bangladesh over the next decades show significant temperature increases for both monsoon and winter periods. The projections for rainfall indicate more rains during monsoon and less during dry periods.

6.1.3   Increased Frequencies of Natural Disasters

Recently an increasing trend of extreme events like cyclones, riverine and coastal floods and droughts have been observed in Bangladesh. Between

1991 and 2000, 93 major disasters were recorded, these resulted in nearly 200 000 deaths and caused US$5.9 billion in damage with high losses in agriculture and infrastructure. Since then, the country has experienced recurring floods frequently. The early monsoon floods in 2008 are part of what the World Meteorological Organization sees as a global pattern of record extreme weather conditions. Some major impacts of climate change are presented in Table 6.1.

6.2   AN OVERVIEW OF CLIMATE IMPACTS ON BANGLADESH AND REST OF SOUTH ASIA

Asia will be one of the most severely affected regions of the world as a result of 'business-as-usual' (BAU) global warming. According to the IPCC, even under its most conservative scenario, sea level will be about 40 cm higher by 2100. This will cause an additional 80 million coastal residents in Asia alone to be displaced. The majority of those displaced will be in South Asia, particularly in Bangladesh. There is a doubt about the extent of sea-level rise at the end of this century, but the IPCC's projection is in the range of 0.5–1 m, which has been regarded as an underestimate. A more realistic assessment, which takes into account the current business as usual scenario, indicates that a 3–5 m rise in sea level is not out of question with a 4–5°C rise in average global temperature, which will hasten the break-up of ice sheets in Greenland and Antarctica.

Sea-level rise will affect the coastal zone of South Asia in many ways, including inundation and displacement of wetlands and lowlands, coastal erosion, increased coastal storm flooding and salinisation. The impacts will vary by location, depending upon the coastal morphology and the extent of human modification. While rapid urbanisation led to the enlargement of natural coastal inlets and dredging of waterways for navigation, port facilities and pipelines, all these exacerbate saltwater intrusion into surface and groundwaters. Thus, built-up areas are more vulnerable than those protected by mangroves, and deltas, low-lying coastal plains, coral islands, beaches and barrier islands are especially at risk. Degradation of coastal ecosystems by human activity will generally aggravate the problems caused by sea-level rise, increasing shoreline retreat and coastal flooding of cities. Moreover, protection by dykes needs to consider not just the extent of average sea-level rise but also the effect of more frequent and intense storm surges. Engineering solutions are not a viable option from protection against sea-level rise, especially for increases greater than a few tens of centimetres. One study estimated that the minimum cost of protection against a metre sea-level rise would be about US500 000 per

Table 6.1   General impacts of climate change in Bangladesh

Effects of climate change	Impacts	Projection
More frequent and severe droughts	• decreased water availability • lead directly to conflict over water resources	IPCC (2007) – by the year 2050 > 1 billion people in Asia adversely affected by climate change
	• ruin harvests, leading to malnutrition and migrations	IPCC (2007) – by the year 2020 75–250 million people exposed to water stress
Acidification of the oceans	• hinder the formation of shells and skeletons of marine organisms, adversely affecting marine ecosystems	
Sea-level rise	• large-scale people migration • increase frequency of floods, storm surges, salt water intrusion, etc. • contaminate fresh water wells and aquifers	World Bank (Dasgupta et al. 2007) – 1 m sea-level rise would affect at least 56 million people
More frequent tropical storms and fires started by lightning strikes	• people move from low-lying areas fleeing the devastation and the loss of farmland • clean water contamination due to saltwater by storm surges	Large-scale people movements are highly likely to lead directly to conflicts as people try to cross borders and settle on land already claimed by others
Loss of biodiversity	• organisms migration • lost of critical 'keystone' species	
	• effect on human socioeconomic systems through agriculture and tourism • loss of irreplaceable natural chemical compounds for pharmaceutical and bioscience research	Outbreaks of cholera, diarrhoea and other waterborne diseases

Direct

Table 6.1   (continued)

Effects of climate change	Impacts	Projection
Indirect 'Other' economic costs	• impact the insurance industry resulting in higher premiums • affect energy generation companies, finally this will pass costs onto consumers • make insurance unaffordable to those who previously afforded	
Higher energy costs	• adverse health outcomes since they increase transport, heating and electricity costs for the health sector	
Donor fatigue	• increased natural disasters and conflicts, spread of tropical diseases, etc. will likely increase energy and other economic costs facing donor countries	pressure on donors' aid budgets

Source: Rahman et al. (2009)

km, but even then about 20–50 per cent of the vulnerable population could not be protected (Tol 2002).

With retreating glaciers in the Himalayas, and with the subsequent loss of fossil water, the water supply of the region will likely cease abruptly. In fact, given the non-linear dynamics of large-scale regional hydrometeorology, flows which may appear to be normal or even increase in the next few decades and therefore fulfil the needs of dry season, could slow down unexpectedly and cause unanticipated disruptions for farmers and urban dwellers (Singh and Bengtsson 2004).

Another big challenge for South Asia is the effect of climate change on monsoonal climate. The south-west monsoon is one of the most significant weather events in the world and delivers about 90 per cent of the annual rainfall for the region. The South Asian region will suffer from serious problems relating to water availability, substantial reductions in the yields of wheat and maize, increases in disease, flooding in some areas and drought in others, and potentially serious disruptions of the entire monsoon cycle. The onset, duration, spatial extent and total precipitation of the monsoon are all critical factors in determining the health of Bangladesh's agricultural sector, in particular, which continues to play a dominant role in the country's economy.

Unfortunately, climate models are generally poor in representing the inter-annual variation of monsoons, in part because of their poor spatial resolution. But they suggest that with a doubling or quadrupling of CO_2 concentrations by the end of the century, the Indian region will receive more average precipitation. There could, however, be substantial changes in the timing of monsoon onset, its spatial distribution and the occurrence of 'breaks', that is to say, periods during the monsoon when there is no rain (IPCC 2007; Mandke et al. 2007; Srinivasan and Joshi 2007). Of greatest concern is the possibility that the monsoon may shift its pattern abruptly and substantially, because of broader changes induced by global warming (Shukla 2007).

While there is some uncertainty of the extent to which regional monsoonal patterns and water availability will be affected in the region, it is clear that the climate in South Asia is quite sensitive to overall changes in the global atmosphere–ocean system, such as sea surface temperature anomalies in the Equatorial Pacific. Substantial changes that are expected elsewhere will greatly raise the risk of abrupt shifts in regional climate. Such low probability, high impact outcomes reiterate the need to use a precautionary approach to climate policy.

6.3   HUMAN IMPACTS AND POTENTIAL FOR DISPLACEMENT

6.3.1   Sea-Level Rise

Certainly, sea-level rise will affect coastal populations by inundation, flood and storm damage, erosion, saltwater intrusion, rising water tables and impeded drainage wetland loss. These will together greatly reduce the ability of these regions to provide their inhabitants with access to their land itself, in some cases, and to many others to their means of cultivation, water resources and fodder, causing severe hardship in terms of livelihood and habitat loss. Sea-level rise and the associated changes in the coastal zone will add burdens to those already poor and vulnerable. Currently almost 65 million people live in the area of about 54 461 square kilometres known as the Low Elevation Coastal Zone (LECZ). The LECZ comprises the coastal region that is within 10 m above average sea level. Bangladesh

Table 6.2   Summary of LECZ

Country	Area of LECZ (sq. km)	Population in LECZ	Urban population in LECZ	Fraction of population in LECZ in cities >5 mill.
Bangladesh	54461	65524048	15428668	33%

Source: www.sedac.ciesin.org.

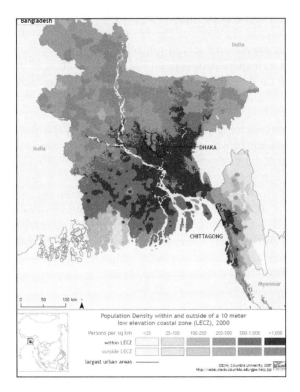

Source: www.sedac.ciesin.org.

Figure 6.1   Population density within and outside the 10 m LECZ in Bangladesh

having a low-lying delta on the Ganges–Brahmaputra plain together with a 700 km coastline, the LECZ in this country is extensive and is presented in Table 6.2 and Figure 6.1. In Bangladesh, most of the vulnerable population (75 per cent) lives in rural areas.

The vulnerability of the coastal population can be expressed in terms of their exposure to stresses such as storm surges and coastal erosion combined with the inadequacy of institutions and infrastructure to cope with the accompanying physical and societal changes. The most vulnerable communities include those having the most exposure to the stresses as well as those with the least capacity to respond and ability to recover (Turner et al. 2003; Adger et al. 2005). The physical changes would themselves take place in abrupt, non-linear ways as thresholds are crossed. In turn, the least resilient communities (for example, those dependent on subsistence fishing) will be the first to experience 'tipping points' in their life systems, so that the only livelihood option available to them will be to abandon their homes and search for better prospects elsewhere. As ever larger numbers of these people pass thresholds in terms of their ability to cope, societal tipping points will be crossed, resulting in the sudden mass movements of entire villages, towns and even cities from coastal regions towards safety.

While the actual triggers of migration are complex, historical evidence of migration from regions experiencing ecological or other stress indicates that population movements tend to take place in waves, often towards regions that are seen as being attractive because of pre-existing family or community contacts, job opportunities and cultural affinity (Myers 2002; Henry et al. 2004; McLeman and Smit 2006). More often than not, the largest recipients of migrants tend to be urban areas, either within or outside the country's borders. Frequently, the bulk of early migrants tend to be relatively young, which creates additional stresses in the remaining populations, thus improving the likelihood of ever larger waves of migrants leaving the vulnerable regions.

6.4   MIGRATION SCENARIOS

The previous sections indicated that climate change likely to trigger mass migration of individuals and their families. This is primarily because of livelihood loss and direct loss of land and homes. It is reasonably certain about the broad trends in physical, social and economic changes over the next 50–100 years for different emissions trajectories, but there are substantial uncertainties when attempts are made to improve scales of spatial and temporal resolution beyond those obtained by most climate models. Furthermore, there are non-linearities and threshold effects to consider when anticipating when and how much migration might occur as a result of the adverse impacts of climate change. Hence, the estimation should be considered as being roughly indicative and by no means exact forecasts of the number of people expected to be displaced from their homes under two different climate change scenarios.

The two scenarios are generally provided for Bangladesh, a business-as-usual (BAU) scenario that results in atmospheric concentrations of CO_2 that exceed 750 ppm by the end of the century and a policy scenario that limits concentrations to below 450 ppm. The BAU scenario causes average global temperatures to rise by 4–5°C, while the policy scenario limits the increase in temperature to below 2°C.

Various conservative assumptions were used to estimate the sea-level rise associated with these global average temperature changes and the corresponding impacts on the residents of South Asia living in the LECZ. First, because of the uncertainty associated with the breakup of land ice in the Antarctic and on Greenland, three possible options are considered for the BAU scenario, 1 m, 3 m and 5 m of sea-level rise in 2100, representing a low, medium and high estimate, respectively. For the policy scenario, an estimate of 0.3 m sea-level rise in 2100 is used, which corresponds roughly to the mid-range of the IPCC scenario.

Furthermore, it is postulated that sea-level rise will take place very gradually in the early years, but will accelerate towards the end of the century, consistent with the understanding that various positive feedback processes will cause ice break-up and melting to gather speed only towards the middle to end of the century. It is also assumed that there is a similar non-linear response to rising average sea levels for communities living along the coast. For instance, at modest levels of sea-level rise, the motivation to leave the region entirely may be relatively low, as people learn to adjust to changing physical and economic conditions. As the average sea level continues to rise, coastal inundation, saltwater intrusion and storm surges will become more intense and people will find it increasingly difficult to stay in their original homes and will look for ways to migrate inland. Figure 6.2 and Table 6.3 show, respectively, how we have modelled the increase in area affected by sea-level rise and the way in which people's migration patterns are impacted upon. Thus, in the BAU cases, where the impacts of sea-level rise are expected to be catastrophic only in later years, it is expected that coping strategies would break down quite soon in the flood zone regions, so that by 2045, the entire population would be forced to migrate inland, primarily to cities. For instance, in the policy scenario, it is also assumed that a certain degree of adaptation is built into the framework, so that some form of evolving coastal protection is included to reduce the impacts of sea-level rise.

The consolidated results for population out-migration in Bangladesh for the two scenarios, including the three cases for the BAU scenario, are

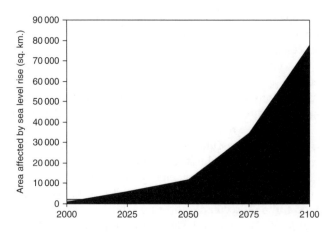

Source: Mondal and Rajan (2009).

Figure 6.2   *Area affected by sea-level rise in Bangladesh for the BAU case where maximum sea-level rise is 3 m in 2100*

Table 6.3   *Estimates of migrants likely to be displaced by sea-level rise in Bangladesh*

Year	Migrants (assuming phased movement)		
	2100 (1 m)	2100 (3 m)	2100 (5 m)
2010	24240	33936	43632
2020	161998	226797	291597
2030	680747	953046	1225344
2040	2742200	3839080	4935959
2050	5730425	8022596	10314766
2060	8786180	12300651	15815123
2070	13287036	18601851	23916666
2080	19915447	27881626	35847805
2090	29676268	41546775	53417282
2100	41611188	58255663	74900139

Source: Mondal and Rajan (2009).

shown in Table 6.3. Note that as many as 75 million people or as few as 41 million could be rendered homeless by 2100 in Bangladesh.

The double burden of globalisation and drought associated with climate change could also be the cause of migration out of several vulnerable areas in the country. While it is far less obvious how to identify the population most likely to migrate from these causes as opposed to the physical reality associated with sea-level rise, one could make simplifying assumptions based on the TERI/CICERO study to focus on the most vulnerable regions and groups of people within them.

6.5   CLIMATE CHANGE STRATEGY AND ACTION PLAN IN BANGLADESH

The design of NAPA (National Action Plan for Adaptation) was a significant start for dealing with climate change impacts in Bangladesh (see Table 6.4). This process has been taken forward, including through the adoption of the Bangladesh Climate Change Strategy and Action Plan (BCCSAP) in 2008, which is the main basis of Bangladesh's efforts to combat climate change over the next ten years. The Climate Change Action Plan is built on six pillars (MoEF 2008) which are:

1. *Food security, social protection and health* – to ensure that the poorest and most vulnerable in society, including women and children, are protected from climate change and that all programmes focus on the needs of this group for food security, safe housing, employment and access to basic services, including health.
2. *Comprehensive disaster management* – to further strengthen the country's already proven disaster management systems to deal with increasingly frequent and severe natural calamities.
3. *Infrastructure* – to ensure that existing assets (for example, coastal and river embankments) are well-maintained and fit-for-purpose and that urgently needed infrastructure (for example, cyclone shelters and urban drainage) is put in place to deal with the likely impacts of climate change.
4. *Research and knowledge management* – to predict the likely scale and timing of climate change impacts on different sectors of the economy and socioeconomic groups; to underpin future investment strategies; and to ensure that Bangladesh is networked into the latest global thinking on climate change.
5. *Mitigation and low carbon development* – to evolve low carbon development options and implement these as the country's economy grows over the coming decades.
6. *Capacity building and institutional strengthening* – to enhance the capacity of government ministries and agencies, civil society and the private sector to meet the challenge of climate change.

*Table 6.4   Suggested adaptation strategies for climate change impacts in
            NAPA for Bangladesh*

1. Reducing climate change hazards through coastal afforestation with community participation.
2. Providing drinking water to coastal communities to combat enhanced salinity due to sea-level rise.
3. Capacity building for integrating climate change in planning, designing of infrastructure, conflict management and land water zoning for water management institutions.
4. Disseminating climate change and adaptation information to vulnerable communities for emergency preparedness measures and awareness raising on enhanced climatic disasters.
5. Constructing flood shelters, and information and assistance centres to cope with enhanced recurrent floods in major floodplains.
6. Mainstreaming adaptation to climate change into policies and programmes in different sectors (focussing on disaster management, water, agriculture, health and industry).
7. Including climate change issues in curriculum at secondary and tertiary educational institution.
8. Enhancing resilience of urban infrastructure and industries to impacts of climate change.
9. Developing eco-specific adaptive knowledge (including indigenous knowledge) on adaptation to climate variability to enhance adaptive capacity for future climate change.
10. Promoting research on drought, flood and saline-tolerant varieties of crops to facilitate adaptation in future.
11. Promoting adaptation to coastal crop agriculture to combat increased salinity.
12. Adaptating agriculture systems in areas prone to enhanced flash flooding in north-east and central region.
13. Adaptating fisheries in areas prone to enhanced flooding in north east and central region through adaptive and diversified fish culture practices.
14. Promoting adaptation to coastal fisheries through culture of salt-tolerant fish special in coastal areas of Bangladesh.
15. Exploring options for insurance and other emergency preparedness measures to cope with enhanced climatic disasters.

Various programmes and sub-programmes have been listed in the BCCSAP (Table 6.5) which are to be implemented by different organisations for coping with the climate change impacts. Responsibility for implementing the various components of the BCCSAP lie with nine ministries and agencies, who are expected to work in partnership with each other and with civil society and the business community. The Ministry of

Table 6.5   Programmes under themes of BCCSAP

Theme/Pillar	Programmes
Food security, social protection and health	• Institutional capacity for research towards climate resilient cultivars and their dissemination • Development of climate-resilient cropping systems • Adaptation against drought • Adaptation in fisheries sector • Adaptation in livestock sector • Adaptation in health sector • Water and sanitation programme in climate vulnerable areas • Livelihood protection in ecologically fragile areas • Livelihood protection of vulnerable socioeconomic groups (including women)
Comprehensive disaster management	• Improvement of flood forecasting and early warning • Improvement of cyclone and storm surge warning • Awareness raising and public education towards climate resilience • Risk management against loss of income and property
Infrastructure	• Repair and maintenance of existing flood embankments • Repair and maintenance of cyclone shelters • Repair and maintenance of existing coastal polders • Improvement of urban drainage • Adaptation against floods • Adaptation against tropical cyclones and storm surges • Planning and design of river dragging works
Research and knowledge management	• Establishment of a centre for knowledge management and training on climate change • Climate change modelling at national and sub-national levels • Preparatory studies for adaptation against sea-level rise • Monitoring of ecosystem and biodiversity changes and their impacts • Macroeconomic and sectoral economic impacts of climate change
Mitigation and low carbon development	• Improved energy efficiency in production and consumption of energy • Gas exploration and reservoir management • Development of coal mines and coal-fired power stations with modern technology • Renewable energy development • Lower emissions from agricultural land

Table 6.5   (continued)

Theme/Pillar	Programmes
	● Management of urban waste ● Afforestation and reforestation programme
Capacity building and institutional strengthening	● Revision of sectoral policies for climate resilience ● Main-streaming climate change in national, sectoral and spatial development programmes ● Strengthening human resource capacity ● Strengthening institutional capacity for climate change management ● Main-streaming climate change in the media

Environment and Forests is responsible for coordinating activities under the Action Plan and intends to establish a Climate Change Secretariat to facilitate this work.

6.6   THE WAYS AHEAD – 15TH CONFERENCE OF THE PARTIES (COP15)

The United Nations Climate Change Conference took place from 7–19 December 2009 in Copenhagen, Denmark. It was held under the 15th Conference of the Parties (COP15) to the United Nations Framework Convention on Climate Change (UNFCCC) and the 5th Conference of the Parties serving as the Meeting of the Parties to the Kyoto Protocol (COP/MOP5). COP15 and COP/MOP5 were held in conjunction with the 31st sessions of the Subsidiary Body for Scientific and Technological Advice (SBSTA31) and the Subsidiary Body for Implementation (SBI31), the 10th session of the Ad Hoc Working Group on Further Commitments for Annex I Parties under the Kyoto Protocol (AWG-KP10) and the 8th session of the Ad Hoc Working Group on Long-term Cooperative Action under the UNFCCC (AWG-LCA8).

The Copenhagen Conference marked the culmination of a 2-year negotiating process to enhance international climate change cooperation under the Bali Roadmap, launched by COP13 in December 2007. Before COP15 there was widespread optimism that even if the outcome was not legally binding, it would include strong positives for the 100 or so developing nations that have done least to cause climate change and are most at risk – the least developed countries, small island developing states and most of Africa. COP15 was not supposed to be about money or politics, but of our future. The most vulnerable countries hoped for a binding agreement that would limit temperature increases to 1.5°C rather than the 2°C favoured by the G20. They wanted an agreement on how to support adaptation to climate change in their countries, with significant funding pledge and technology transfer from industrialised countries, and a 'Reducing Emissions from Deforestation and Forest Degradation (REDD)' deal that would pay nations with major forestry resources to reduce emissions from deforestation.

Towards the end of the COP15 negotiations, the talks were going on in two completely separate directions. First, negotiations among all 192 parties to the UNFCCC continued. Second, and behind closed doors, a select group of about 25 world leaders came up with the Copenhagen Accord, into which most of the vulnerable countries had very little input. During the closing COP plenary, which lasted nearly 13 hours, what many characterised as 'acrimonious' discussions ensued on the transparency of the process that had led to the conclusion of the Copenhagen Accord and on whether the COP should adopt it. Most negotiating groups supported its adoption as a COP decision in order to operationalise it as a step towards a 'better' future agreement. Some developing countries, however, opposed the Accord reached during what they characterised as a 'non-transparent' and 'undemocratic' negotiating process. During informal negotiations facilitated by UN Secretary-General Ban Ki-Moon during the night and early morning of the last day, parties agreed to adopt a COP decision whereby the COP 'takes note' of the Copenhagen Accord, which was attached to the decision as an unofficial document. Parties also agreed to establish a procedure whereby countries supporting the Copenhagen Accord can accede to it. Though the Copenhagen Accord immediately faced strong criticism, the agreement did include a 2°C target and many other important provisions. Indeed, many saw the Copenhagen Accord as a concise document containing an outline of a future framework to address climate change (Hossain 2009).

Nevertheless, its provisions on mitigation by developed countries are widely seen as 'clearly weak' and 'a step backwards from the Kyoto Protocol'. Developed countries do not commit themselves to legally binding emission reductions. Similarly, there is no quantification of a long-term global goal for emission reductions, or specific timing for global emissions to peak. Instead, the agreement suggests a bottom-up approach whereby developed and developing countries submit their pledges for information purposes to the Convention, a method advocated most prominently by the United States.

With regard to mitigation actions by developing countries, the Accord does not contain any quantified emission reduction objectives and mainly elaborates on the monitoring, reporting and verification (MRV) of developing country actions, one of the major stumbling blocks in the negotiations leading to Copenhagen. MRV of unsupported actions are suggested to be done domestically and reported to the Convention through national communications. The Accord, however, does contain some language, reportedly a compromise between the United States and China, stating that there will be some provisions for 'international consultations and analysis', a concept yet to be defined. Those actions supported by international finance, technology transfer and capacity building will, however, be subject to international MRV.

The most successful part of the Accord relates to short- and long-term financing. Developed countries and Bangladesh went to Copenhagen with clear promises to fund mitigation and adaptation actions. According to the Copenhagen Accord, US$30 billion for the period 2010–12 will be provided, and long-term funds of a further US$100 billion a year by 2020 will be mobilised from a variety of sources. However, it lacks essential details such as where this money will come from loans or grants. The Accord also establishes four new bodies: a mechanism on REDD-plus, a High-Level Panel under the COP to study the implementation of financing provisions, the Copenhagen Green Climate Fund and a Technology Mechanism. Furthermore, the Accord contains a reference to possibly limiting temperature increase to below 1.5°C, as advocated by many small island developing states and others, although only with regard to the future assessment of the implementation of the Accord. However, the biggest disappointment in Copenhagen was one of leadership and, perhaps, to save the planet we should start looking for true climate leadership more importantly than anything else.

6.7   CONCLUSIONS

The magnitude of the impacts of climate change are uncertain. The understanding of the phenomenon will further deepens with more knowledge of the latest developments and experiences in other parts of the world. Hence, the Strategy and Action Plan will require periodical revision. The following enhancements should be considered by the Government of Bangladesh for their policies and programmes.

Adopt meaningful, achievable climate change targets: Although the focus of the action plan of Bangladesh is on low carbon development, the emissions are actually negligible. Bangladesh produces approximately 0.2 per cent global CO_2 so the government must be careful in setting out targets considering our growing economy.

Pursue strong, binding emissions targets in international negotiations: In international climate change negotiations, the Bangladesh government should support strong binding emissions reduction targets for developed countries that will keep global warming below 2°C, including emission reduction targets of 25–40 per cent below 1990 levels by 2020, and at least 80 per cent below 1990 levels by 2050.

Ensure commitment of developing countries' fair share to climate change adaptation: The Bangladesh government should strongly negotiate for increasing aid directed towards helping developing countries such as Bangladesh to improve energy efficiency, to adopt energy-efficient production processes, to adopt renewable energy technologies and to adapt to climate change through measures such as disaster preparedness planning and improving food and water security.

Education, training and public awareness: The Bangladesh government should develop and implement educational and public awareness programmes on climate change and its effects. The public should have access to information on climate change and its effects and should participate in addressing the issue and develop adequate responses. The government should train scientific, technical and managerial personnel on climate change and its effects; and programmes should include strengthening of national institutions and the exchange of personnel to train experts in this field.

Seeking more support for climate change mitigation and adaptation research: The Bangladesh government should look for increased funding support for research into innovative technologies including renewable energy, understanding climate change dynamics, carbon capture and sequestration, energy efficiency, crop varieties and other adaptation and mitigation innovations.

Encourage environmental solutions in other countries: Bangladesh should support and play an advocacy role for global, regional, national and local efforts to address climate change through leading-edge biosequestration programmes, including agricultural diversification, reforestation and reduction of deforestation.

Collaborate with our neighbours who are victims of climate change: The Bangladesh government should take more initiatives for better collaboration with our neighbours for jointly dealing with the climate change impacts and implement adaptation strategies.

REFERENCES

Adger, W., T. Hughes, C. Folke, S. Carpenter et al. (2005), 'Social-ecological resilience to coastal disasters', *Science*, **309**: 1036–9.
Ahmed, A.U. and S. Alam (1999), 'Development of climate scenarios with general

146   *Climate change and growth in Asia*

circulation models', in *Vulnerability and Adaptation to Climate Change for Bangladesh*, Dhaka: BUP.
Dasgupta, S., B. Laplanate, C. Melser, D. Wheeler and J. Yan (2007), 'The impact of sea level rise on developing countries: a comparative analysis', World Bank Research Working Paper 4136, Washington DC.
Henry, S., V. Piché, D. Ouédraogo and E. Lambin (2004), 'Descriptive analysis of the individual migratory pathways according to environmental typologies', *Population & Environment*, **25** (5): 397–422.
Hossain, M. (2009), '"Wild roller coaster ride" at COP15: us vs. them', *The Daily Star*, 21 December, Dhaka.
Huq, S., A.U. Ahmed and R. Koudstaal (1996), 'Vulnerability of Bangladesh to climate change and sea level rise', in T.E. Downing (ed.), *Climate Change and World Food Security*, NATO ASI Series, I 37, Berlin, Heidelberg: Springer-Verlag, pp. 347–79.
IPCC (2007), *Climate Change 2007: Impacts, Adaptation and Vulnerability*, Fourth Assessment, Cambridge, UK: Cambridge University Press.
McLeman, R. and B. Smit (2006), 'Migration as an adaptation to climate change', *Climatic Change*, **76** (1): 31–53.
Manabe, S., R.J. Stouffer, M.J. Spelman and K. Bryan (1991), 'Transient responses of a coupled oceanatmosphere model to gradual changes of atmospheric CO_2, Part I: annual mean response', *Journal of Climate*, **4**: 785–818.
Mandke, S.K., A.K. Sahai, M.A. Shinde, S. Joseph et al. (2007), 'Simulated changes in active/break spells during the Indian summer monsoon due to enhanced CO_2 concentrations: assessment from selected coupled atmosphere–ocean global climate models', *International Journal of Climatology*, **27**: 837–59.
MoEF (2008), 'Bangladesh Climate Change Strategy and Action Plan 2008', Dhaka, Bangladesh: Ministry of Environment and Forests, Government of the People's Republic of Bangladesh.
Mondal, M.K. and S.C. Rajan (2009), 'Climate migrants in Bangladesh: estimates and solutions', in M.H. Rahman et al. (eds), *Climate Change Impacts and Adaptation Strategies for Bangladesh*, Dhaka: ITN, BUET, pp. 225–35.
Myers, N. (2002), 'Environmental refugees: a growing phenomenon of the 21st century', *Philosophical Transactions: Biological Sciences*, **357** (1420): 609–13.
Rahman M.H., M.A. Noor and A. Ahmed (2009), 'Climate change related policies and strategies: Bangladesh perspective', in M.H. Rahman et al. (eds), *Climate Change Impacts and Adaptation Strategies for Bangladesh*, Dhaka: ITN, BUET, pp. 12–25.
Shukla, J. (2007), 'Monsoon mysteries', *Science*, **318** (5848): 204.
Singh, P. and L. Bengtsson (2004), 'Hydrological sensitivity of a large Himalayan basin to climate change', *Hydrological Processes*, **18** (13): 2363–85.
Smith, J.B., A. Rahman and M.Q. Mirza (1998), 'Considering adaptation to climate change in the sustainable development of Bangladesh', Report to The World Bank by Stratus Consulting Inc., Boulder, CO.
Srinivasan, J. and P. Joshi (2007), 'What have we learned about the Indian monsoon from satellite data?', *Current Science*, **93** (2): 165.
Tol, R. (2002), 'Estimates of the damage costs of climate change. Part II: Dynamic estimates', *Environmental and Resource Economics*, **21** (2): 135–60.
Turner, B., R. Kasperson, P. Matson, J. McCarthy et al. (2003), 'A framework for vulnerability analysis in sustainability science', *Proceedings of the National Academy of Sciences*, **100** (14): 8074–9.

7. Climate change, vulnerabilities and South Asia: issues, challenges and options

M. Adil Khan

> So if we carry on as we are, Bangladesh will enter its endgame . . . The head-stone would read, Bangladesh, 1971–2071: born in blood, died in water.
>
> Hari 2008

7.1 CONCEPTS AND DEFINITIONS

The Fourth Assessment Report by the Intergovernmental Panel on Climate Change (IPCC) states that '[W]arming of the climate system is unequivocal, as is now evident from observations of increases in global average air and ocean temperatures, widespread melting of snow and ice and rising global average sea level' (2007).[1] Climate change affects everyone and cuts across sectors – rich and poor, rural and urban, farmers and industrialists, public and private, and central and local governments. The poor in developing countries are most vulnerable where population density is high, and there is high malnutrition, lack of sanitation and water supplies, weak infrastructures (schools, buildings, bridges), inadequate or no social support and limited income opportunities (Eakin 2005; IPCC 2007; WESS 2008).

7.1.1 Conceptualising Climate Change

'Climate change' is often referred to as changes in climatic averages and variability brought about by global warming. Independently of global warming, climate change on seasonal, inter-annual, decadal and multi-decadal timescales takes place on a regular basis. Seasonal changes are so reliable that environmental and socioeconomic systems tend to adjust themselves well to these changes. However, even if extreme weather conditions occur on inter-annual (for example, floods, droughts), decadal (for example, tsunamis), or multidecadal (for example, earthquakes)

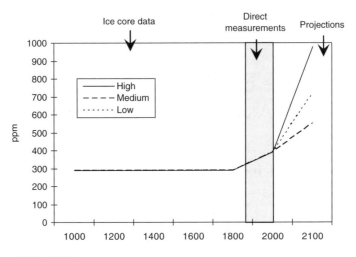

Source: WHO (2003).

Figure 7.1   Atmospheric concentrations of CO_2

timescales, environmental and socioeconomic systems run the risks of getting out of sync. In the longer term, the distinction between 'normal' climate change and that caused by global warming is hard to define. A normal climate under normal circumstances may change over a period of several decades, while 'climate change' is human-created excessive greenhouse gas (GHG)[2] emissions heating up the atmosphere and causing drastic changes in climatic conditions (IPCC 2007). In recent times, the rate at which the climate is changing is unprecedented and this includes rapid change in temperature, rise in sea level, change in precipitation patterns, increased glacial and permafrost melting and increased intensity, frequency and length of extreme weather conditions such as floods, droughts and hurricanes.

Public concern over the problem of global warming brought climate change into the scientific discourse and international political agenda in the mid-1980s. To collect and highlight in the public domain up-to-date scientific information on climate change, the World Meteorological Organization and the United Nations Environment Programme (UNEP) established the International Panel on Climate Change (IPCC) in 1988 and the United Nations Framework Convention on Climate Change (UNFCC) in 2002. The IPCC's First Assessment Report in 1990 highlighted the threat of climate change and identified anthropogenic increases in carbon dioxide (CO_2) as the most significant contributor to global warming (see Figure 7.1).

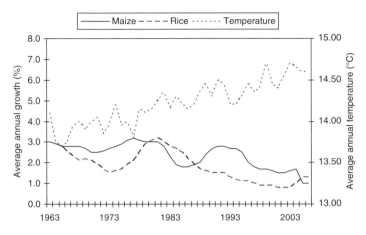

Source: World Bank (2008) and Goddard Institute for Space Studies (NASA 2005).

Figure 7.2   Global warming and declining productivity of food crop

The difference between *seasonal changes* and *climate change* is that while the former is nature induced, gradual and somewhat predictable, and thus adaptations are relatively easy, the latter are *human induced* and the effects are more drastic and adaptations are far more challenging.

Effects of climate change on the economies of countries are likely to be multi-faceted and it is conceivable that developing countries are going to be the worst sufferers. Figure 7.2 demonstrates the inverse relationship between global warming and average annual growth of food crops – the higher the temperatures the lower the growth of the food crop.

Indeed, climate change induces changes such as those outlined above and these hazards pose unprecedented risks and expose people, especially the poor, to numerous vulnerabilities.

As is obvious, climate change-induced effects also put at risk the timely achievement of the goals of the Millennium Declaration 2001, the globally agreed eight millennium development goals (popularly known as MDGs) that envisage, among other things, reduction of poverty by half and achievement of important educational, environmental, health and gender development goals by 2015.[3]

7.1.2   Climate Change Vulnerabilities[4]

Climate change-induced vulnerabilities include a range of risks and in this chapter these risks are categorised broadly as:

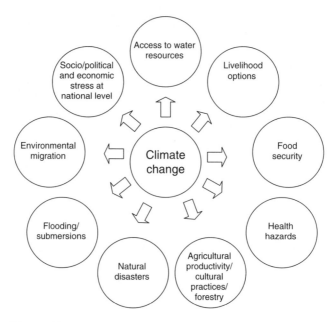

Source: Khan (2009).

Figure 7.3   A framework of climate change vulnerabilities

1.   Physical and biophysical;
2.   Economic and social; and
3.   Political.

Intensity of vulnerability arising out of climate change depends on a country or a region's geo-physical location and its existing socioeconomic conditions. Low-lying coastal areas and arid and semi-arid regions are most vulnerable. Figure 7.3 presents various elements of multi-faceted dimension of climate change-induced vulnerabilities (Khan 2009).

   Figure 7.3 demonstrates two interesting phenomena that climate change vulnerabilities that include uncertainties with food security and agricultural productivity, health hazards, natural disasters, flooding and submersions, environmental migrations, sociopolitical and economic stress, dwindling accesses to water, livelihood options, etc. are not only multi-faceted, they are also interlinked. For example, natural disasters have the potential to cause health hazards and again health hazards will influence livelihood options and so on and so forth. Similarly, loss of agricultural productivity will cause food deficits and thus hunger, and consequently, may contribute to socioeconomic and political stress and so forth.

The implications of a multi-faceted interlinking characteristic of climate change vulnerability are that those who are threatened by these are prone to be subjected to what can be termed as a *vulnerability trap*.

Table 7.1 demonstrates how various climate change-induced sectoral vulnerabilities impact the physical/ biophysical as well as socioeconomic and political elements of a society.

In summary, what is obvious is that the climate change vulnerabilities are multi-dimensional and the extent and intensity of negative impacts of climate change will very much depend on a country or a community's existing overall socioeconomic and physical/ecological conditions, as well as on the rate and intensity of future global warming. Furthermore, due to their limited coping capacities poorer nations are likely to be disproportionately exposed and thus be more vulnerable to climate change-induced because disasters:

1. Developing countries often do not have the required resources and thus are ill-prepared in terms of coastal protection, early warning and disaster response systems, victim relief and recovery assistance (GEF 2001);
2. For many countries, climate change is only one of the many environment problems they have to cope with;
3. Proportionately, recovery costs are also higher for developing countries – whilst developed countries pay 0.1 per cent of GDP in losses, developing countries pay 3 per cent or sometimes as much as 15 per cent as seen with hurricanes in the Caribbean; and
4. Developing countries also experience a greater loss of life; 90 per cent of all deaths – for example, the risk of drowning in Fiji due to dyke failure is 1 in 100 000 whereas in the Netherlands it is 1 in 10 million (Olsthoorn et al. 1999).

Again, within the poorer nations, the poorer communities are at a much greater risk and their climate change vulnerabilities seem to stem from a number of factors including (Khan 2009a):

1. As they live at the margin of society – many in environmentally degraded and vulnerable locations – poor communities are more vulnerable to extreme weather events, like those associated with climate change;
2. Their physical location, lack of services and infrastructure poor building structures and so forth all increase their vulnerability to flooding, storm surges and cyclonic wind and rain (in Bangladesh, for example, 15 per cent of total land is subject to flooding and is disproportionately

Table 7.1   Sectoral and cross-sectoral implications of climate change

Sector	Sector level impacts	Physical and biophysical	Socioeconomic and political
Agriculture	Reduction in cereal crop yields; affect farm animals (quality and quantity of output produced); increased prevalence of pests, weeds and diseases. However, some crop yields may increase due to CO_2 fertilisation; longer growing season in high latitude	Increased desertification; loss of soil fertility; changes in flora and fauna; flooding and increased salinity of water, etc.	Food crisis; hunger; malnutrition; rise in poverty, inequality and internal disharmony
Health	Heat stress and heat related mortality; intense winter deaths; prevalence of vector-borne diseases (malaria and dengue fever); food and nutritional deficiencies	Overall poor health especially for women and children	Increased health costs; high mortality; lowered life expectancy; increased infant and maternal mortality and low labour productivity
Water resources	Change in water volume, timing and flow; increase in salinity in the inland water bodies (e.g. rivers, lakes, ponds); change in water source (e.g. from rain-fed streams to groundwater); decrease in water quality; high water temperature affects aquatic ecology and prevalence of water-borne diseases.	Uncertainty of availability of water and reduction in water quality and access; change in aquatic ecology; increase in water-borne diseases	Lower availability and access to food, fisheries, etc.
Fisheries and birds	Alterations to the conditions of habitat and ecosystem; changes in migration patterns; changes in nesting and reproduction behaviours; loss of species that are slow to adapt to climate change	Vast biophysical changes including changes in behaviours and habitats of animals and other species	Uncertainty of livelihood options/ food sources; increased poverty, etc.

Table 7.1   (continued)

Sector	Sector level impacts	Physical and biophysical	Socioeconomic and political
Settlement, transportation and trade	Malfunctioning infrastructure; rapid deterioration of roads and paths; disruption of various signals (e.g. cell signals, radio waves); dislocation of transportation systems and disruption in transfer of goods and services (e.g. road smog, overcast sky); reduction of tourism due to extreme summer or long winter; increased energy demand for space cooling or space heating	Infra-structural disorder and imbalances	Loss of trade, income and productivity; high energy demand; pressure on an existing weak service delivery capacity; increase in crime, etc.
Extreme weather events	Higher frequency and severity of extreme weather events (hurricanes, floods and storms) likely to damage infrastructure; weaken capital stocks; interrupt daily economic activities; cause health difficulties, injury and deaths of humans and animals, etc.	Drastic changes in physical/ biophysical conditions	High cost of relief, rehabilitation, including high costs of adaptation and mitigation; loss of livelihood options and income; increased political stability, etc.
Climate migration	Alterations to eco-system; submersion of low-lying areas and increased risks to livelihood options will induce climate migration, firstly within the affected country from the affected zones to safer areas and eventually, across national borders	Internal displacements; severe pressure on infrastructure and employment options; security threats	Economic and political instability including, where relevant, cross-border illegal migration

occupied by people living in a marginal existence (IPCC 2001));

3. Poorer settlements also lack the infrastructure of fire services, dykes, early warning systems (EWS), drains, and so forth, which help cope with a disaster;
4. The poor do not have the resources to invest in disaster-proof buildings, which increases the risk of them losing their shelter; and
5. Poorer communities also have limited means to cope with the losses and damage inflicted by natural disasters.

Also among the poor, the most vulnerable are the rural smallholder agriculturalists, fishing communities, pastoralists, wage labourers, particularly those living in remote/coastal agricultural lands, urban poor and refugees and the displaced. An in-depth understanding of this socio-matrix of climate change vulnerabilities is key to finding and designing options relevant to preparedness, adaptation and mitigation (PAM).

7.1.3　A Demand Side or a Lifestyle Perspective on Climate Change

Most coping initiatives of climate change vulnerabilities tend to focus on what can be termed supply side solutions that include improved preparedness, various adaptation measures (mostly infrastructure development-related interventions) and mitigation options – through cuts in carbon emissions at the enterprise level.

While these measures are important and must be pursued, equal attention must also be given to the aspects of lifestyle or the demand side perspectives that induce global warming and cause climate change. It is important to recognise that no amount of supply side interventions (green technology, emission cuts, improved adaptations and so forth) is going to help until the demand side challenges – the lifestyle issues that promote consumerism and materialism as end goals of development and thus put continuous pressure on the environment and contribute to global warming – are also tackled at the same time. Consumerism and materialism, a post-Industrial Revolution capitalist mode of development and, as far as the developing countries are concerned, a colonial and neo-colonial phenomenon, was further deepened through the current globalisation processes. Excessive consumerism has not only become part of contemporary value systems right across the globe, and thus an aspired lifestyle option, it has equally influenced the notion of development as a means of achieving such lifestyles, marginalising value systems and cultures that promoted conserving consumption in the recent past.

As far as developing countries are concerned, colonial exchange arrangements and the altered administrative and production systems that accompanied these arrangements seem to have replaced their traditional values of conserving lifestyles with a growth model that is excessively consumerist and thus has become climate risky. On the virtues of conserving consumerism, Blackwell and Searbook (1993) note that 'Popular traditions of frugality were not ideologies, they were living practices. They were the way ordinary women and men carried out their daily lives and taught their children to follow them. That all this should have been discarded overnight was a grievous loss, and grievously we are paying for it.' These authors also argue that re-evaluation and possible re-invention of these traditions has nothing or little to do with a desire to return to a 'life of penny pinching misery and privation upon people', rather a 'wish to restore a sense of balance against the celebration of waste, a sense of judgement against the glorification of the superfluous.'

The evolving climate change threats are challenging the world to re-examine the validity and sustainability of the consumerist value system and, at the same time, explore options of re-enacting a value system that stresses moderation in consumption and, consequently, deters further decay of the environment.

In summary, this chapter attempts to examine the effects of climate change within the contexts of multi-faceted dimensions of vulnerabilities unique to South Asia. Termed as PAM, the chapter also discusses the opportunities and difficulties of a set of remedial actions, and finally, as a universal antidote to climate change advocates lifestyle changes through re-invention of a climate friendly value system that is unique to many developing countries, especially South Asia.

7.2   CLIMATE CHANGE AND SOUTH ASIAN VULNERABILITIES

The climate change vulnerabilities in South Asia have been examined at three levels:

1.   Macro-economic;
2.   Sectoral; and
3.   The vulnerabilities emanating from sea-level rise.

7.2.1   Macro-economic Vulnerabilities

The South Asian region is the poorest and the most climate change vulnerable region in the world. The region's vulnerability stems from a variety

Table 7.2   Selected socioeconomic indicators of South Asia

Country	Daily per capita calorie supply	% of people without sustainable access to improved water sources in 2000	Malaria cases (per 100 000 persons) in 2000	% of people living below US$1 a day (most recent during 1990–2002)
Bangladesh	2201	3	40	36
Bhutan		38	285	
India	2417	16	7	43.7
Nepal	2264	12	58	13.4
Pakistan	2262	10	58	13.4
Sri Lanka	2411	2	1110	6.6
Data source	WRI	UNICEF, UNDP HDR	UNDESA, WHO, UNDP, HDR	WB, UNDP, HDR

Notes:
World Resources Institute (WRI)
United Nations Children's Fund (UNICEF)
United Nations Development Programme (UNDP)
United Nations Department of Economic and Social Affairs (UNDESA)
World Health Organization (WHO)
World Bank (WB)
Human Development Report (HDR)

Source: Kelkar and Bhadwal (2008).

of factors that are both ecological and socioeconomic in nature. It is the latter that risks its coping capacity most.

Table 7.2 highlights generic socioeconomic challenges of South Asia countries.

In addition to the above, South Asia's existing development challenges also include the following (compiled from Mahbubul Huq Human Development Centre 2006):

- The region's share in world population is 22 per cent but it contains more than 40 per cent of the world's poor;
- Nearly half a billion people live below the poverty line and three-quarters survive below US$2 a day;
- A total of 62 per cent of the region's population is without sanitation and 46 per cent of children under 5 years of age are malnourished;

- Although gender gaps are closing in the South Asian region, women are still among the most illiterate in the world;
- Although in recent years the region has experienced impressive economic growth, inequality is on the rise, so is regional disparity;
- Rural poverty has remained high and in some countries such as Nepal, Pakistan and Sri Lanka, it has, in fact, gone up in recent times;
- Although in recent times micro-credit schemes have helped the poor, a general lack of access to affordable credit remains a major cause of continuing poverty; and
- Poor governance standards cause failures in public service delivery that affect the poor most.

From the climate change vulnerability perspective, these weak socioeconomic and governance conditions that are currently experienced by South Asian countries are likely to affect their people in two interlinking ways:

1. That poor socioeconomic conditions will make an existing vulnerable situation worse; and
2. That an existing weak governance situation shall render the task of implementing a suitable adaptation strategy daunting.

7.2.2 Sectoral Vulnerabilities

Presented below is a brief overview of South Asian vulnerabilities specific to climate change (compiled from Kelkar and Bhadwal 2008):

- *Food security*: Temperature rise of 1.5°C could reduce wheat yields by 2 per cent and rice yields by 3–15 per cent in central India; in Pakistan, in arid and semi-arid areas, wheat yields could be reduced by 6–9 per cent; in Sri Lanka rice output by 6 per cent (tea production will also decline); and in Bangladesh, during 1962–88 the country lost 0.5 million tons of rice to flood annually, accounting for almost 30 per cent of its total food grain import, climate change-induced natural hazards that are expected to be more frequent and fierce and are likely to make the situation of food deficit much worse in Bangladesh.
- *Access to and availability of water*: By 2050, 2.5 billion people in South Asia will be affected by water stress and scarcity, this is without accounting for climate change.
- *Flooding/inundations*: Due to sea-level rise about 130 million people living in the Low Elevation Coastal Zones (LECZ) of Bangladesh, India and Pakistan are likely to be threatened by inundation and

97 per cent of these reside in Bangladesh and India, with roughly equal numbers each. Countries like the Maldives and Sri Lanka are vulnerable to total or near total submersion.

- *Health hazards*: Outbreaks of malaria and waterborne diseases loom large, especially in Bangladesh, Nepal and Bhutan.
- *Migration*: Climate change-induced migration initially within countries, mainly to cities then across national borders, is a likely prospect. Depending on the level of sea-level rise (worst scenario of 5 m under a 'business as usual (BAU)' situation or 0.3 m scenario under policy reform scenario), migration will vary from 100 per cent to 20 per cent respectively. About 75 million from Bangladesh are particularly vulnerable, rendering the nation virtually a non-viable entity in future and, most alarmingly, may subject the neighbouring countries to massive involuntary immigration.
- *Vulnerable communities*: In the South Asian region, fishing communities, landless labour, the marginal farmers and people living in LECZs are the most vulnerable to the effects of climate change and these number roughly 130 million people. In terms of area, this comprises nearly one-third of Bangladesh.

Table 7.3 highlights a country-specific summary of climate change vulnerabilities of South Asia (modified from Kelkar and Bhadwal 2008).

It is evident from Table 7.3 that in one form or another each of the seven countries of South Asia are threatened by climate change induced vulnerabilities and, among these, Bangladesh faces the worst of the risks. Although, at this stage, the precise physical impacts of climate change are difficult to estimate, the social effects of physical and biophysical changes are easy to anticipate and these are likely to be quite serious.

The IPCC (2007) estimates that even under the most conservative scenario, the sea level in 2100 will be about 40 cm higher than today, which will cause an additional 80 million people of coastal Asia to be subjected to flooding and the majority of the flooded areas will be in South Asia, particularly in India and Bangladesh. The same study estimates that a 1 m sea-level rise would result in 6000 sq. km of the coastal area of India alone being flooded. In Bangladesh, the entire southern coastal belt is likely to be affected.

7.2.3   Nature of Vulnerabilities Emanating from Sea-Level Rise

As is obvious, the sea-level rise will affect the coastal population and their habitats in a number of ways, including inundation, flooding, storm damage, erosion, salt water intrusion, rising water tables and impeded

Table 7.3   Country-specific vulnerabilities of climate change in South Asia

Country	Vulnerability to climate change
Bangladesh	**Water resources** Increased coastal and inland flooding; enhanced winter droughts. **Sea-level rise** Submersion of large areas of LECZ in the south of the country; saline water intrusion; changes in coastal morphology; threats to existing flood control and cyclone protection infra-structures, etc. **Agriculture** The estimated impact on rice yield is expected to vary between –6% to + 14% depending on different climate change scenarios; food crisis due to loss of production/productivity (Bangladesh lost 0.5 tons of rice to annually to flooding during 1962–88, constituting 30% of country's average food import).
Bhutan	**Water resources** The availability of water in Bhutan is heavily dependent on heavy rainfall, glaciers or snow; global warming may alter the pattern of snow-fed water flows leading to reduction in water flows and in the peak season increase in flows and sediment yields affecting its hydro-power generation, urban water supply and agriculture, including increased soil erosion, etc. **Agriculture** Upland crops are highly vulnerable to temperature change – a 2°C temperature increase is likely to shift the cultivation zones to a higher elevation and the accompanied increase in the frequency of storms and flooding in the Himalayas is likely to worsen the situation even more.
India	**Agriculture** Wheat yields in central India may drop by 2% in a pessimistic climate change scenario; temperature rise of 1.5°C and 2 mm increase in precipitation could result in a decline in rice yields by 3% to 15%. **Water resources** Climate change warming is likely to increase glacial melting and thus increase water flow in the rivers initially, followed by a decrease in and drying up of the water flow. Although increased water flow could help hydro-power generation, it could equally increase flooding, crop losses, etc. India is already projected to experience water stress by 2050 – climate change conditions are going to make the situation even worse. **Health** Climate change is likely to alter the distribution of vector species (for example, mosquitoes) and may increase the spread of diseases

Table 7.3   (continued)

Country	Vulnerability to climate change
	to new areas that lack a strong public health infrastructure. Malaria and other diseases may invade new high altitude areas.
Maldives	**Water resources** Sea-level rise is likely to affect drinking water sources. **Ecosystem and biodiversity** Mass bleaching of coral reefs is a real possibility. **Inundation and beach erosion** Over 80% of the land area is less than 1 m above mean sea level subjecting the country to inundation and beach erosion. **Health** Although in recent years the country achieved high health standards, climate change may change all that and may result in the outbreak of water-related and waterborne diseases.
Nepal	**Water resources** Glacial melt is expected to increase which would lead to increased summer flows in some rivers for a few decades followed by a reduction in flow as upper glaciers disappear. **Agriculture** Soil loss, an on-going problem, is likely to get worse and a rise in temperature would affect wheat and maize production negatively. **Health** The subtropical regions are predicted to be particularly vulnerable to malaria and kalaazar outbreaks.
Pakistan	**Agriculture** Crops such as cotton, wheat, mango and sugarcane, are likely to be the worst affected by the rise in temperature. **Infrastructure** Periodic flooding and tidal waves caused by temperature rise are likely to threaten the Karachi port.
Sri Lanka	**Water resources** It is indicated that much of the water from heavy rainfall will be lost as run-off to the sea. Severe erosion is also predicted. **Agriculture** Temperature rise and extreme weather are likely to affect grain, tea and coconut production. **Health** Increase in malaria predicted.

Source: Kelkar and Bhadwal (2008) (modified).

Table 7.4   Spatial distribution of LECZ and population living in LECZ in South Asia

Country	Area of LECZ ('000 sq. km)	Population in LECZ (mill.)	Urban population in LECZ (mill.)	Fraction of urban population in LECZ in cities exceeding 5 mill.
Bangladesh	54.5	65	15	33%
India	81.8	63	31	58%
Pakistan	22	4	2	92%
Sri Lanka	5	2	0.96	5

Source: sedac.ciesin.org.

drainage wetland loss (Byravan and Rajan 2008). Since the South Asian region is home to the world's largest number of poor people, many of these living in the coastal zone, climate change-induced sea-level rise is likely to make the conditions of these people even worse. Byravan and Rajan (2008) reveal that the three South Asian countries – Bangladesh, India and Pakistan – share a coastline that is a LECZ that is home to nearly 130 million people and the that bulk of the LECZ people (nearly 97 per cent), live in Bangladesh and India, with equal numbers in each being directly vulnerable to a rise in sea level.

Table 7.4 presents the spatial distribution of the LECZ and the population living in the LECZ in South Asia.

It is also evident from the Table 7.4 that in Bangladesh 70 per cent of the LECZ vulnerable people are rural, whereas in India the proportion of rural LECZ is about 50 per cent.

The stress of climate change for the rural population is expected to be much different from that of the urban LECZ people. Among these, fishing and coastal agriculturalists that are already quite poor and, therefore, are least resilient to disaster-related losses are likely to be the hardest hit. Faced with these dire prospects many may migrate. Referring to their situation, Byravan and Rajan (2008, p. 8) argue that 'as ever larger numbers of these people pass thresholds in terms of their ability to cope societal tipping points will be crossed, resulting in the sudden movements of entire villages, towns and even cities in coastal regions towards safety'.

As far as South Asia is concerned the possibilities of huge climate migration, first to urban areas within the affected countries, and later across the borders, are virtually inevitable. It is estimated that a 3–4 m rise in average sea level by the end of the century would effectively depopulate the major coastal towns of South Asia, thus putting more pressure on already overburdened cities located in safe areas of these countries. Some estimates also suggest that climate change vulnerabilities will affect areas that are experiencing the negative trade effects of globalisation, 'doubly exposing' them to both processes and, thus, making them more vulnerable (O'Brien et al. 2004).

In present times, two scenarios are predicted for sea-level rise, a 4–5°C rise in temperature with business-as-usual (BAU) meaning no action on GHG emission and a 2°C for policy change (PC) meaning significant cuts in carbon emissions In either case, the rise is likely to take place gradually in the early years causing relatively slower migration of people. However, as the sea level starts to rise more rapidly the migration rate will accelerate putting unprecedented pressure on human and national/regional coping capacities.

It is estimated that under a BAU situation – a likely scenario due to COP15's failure to obtain binding commitments to cut GHG emissions – the entire population of the South Asian LECZs will be forced to migrate by 2045. In this regard, Byravan and Rajan (2008, p. 16) surmise that, 'Given the proximity of Bangladesh to India and large land area that would be inundated, it is also likely that the bulk of these people (nearly 120 million in the worst case BAU scenario) will end up being migrants in India.'

In summary, the physical, geo-physical and social costs of climate change in South Asia are enormous. It is evident that emanating from climate change a myriad of interlinking factors influences the extent of vulnerabilities and the depth of insecurity of human systems. Implicit in the analysis is also the relationship that exists between vulnerability and insecurity – the more vulnerable a community is, the greater the insecurity. A full understanding of the community socio-matrix is, therefore, key to formulation of a strategy that can adequately addresses the aspects of climate change PAM in South Asia.

7.3 PREPAREDNESS, ADAPTATION AND MITIGATION (PAM) STRATEGY: A FRAMEWORK FOR SOUTH ASIAN CLIMATE ACTION

It has been argued above that to meet the challenges of climate change vulnerabilities a comprehensive strategy, referred to here as a PAM strategy, tailored to the unique needs and the cultural context of each of the affected South Asian communities, is a *sine qua non*. Figure 7.4 presents an operating framework for PAM.

'Preparedness' measures include, but are not limited to, the following:

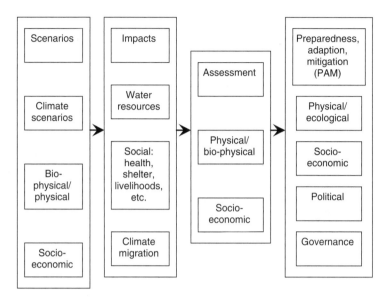

Figure 7.4 An operating framework of PAM

1. Establishment of an early warning system;
2. Making provisions for post-disaster shelter, health, water, food, credit; and
3. Organising appropriate livelihood recovery measures.

Preparedness initiatives also warrant interactions among various stake-holders including the scientific community and, most importantly, a decentralised governance system and community engagement process that would guarantee greater accountability and ownership to the actions planned. It is imperative that adoption of a suitable preparedness strategy will very much depend on the understanding of the depth and extent of climate change hazards and the vulnerability these hazards are likely to cause to the affected area, the community and individual households. A general concept of vulnerability is the notion that the vulnerable condition of a system is reflective (or a function) of the exposures and sensitivity of that system to hazardous conditions and the ability or capacity to resist the negative effects while coping, adapting or recovering from the risky condition (IPCC 1996; Kelly and Adger 2000; Leichenko and O'Brien 2002; OECD 2008). Depending on the focus of the discussion and the field of study, these concepts are labelled and emphasised differently. For example, the examination of social vulnerability of climate change would warrant, among other things, the understanding of the enabling

environment that defines the individual or group capacity to join governance systems, local as well as national. This is important because quality
of governance influences decision-making processes and their impacts as
well as the group capacities to access resources.

'Adaptation' is defined as the response to climate change in terms of
organisation of lives and livelihoods. It also means adapting socioeconomic and other production systems sensitive to emerging climatic conditions. For example, in agriculture, an adaptation strategy could include
changes in cropping patterns, intensity, crop location, irrigation, fertiliser
use and new infrastructure development. Similarly, in the water resources/
energy sector this may mean new and integrated water resource management techniques, a shift to green energy and eco-friendly land use. Similar
attention will also need to be given to the issues of health, shelter, resettlement (for the climate migrants/refugees).

Mitigation refers to a cut in GHG emissions through the introduction
of alternative and sometimes costly technological options. As the biggest
GHG emitters, the industrialised developed nations are expected to bear
the brunt of mitigation costs both for themselves as well as for others,
especially those who lack technology. However, this is a contentious issue.

Although on a per capita basis, the United States and other industrialised nations appear to be the worst polluters, in absolute terms, China
comes second after the United States. The industrialised developed nations
fear that in the absence of parity in GHG emission cuts, which involves
substantial costs which also increases production costs, will put them at a
disadvantage vis-à-vis those who would not cut emissions, especially the
growing economies of China, India, Brazil and South Africa.

Table 7.5 presents the situation of per capita emission of CO_2 of selected
South Asian countries vis-à-vis the rest of the world.

It is quite obvious from Table 7.5 that, from a regional perspective,
South Asia pollutes the least of all, especially Bangladesh, and yet South
Asia faces the worst risks and Bangladesh, the least polluting country,
faces the gravest of threats.

Each country's ability to adapt to climate change vulnerabilities is linked
to its existing financial, institutional and technological capacities. As they
are already economically and/or otherwise significantly constrained there
is little doubt that comprehensive climate change adaptation will warrant
significant doses of financial and technological support from outside.
Equally, the issue of climate migration will require major political rethinking and cooperation on a regional, not merely a country basis.

Furthermore, while each nation has to devise its own PAM solutions
relevant to its own local conditions, there is also a need for a framework
that links global (on the issues of mitigation or GHG cuts and financial

Table 7.5   South Asia from the polluting perspective

Country	Population (mill.)	Per capita CO_2 emission (tons)
United States	302	19
Russia	142	11
Japan	128	8
China	1318	4
India	1132	1.8
Bangladesh	150	0.3
Rest of Asia	1560	2

Source: Khan (2009b).

and technological assistance) with regional (climate migration, water and energy sharing and so forth) with national (preparedness, adaptation and so forth) and national with local and vice versa. In this comprehensive PAM framework the community should continue to play an important role not just as passive recipients of assistance but as active participants in every aspect of decision-making – from national level policy making to community level interventions and vice versa – and help by shaping policies for present and future sustainability.

Finally, there is no one-size-fits-all recipe for PAM initiatives. Based on its own national capacities and community dynamics each country has to devise its own PAM strategy. Diverse community characteristics and their varied expectations indicate the importance and necessity of complex community engagement processes conducive to PAM planning. Countries also need to leverage funding from all sources – local, national, private, donors and so forth.

7.3.1   Implementing PAM

As a follow up to the Bali agreement, almost all of the South Asian countries have developed national climate change strategies. Kelkar and Bhadwal (2008) also list a range of preparedness and adaptation measures relevant to agriculture, water resources management, flood control and drought mitigation and mountain development. But to what extent these initiatives are conducive to a comprehensive PAM strategy or are merely responses to short- to medium-term development needs is difficult to assess at this stage. In this regard, Kelkar and Bhadwal (2008, p. 38) indicate that while many South Asian public sector programmes 'are relevant for strengthening adaptive capacity to climate change, they do not as yet explicitly incorporate the increased risks due to climate change'. This may be due to the fact that a comprehensive PAM strategy would require a long-term strategic plan and the benefits of such plans are not accruable in the short- to medium-term – a condition that is neither conducive to nor much of an incentive for the short life cycle of political governance of any country. Furthermore, weak commitment to formulation of a comprehensive PAM strategy may also be due to the following factors:

1. Both the extent and impacts of climate change are yet to be fully understood, mapped and properly costed;
2. Inadequate decentralisation of public governance and low institutional capacity to link national with local and local with the community, and vice versa, compromise a bottom-up planning process, vital to climate change planning;
3. Inadequate resources and lack of required technical know-how jeopardize development of suitable adaptive infrastructure; and
4. Absence of meaningful regional cooperation – geo-politics and the political mind-set of inter-country rivalries continue to obstruct progress in and collective visioning of a regional framework vital to address the hazards of climate change migration, especially those that relate to cross-border migration.

7.3.2 The Issue of Regional Cooperation

While each country in South Asia must devise its own strategy to tackle climate change vulnerabilities and match its own unique requirements, several aspects of regional cooperation, especially those that relate to sharing and management of common resources, such as equitable sharing of water resources as well as that of cross-border environmental migration, are key to tackling the looming risks of climate change in the region. The threat of environmental migration is especially high from the LECZ countries and the countries that constitute the lower riparian zones of major river systems that are particularly vulnerable. For example, Bangladesh is particularly affected by both of these risks. Increased global warming accompanied by sea-level rise puts the lives of 75 million at serious risk. Similarly, morphological changes caused by construction of dams and other water retention structures in the upper riparian (in this case, by India) are damaging its existing fragile ecosystem and depleting further the livelihood options of millions of people. Future repercussions of lack of meaningful and equitable cooperation in both of these aspects, displacements caused by both sea-level rise and equitable water sharing, are likely to be quite costly for the entire region, especially the upper riparian countries.

Several intergovernmental and Civil Society Organization (CSO) regional cooperation frameworks, such as the South Asian Association of Regional Cooperation (SAARC), the World Bank funded South Asian Cooperative Environment Programme (SACEP), Bay-of-Bengal Initiative for Multi-Sectoral Technical and Economic Cooperation (BIMSTEC), Climate Action Network–South Asia (CANSA) and Indian Institute of Tropical Meteorology (IITM) that supplies weather-related information to all the countries, do exist but most of their initiatives are either not relevant to or are politically disinclined to mainstream the climate change issues at the regional level.

In South Asia, in the face of induced morphological changes in upper riparian countries that adversely affect lower riparian countries and gradual inundation of coastal areas caused by increased global warming, the prospect of an eventual involuntary and illegal cross-border migration from affected countries to less affected ones cannot be ignored and is almost a fact of life. Yet, there is hardly any strategic thinking at the regional level. The issue is either not fully understood or deliberately ignored by political leaderships of the concerned countries. In this regard, Byravan and Rajan (2008, p. 21) observe that:

> With a 5 metre sea level rise, there will be about 125 million climate migrants in this region alone with little or no legal standing . . . In fact the 75 million or so from Bangladesh will be especially vulnerable, as their entire nation-state becomes non-viable as an entity, with most of its land inundated and its economy defunct.

A European Union-like South Asian Union that would allow free movement of people and capital may be the answer.

In general, what is becoming evident is that for implementation of an effective PAM South Asian countries must pursue interventions that are both country-specific as well as regional. One without the other will not achieve the desired results. Implementation of a suitable PAM strategy will also require significant global cooperation.

7.4   GLOBAL COMMITMENTS AND SOUTH ASIA

There are two global commitments that are relevant to tackling the risks of climate change in South Asia:

1. Making adequate resources and technology available for funding and supporting the implementation of a suitable PAM; and
2. Immediate and drastic emissions cuts by all, especially by the polluting nations – this is generic to all.

7.4.1 Funding PAM

If the poorer countries of South Asia are to implement a suitable PAM strategy, they require massive doses of external funding, especially from the richer countries, and this is in addition to the funding currently committed for on-going development of these countries. According to a recent estimate (Mufti 2009) of the total world population of 6.11 billion, 1.35 billion live in the South Asian region of whom 43 percent (540 million) live in absolute poverty.

Of South Asia's total poor, nearly 40 per cent or 360 million live in the rural areas and the rest, 80 million, in the urban areas. Urban poverty is, to a considerable extent, a spillover of rural poverty. It is conceivable that climate change risks will simply aggravate this situation even more and induce further rural–urban migration of the poor warranting urgent action to implement a suitable PAM strategy in affected areas so as either to halt or reverse current migration trends. But the question is: whether the richer countries who are also the worst polluters are ready to commit the funding at a level required to implement a comprehensive PAM strategy in the region?

The COP15 has promised mobilisation of US$100 billion for climate change activities per annum from 2020 and the developed countries have promised, under certain conditions, a fund of US$10 billion per annum for mitigation activities from 2010 to 2012. These are positive outcomes of COP15 although, if past history is a guide, one would notice how most rich countries, far from fulfilling their commitments, have shied away from initiatives, such as the funding of the Millennium Development Goals (MDGs).

It is also true that the current financial crunch and domestic financial crises of their own make it somewhat difficult for the richer nations to mobilise additional resources – the budget deficit of the United States is projected at 13.6 per cent of GDP in 2009 and an annualised contraction of the Japanese economy is estimated at 14.2 per cent. It has been suggested, and with some justification, that in times of economic difficulties, the best way to generate income is by saving, especially by cutting wasteful expenditure such as defence spending.

Similarly, attention must also be given to the aspect of greater savings and better use of resources within the South Asian countries themselves. Civil wars, internal conflicts, improper use of scarce national resources, lax tax systems, corruption and so forth seem to significantly stifle optimisation of both mobilisation as well as the use of resources in most of these countries. Greater political acumen in conflict resolution, transparency and accountability in public governance and improved technical know how are key to improving the South Asian regions accessibility to and utilisation of resources.

7.4.2 Limiting Emissions

Considering the magnitude of risks faced by the South Asian region, especially the LECZ and the arid and semi-arid zones of these countries, no tangible progress is possible without drastic global reduction of GHG emissions. Adoption of rigorous mitigation measures such as drastic cuts in CO_2 emissions by both developed and developing polluting nations is a *sine qua non.* This is important for two reasons – firstly, a CO_2 emission cut will help in arresting rising trends in global warming and thus offer planners a more predictable set of scenarios to work with to tackle climate change vulnerabilities more strategically – especially on preparedness and adaptation measures; and secondly, a decline in global warming will also make adaptation planning more predictable and less costly to implement.

The outcome of the COP15 in Copenhagen indicates that, far from reaching an agreement on time-bound emission targets, the world leaders left the meeting with a note of intent and not a commitment, thus rendering the goal of drastic and immediate emission cuts unattained.

Industrialised nations are required to cut emissions by 25–40 per cent during 1990–2012 but as per the current trend, only 10 per cent is achievable by 2020. Growing developing countries such as China and India – who themselves are not big polluters in per capita terms, although in total terms China is the second largest polluter – argue that emission cuts at this stage would stunt their growth and increase poverty and thus stress that it is the developed countries of the West, the worst polluters in per capita terms, that should bear the brunt of responsibilities and agree to drastic GHG emission cuts. However, developed countries argue that while they are willing to make some adjustments in their CO_2 emissions countries such as China, India, Brazil and South Africa – the emerging developing countries that contribute to significant GHG emissions – must also take similar drastic actions. Is there a way out of the gridlock of rich country/poor country debate?

7.4.3 A Lifestyle or Demand Side Perspective on Emissions Cuts

Chakravarty et al. (2009) of the Princeton Environment Institute argue that instead of setting targets of emissions cuts on the basis of high energy use wealthy countries – something that is proving to be quite contentious and is unnecessarily miring the discussions into a rich country/poor

*Table 7.6   Energy consumption: total energy consumption per capita
(units: kgoe per person)*

	2005	2000	1990
World	1778.0	1657.0	1668.0
Region			
Asia (excluding Middle East)	1051.5	865.2	775.8
Central America & Caribbean	1365.9	1266.3	1243.1
Europe	3773.4	3580.8	4080.4
Middle East & North Africa	1765.5	1531.5	1184.6
North America	7942.9	8157.9	7686.3
South America	1151.2	1123.8	970.1
Developed countries	4720.0	4622.6	4755.8
Developing countries	975.9	807.5	684.6
High income countries	5523.6	5468.7	4906.0
Low income countries	491.8	457.3	431.5
Middle income countries	1509.3	1252.9	1365.4

Source: OECD/IEA (2007, 2008).

country debate – it may be more useful to target the polluting wealthy, the real polluters in each country instead. This school of thought believes that since most of the world's carbon dioxide comes from wealthy individual polluters (numbering approximately 700 million people, worldwide), the issue of lifestyle along with a country's average energy use must also be factored in as an equitable and a long-term deterrent to preventative actions on climate change.

Due to their high consumerist and materialist lifestyle, per capita use of energy in the West is far greater than that of Asia, particularly South Asia. Table 7.6 presents the per capita use of energy by region.

Table 7.6 reveals that in comparison to North America and Europe (the countries that constitute the 'West'), the Asian region, especially the least developed countries (LDCs) in the Asian region, consumes much less energy. In 2005, while North America consumed 7942.9 kilograms of oil equivalent (kgoe) of energy, Asia (minus the Middle East) consumed 1051.5 kgoe per person and the low income countries of Asia 491.8 kgoe. Again, when one compares North American per capita consumption of energy with that of India and Bangladesh (the two countries that are likely to be worst hit by climate change) the figure stands at 491 (16 times higher than) and 171 (46 times higher than) kgoe per capita respectively (OECD/IEC 2007). In other words, in 2005, in comparison to India and

Bangladesh, the United States consumed 16 and 46 times more energy per unit than these two countries, respectively. However, it also appears that some of the developing countries, including India and China, are not exactly lagging behind in Western-type consumerist behaviour. For example, the 6 August 2009 edition of *The Independent* ('A must-have revolution: how shopping became India's new religion') reports that, in the year 2000, India only had three Western-type shopping malls in the entire country – now it has 350. In 2030, China's GDP will equal that of the United States and at its current rate of energy consumption will require 98 million barrels of oil a day, compared to world capacity of 85 million in that year. In terms of lifestyle perspective, can South Asia afford to continue along the same path?

In terms of lifestyle reform, South Asians may even have an advantage over the others. Until recently, the South Asians, through their various religious and cultural practices – Hinduism, Buddhism, Islam, Jainism – pursued a value system that was steeped in the principles of conserving consumption.[5] All these changed with the advent of European colonisation of the region and the subjugation of its local traditional values of a frugal lifestyle was replaced by a consumerist materialist value system. Implemented within the framework of colonially induced and post-colonial unequal exchange relationships and inculcated within the myth of a cultural superiority, these arrangements did two things to the region:

1. Turned the region into a cheap source of raw materials for their manufacturing sectors; and
2. By creating a lifestyle value shift, created a market for their products.

Even though the region, as a whole, achieved its political independence a while ago, the lifestyle goals altered through the colonial interventions and, later, through promotion of a consumerist growth model continue to affect and marginalise the region's own traditional conserving value system. Yet the founding fathers of some of the countries of the region, for example, India, were not too oblivious of the long-term dangers of a consumerist/materialist model of development. On the eve of the country's independence in 1947, when the departing Viceroy of India Lord Mountbatten asked Mr Gandhi whether one day he would like see India develop as England, Mr Gandhi replied saying, 'I don't think so, you see it took England half the planet's resources to develop in the manner it has, imagine how many planets India would need to come to this stage.' The challenges of supply side solutions, especially those that relate to emissions cuts, are numerous and these range from political commitment to technology. Therefore, rather than focussing attention on emissions cuts by the polluting wealthy – something that is proving to be contentious and, if COP15 and its aftermath is any guide, largely unattainable – there may be an opportunity to focus on the demand side or lifestyle perspectives of climate change and advance actions at two levels – tax wealthy polluters and, at the same time, re-invent and internalise value systems that act as a natural motivator to adopt a climate friendly lifestyle.

7.5 CONCLUSIONS

Climate change is an issue that has global, regional and in-country ramifications and, therefore, strategies must be sought within mutually beneficial frameworks of mutual cooperation and support, both within and across nations.

Of all the regions, the South Asian region is most vulnerable to climate change impacts both in terms of the number of people that are likely to be affected as well as the magnitude of economic, social and political vulnerabilities that the region faces.

As is obvious, there is no quick fix nor is there a one-size-fits-all panacea. In addition to relevant in-country measures, the climate change solutions in South Asia must seek a regional cooperation framework that promotes equitable sharing of common resources and offers freer mobility of both capital and people within the region. A suitable in-country PAM strategy accompanied by regional cooperation has not only the potential to make country interventions more effective but, by adopting a regional strategy, could by reduce one of the looming risks of climate change – large-scale involuntary and illegal cross-border environmental migrations.

Within countries, especially those that are facing the worst climate change hazards such as Bangladesh, there is an urgent need to leverage the government, civil society organisations, scientists, donors and, indeed, the community together to find solutions that are knowledge-based, accountable and transparent. In addition, efforts must also be made to map out completely climate change vulnerabilities in terms of each nation's financial and technical capacities; physical-ecological conditions; and socioeconomic situation. This is important to plan appropriate interventions and allocation of necessary resources.

Implementation of a people-centric PAM strategy would also require significant decentralisation and empowerment of the communities and inclusion of the latter in all planning decisions. In recent years most South Asian countries have made progress in political decentralisation of public governance and this is helpful for planning PAM. However, some also report that, despite this progress in political decentralisation, the aspects of 'fiscal and administrative decentralization still lag behind' (World Bank 2004). Absence of full decentralisation of public governance that has traditionally hampered development and service delivery may equally weaken implementation of measures relevant to PAM, especially those related to preparedness and adaptation.

It is also noteworthy that in terms of preparedness and adaptation initiatives, many countries, including the donors, seem to focus more on ad hoc infrastructure development and not on a comprehensive PAM strategy. Such piecemeal initiatives have little or no chance of succeeding, especially if these initiatives are undertaken in conditions of weak decentralisation and inadequate or non-existent community participation in the decision-making.

Finally, the world as a whole must also learn to address the climate change challenges more from the demand side or lifestyle perspective than from the supply side technology-based control perspectives. In this regard, re-invention and revival of the South Asian value system that glorifies and not stigmatises conserving consumption must be given some serious thought, to act to mitigate further global warming. This may also mean a paradigm shift in the notion of 'development' – shifting the concept from its current consumerism and materialistic underpinnings, to a more conserving model of development that stresses sustainable human development, a framework that assists intra and inter-general equity in the use and distribution of resources.

In summary the key climate change challenges that confront South Asian countries include:

1. Mapping comprehensive PAM strategies that will help minimise risks and maximise preparedness as well as adaptations within countries;
2. Regional level political commitment to tackling the challenges of environmental migration, both within and beyond the political boundaries of the countries; and
3. Abandonment of colonially induced and neo-colonially entrenched values of consumerism and materialism and recreate South Asian values that promote and honour a conserving lifestyle?

The general trend of the analysis presented above demonstrates that even though the climate change crisis is real and looms large in South Asia there are also opportunities that can be exploited to minimise risks significantly. It is evident that persistent global-level advocacy for emissions cuts, regional cooperation in the use of common resources such as water and on issues of environmental migration, a bottom-up planning and implementation of a comprehensive PAM strategy and, indeed, re-enactment of a

South Asian value-oriented conserving development consumption model lie at the heart of tackling some of the looming climate change vulnerabilities in the South Asian region.

NOTES

1. The IPCC Fourth Assessment Report predicts that under current trends and relative to the year 2000, greenhouse gas emissions could rise by 25 per cent by 2030 and that the earth could warm by 3°C within this century. Even a temperature growth of 1–2.5°C could have serious environmental effects that would reduce crop yields in tropical areas, lead to hunger and famine, spread of climate-sensitive diseases like malaria and cause the extinction of 20–30 per cent of all plant and animal species. By 2020, up to 250 million people in Africa could be exposed to severe water and food stress. Over the course of the century, millions of people living in the catchment areas of the Himalayas and Andes face increased flooding due to melting of glaciers of these mountain ranges. Also, rising sea levels will lead to inundation of coasts worldwide with some small island states possibly facing complete submersion. It is estimated that the cost of adaptation could amount to at least 5–10 per cent of global GDP. People living in cyclone-prone areas now face possible increased severity and frequency of events, along with the associated risks to life and livelihood. In recent times, however, errors with regard to IPCC's projected timing of the melting of the Himalayan glaciers have been acknowledged – but this inadvertent mistake does not seem to affect the projections concerning the on-going phenomenon of human induced global warming and its negative effects.
2. Greenhouse gases trap heat in the atmosphere and are essential for sustaining life on earth. However, anthropogenic sources compound the effect to dangerous levels. There are many greenhouse gases, such as carbon dioxide, methane, nitrous oxide, tetrafluoromethane, hexafluoroethane and sulfur hexafluoride. Of these, carbon dioxide, a by-product of burning fossil fuels, has received the most attention.
3. The eight MDGs are:
   (1) Eradicating poverty and hunger;
   (2) Achieving universal education;
   (3) Promoting gender equality and empowerment of women;
   (4) Reducing child mortality;
   (5) Improving maternal and child health;
   (6) Combating HIV, AIDS, malaria and other diseases;
   (7) Ensuring environmental sustainability; and
   (8) Developing a global partnership for development.
   Also see www.undp.org/mdg/basics.shtml.
4. For a more comprehensive understanding of climate change-related vulnerabilities see Füssel (2005). By using the United Nations definition of vulnerabilities (2004) Füssel describes climate change vulnerabilities as:
   (1) *Physical factors* which describe exposure of vulnerable elements within a region;
   (2) *Economic factors* which describe the economic resources of individuals, population groups and communities;
   (3) *Social factors* which describe the non-economic factors that influence the well being of communities – education, health, security, demography, access to human rights, resources and governance.
   Also see World Food Programme (2004).
5. For example, while both Hinduism and Islam strongly advocate the shunning of extravagance in lifestyle matters, Buddhism prescribes a value system that is synonymous to UNDP's concept of *sustainable human development* – pursuing development within the parameters of inter- and intra-generational equity.

REFERENCES

Blackwell, T. and J. Searbook (1993), *Revolt Against Change: Towards Conserving Radicalism*, London: Vintage.

Byravan, S. and S.C. Rajan (2008), 'The social impacts of climate change in South Asia', *Social Science Research Network*, available at http://ssrn/abstract=1129346.

Chakravarty, S., A. Chikkatur, H. de Coninck, S. Pacalaa, R. Socolow and T. Massimo (2009), 'Sharing global CO_2 emission reductions among one billion high emitters'; doi:10.1073/pnas.0905232106.

Eakin, H. (2005), 'Institutional change, climate risk, and rural vulnerability: cases from Central Mexico', *World Development*, **33** (11): 1923–38.

Füssel, Hans-Martin (2005), *Vulnerability in Climate Change Research: A Comprehensive Conceptual Framework*, UC Berkeley: University of California International and Area Studies, available at http://www.escholarship.org/uc/item/8993z6nm.

Global Environmental Facility (GEF) (2001), *GEF Annual Report 2001*, Washington DC: Global Environmental Facility.

Hari, J. (2008), 'Bangladesh is set to disappear under the waves by the end of the century', *The Independent*, UK.

IPCC (1996), *Climate Change 1995: Economic and Social Dimensions of Climate Change*, Cambridge, UK: Cambridge University Press.

IPCC (2001), *IPCC Third Assessment Report. Climate Change: The Scientific Basics*, Geneva: UNEP.

IPCC (2007), *Climate Change 2007: Impacts, Adaptation and Vulnerability*, Working Group II contribution to the Fourth Assessment Report of the Intergovernmental Panel on Climate Change (IPCC), Cambridge, UK: Cambridge University Press.

Kelkar, U. and S. Bhadwal (2008), 'South Asian regional study on climate change impacts and adaptation: implications for human development', Human Development Report 2007/2008; Fighting climate change: human solidarity in a divided world, Human Development Report Office, occasional paper.

Kelly, P.M. and W.N. Adger (2000), 'Theory and practice in assessing vulnerability to climate change and facilitating adaptation', *Climatic Change*, **47** (4): 325–52.

Khan, M.A. (2009a), 'Climate Change, Vulnerabilities and Communities', paper presented at the United Nations Expert Group Meeting on 'Civic Engagement in climate change governance', World Civic Forum, Kyung Hee University, Seoul, Republic of Korea, 5–7 May.

Khan, M.A. (2009b), 'Climate change and vulnerabilities: challenges and options for South Asia', paper presented at the International Workshop on Climate Change and Growth in Asia, Griffith Asia Institute, Griffith University, Brisbane, 8 September.

Leichenko, R.M. and K.L. O'Brien (2002), 'The dynamics of vulnerability to rural change', *Mitigation Strategies for Global Change*, **7**, 1–18.

Mahbubul Huq Human Development Centre (2006), 'Poverty in South Asia: challenges and responses', Human Development in South Asia Report 2006, Oxford, UK.

Mufti, I. (2009), 'South Asia poverty eradication paradigm', Johannesburg: CIVICUS.

NASA (2005), 'Global temperature anomalies in 0.01°C', Goddard Space Flight Center, Earth Sciences Directorate.

O'Brien, K., R. Leichenko, U. Kelkar, H. Venema et al. (2004), 'Mapping vulnerability to multiple stressors: climate change and globalization in India', *Global Environmental Change*, **14** (4): 303–13.

Olsthoorn, A.A., T.E. Dowing, M.J. Gawith, R.S.J. Tol and P. Vellinga (1999), 'Introduction', in T.E. Dowing, A.A. Olsthoorn and Richard S.J. Tol (eds), *Climate, Change and Risk*, London: Routledge.

OECD (2008), *Economic Aspects of Adaptation to Climate Change: Costs, Benefits and Policy Instruments*, Rome: OECD.

OECD/IEA (2007), *Energy Balances of Non-OECD Countries (2007 edn)*, Paris: IEA.

OECD/IEA (2008), *Energy Balances of OECD Countries (2008 edn)*, Paris: IEA.

United Nations (2004), *Living with Risks: A Global Review of Disaster Reduction*, Geneva: United Nations.

WESS (2008), *World Economic and Social Survey: Overcoming Economic Insecurity*, Geneva: United Nations.

WHO (2003), *Climate Change and Human Health – Risks and Responses*, Summary, Geneva: WHO.

World Bank (2004), *Decentralization in South Asia*, The World Bank: Washington, DC.

World Bank (2008), *World Development Report 2008: Agriculture for Development*, Washington DC: World Bank.

World Food Programme (2004), 'Vulnerability analysis and mapping: a tentative methodology', available at http://www.preventionconsortium.org\files/wfp_vulnerability.pdf

8. 'Harmony' in China's climate change policy

Paul Howard

8.1 INTRODUCTION

Under Hu Jintao's leadership of the Chinese Communist Party (CCP), the Chinese Government's response to climate change and other environmental issues will continue to be framed within the context of China's quest for 'harmony' that features a 'balanced' relationship between 'man and nature' and between economic growth and the environment.

International climate change negotiations are inherently complex, largely due to variations in existing political, economic, social and even cultural contexts. This complexity is not exclusively confined to negotiations at the level of the state or within supranational organisations. For, even within states, local contexts preclude a 'one size fits all' approach to the formulation and implementation of pollution measures. Within the People's Republic of China (PRC), great variances in context exist not only between geographic areas, but also between ethnic groups, socioeconomic background and any number of other elements. Overarching this intra-national variance though is a state apparatus which must function to serve its constituents.

China's current leadership is well aware of the need to both serve the citizenry and maintain positive foreign relations. This need to consider both the needs of the citizenry along with the maintenance of cordial foreign relations is central to China's action and negotiations on climate change. However, it is the domestic audience that remains the foremost priority for the CCP. For, it is the legitimacy of the CCP in the eyes of the Chinese people that is crucial to the party's long-term future. Increasing concern within China about the state of the environment means that environmental policy is increasingly prominent in terms of CCP legitimacy. For, if the CCP is to be continued to be perceived as looking after the needs of the people, then it follows that it must be seen to be looking after 'the people's' environment.

Until recent years, it had primarily been economic achievement that had largely, or almost exclusively, defined the CCP's legitimacy. However, the Party's explicit goal of creating a 'harmonious society' is increasingly defining the legitimacy of the CCP. Subsequently, I argue that this new emphasis on creating a 'harmonious society' and 'harmonious' relations presents the global environmental movement with increased opportunity for non-governmental organisations (NGOs) and other civil society actors concerned with environmental issues in general and, more specifically, with the issue of climate change, to engage with the political process to effect change. In shifting the emphasis to 'harmonious society' and explicitly stating the need for the party to be more responsive to the public's concerns, the CCP has simultaneously both redefined the terms of its legitimacy and raised the expectations among the citizenry that there will be increased opportunity for freedom of expression and, consequently, associational activity.

This shift in emphasis to the explicit goal of a 'harmonious society' cannot be understood in isolation. For, rather than simply departing from the previous leadership's goals, the CCP has been careful to shift political emphasis, where required, whilst acknowledging the contribution of past leadership. To understand the CCP's current policy goals in relationship to the environment, it is essential to have an understanding of the historical context from which such goals are drawn. Consequently, in order to adequately address this issue, I will cover the following points:

- The changing political narrative of the PRC and the link this has to personal legacies of its leaders.
- The concept of 'harmonious society' and the way it has been personalised by Hu Jintao.
- Rhetoric or reality? Is 'harmony' a genuine aspiration of the PRC or a means of diversion from a separate underlying agenda?
- The goal of 'harmony' in the context of the issue of climate change.
- How NGOs may most effectively deal with China on the issue of climate change and other environmental issues within the context of the PRC's political narrative.

In covering these main points, my intention is, at the very least, to raise awareness and hopefully facilitate a greater understanding of the current political narrative among civil society actors who operate or wish to operate within the Chinese sociopolitical context.

8.2   POLITICAL NARRATIVE AND LEADERS' LEGACIES

The PRC has been adaptable in its approach to the maintenance of its legitimacy. This is evident in the changes in political narrative that have come to be associated with the PRC's leaders. As I provide some background to the way that narrative shift has taken place under various leaders, it is important to note the fluidity of the state narrative and the connection that the historical fluidity of the political narrative has to the CCP's legitimacy in the context of the PRC today. For, as Ron Keith (2009, p. 111) has succinctly observed, Jiang Zemin 'with Deng's borrowed prestige' developed a political strategy that was 'predicated explicitly on change within continuity'. Further, when Hu Jintao replaced Jiang as CCP leader, he rolled the 'three represents' into a bigger policy synthesis.

There has been a great deal of personalisation in the national political narrative by the PRC's leaders since its formation in 1949. By personalisation, I refer not to the idea of 'personality cult' as such, but rather to the clear association of the respective Party leaders with the state political narrative. Mao Zedong who ruled the PRC from its inception in 1949 until his death in 1976 is associated with 'class struggle' and 'Mao Zedong thought'. The major actor during China's reform period and modernisation (1978–early 1990s), Deng Xiaoping, in a relatively short time frame, focussed the energies of the state apparatus and the citizenry toward modernisation of the economy. As integral parts of the modernisation process, the notions of 'opening to the outside' and the development of 'socialism with Chinese characteristics' became synonymous with Deng. More recently, Jiang Zemin was associated with 'The Three Represents' and now Hu Jintao is creating his own political narrative and legacy, that of 'harmonious society'.

8.3   HU JINTAO AND 'HARMONIOUS SOCIETY'

Heberer and Schubert (2006, p. 20) have asserted that the theme of 'harmonious society' is 'a contemporary revival of the traditional Confucian ideal of the 'great Harmony' *(datong)* which they explain as being 'a society characterized by social equality and political harmony as opposed to the dangers of a neo-liberal market society characterized by consumerism, material wealth and the maximization of profit'. Following from this, Heberer and Schubert (2006, p. 20) essentially argue that the intention of the goal is to increase the 'middle strata' and, consequently, reduce the number of disadvantaged people in society so that all can live in 'harmony'. Heike Holbig (2008) has asserted that the various doctrines espoused under successive leaders of the PRC all have Confucian roots and sees the 'harmonious Socialist society' concept as a reinterpretation of Jiang Zemin's 'Three Represents'. Holbig (2008, p. 27) argues:

> From the perspective of maintaining political legitimacy, Hu Jintao's people centred policy, with its Confucian–Communist blend of imperial and Maoist doctrines, thus appears as a rational reaction to what seems to have been perceived as a looming legitimacy crisis in the wake of Jiang Zemin's elitist redefinition of the common interest.

It is pertinent to note, though, that the need to act in the interests of the people to ensure the CCP's legitimacy was clearly recognised by Jiang Zemin. For example, in forwarding his 'Three Represents', Jiang (CPC 2006) asserted that the Party had maintained 'the people's support' during 'the historical periods of revolution, construction and reform' because it had 'always represented the development trend of China's advanced productive forces, the orientation of China's advanced culture, and the fundamental interests of the overwhelming majority of the Chinese people'.

It is the third of the 'Three Represents', namely the need for the Party to 'represent' 'the fundamental interests of the overwhelming majority of the Chinese people' that resonates strongly with Hu Jintao's 'harmonious society'. This theme of 'harmony' is filtered into all aspects of governance and China's international relations, even touching on issues of environmental sustainability. In short, the domestic and international policies the PRC pursues should not be considered as disconnected. Rather, the goal of creating a 'harmonious society' at home will shape the way in which the PRC negotiates and cooperates internationally.

8.4   RHETORIC OR REALITY?

It is natural, of course, to be cynical of government's true motivations when the political narrative is formed on seemingly Utopian language such as that encapsulated by Hu Jintao's 'harmonious society'. It is then pertinent to consider if this theme of 'harmony' is grounded in reality or is merely rhetoric that is employed by the central government to persuade domestic and international audiences of their virtuous intent. To address this question first requires an examination of the legitimacy of the CCP and the role that 'harmonious society' plays in the domestic sphere.

Essentially, until recent years, the legitimacy of the CCP had largely come to be both defined and reinforced by economic performance. Robert Weatherley (2006, p. 160) notes that greater emphasis 'has been placed on legal rational and electoral legitimacy' in an effort to 'strengthen the basis of CCP legitimacy'. Whilst this is undoubtedly true, the legitimacy of the CCP is increasingly coming to be defined by a fuller measure of, if you like, 'quality of life'. Of course, economic development is part of the picture, but many citizens' expectations have grown along with the country's foreign reserves and GDP. Because of this shift in expectations, the notion of 'harmonious society' is opportune. It is opportune because the government has neatly redefined the parameters of its legitimacy to suit a changing social landscape and expectations. Of course, the many inequities that exist within that changing social landscape make the CCP's task of maintaining its legitimacy problematic. However, many of Hu Jinato's statements and speeches, such as his report to the 17th National Party Congress reflect the CCP leadership's awareness of the need for an inclusive approach to policy implementation and official ideology that accounts for the inequities.

The explicit desire for a 'harmonious society' is therefore both rhetoric and reality. Hu Jintao has often deployed the phrase to persuade the public to accept that he and the CCP are determined to supply this 'harmonious society'. In that sense, it is rhetoric. From the CCP's standpoint, the term 'harmonious society' is both encompassing enough and vague enough to be malleable to suit changing circumstances. However, it is at the same time glaring political reality that if the CCP is not seen to deliver the people a better quality of life (that is, in terms of a 'harmonious society') in years and decades to come, then the legitimacy of the party will be compromised. Whilst he did not specifically talk of Party legitimacy, Hu Jintao's speech at the 17th National Party Congress (2007) finished by linking the Party's ideology and goals with the interests of the people:

> hold high the great banner of socialism with Chinese characteristics, rally more closely around the Central Committee, unite as one, forge ahead in a pioneering spirit, and work hard to achieve new victories in building a moderately prosperous society in all respects and write a new chapter of happy life for the people!

8.5 THE QUEST FOR 'HARMONY' AND CLIMATE CHANGE

Earlier this year, Hu Jintao's chief representative on climate change wrote that climate change eclipsed the global financial crisis (GFC) asserting that 'climate change is a more far-reaching and serious challenge' and highlighting China's commitment to addressing the issue by pointing to environmental measures accounted for in the economic stimulus package designed in the midst of the financial crisis (Kohn 2009).

At the opening of the 17th CCP National Congress (Xinhua 15 October 2007), Hu Jintao highlighted the need for the Chinese government to 'promote a conservation culture by basically forming an energy- and resource-efficient and environment-friendly structure of industries, pattern of growth and mode of consumption'. He asserted: 'Awareness of conservation will be firmly established in the whole of society', a remark which one delegate noted was a clear link to the concept of 'harmonious society' (Xinhua 15 October 2007).

At that 17th National CCP Congress, an amended Party constitution was adopted. The 'five balances',[1] embedded in the constitutional amendment included the explicit reference and prioritisation to the need to balance development with environmental considerations as follows:

> The Party works to balance urban and rural development, development among regions, economic and social development, relations between man and nature, and domestic development and opening to the outside world, adjust the economic structure, and transform the pattern of economic development. It is dedicated to building a new socialist countryside, taking a new path of industrialization with Chinese characteristics, and making China an innovative country and a resource-conserving, environment-friendly society. (IDCPC 2008)

The reference in the amended constitution to 'a new path of industrialization with Chinese characteristics' is further evidence of the flexibility of the CCP to respond to changing social dynamics. Furthermore, as part of the evolving political narrative, the need to address the issue of climate change dovetails neatly with the 'quest for harmony' as is supported in the constitutional amendment that defines the need to 'balance', among other things, 'relations between man and nature'.

Admittedly, this constitutional amendment is not in itself an explicit reference to climate change. However, in regard to climate change, a 2007 paper 'China's National Climate Change Programme' prepared for the National Development and Reform Commission, People's Republic of China (2007, pp. 4–6), identified a number of potential trends due to climate change identified by Chinese scientists which included the following:

- The nationwide annual mean air temperature would increase by 1.3~2.1°C in 2020 and 2.3~3.3°C in 2050 as compared with that in 2000.
- The warming magnitude would increase from south to north in China, particularly in north-western and north-eastern China where significant temperature rise is projected.
- It is estimated that by 2030, the annual temperature would likely increase by 1.9~2.3°C in north-western China, 1.6~2.0°C in south-western China and 2.2~2.6°C in the Qinghai-Tibetan Plateau.

- Precipitation in China would possibly increase during the next 50 years, with a projected nationwide increase of 2~3 per cent by 2020 and 5~7 per cent by 2050. The most significant increase might be experienced in south-eastern coastal regions.
- The possibility of more frequent occurrences of extreme weather/ climate events would increase in China, which will have immense impacts on socioeconomic development and people's lives.
- The arid area in China would probably become larger and the risk of desertification might increase.
- The sea level along China's coasts would continue to rise.
- The glaciers in the Qinghai-Tibetan Plateau and the Tianshan Mountains would retreat at an accelerated rate, and some smaller glaciers would disappear.

Given these potential developments, the paper goes on to explicitly outline the need to address the threat of climate change and the need for action to curb greenhouse gas emissions (GHG) globally. In terms of China's domestic response to climate change, a paper issued in 2008 by the State Council (2008), 'China's Policies and Actions for Addressing Climate Change', concludes:

> China is now in a crucial period in building up a moderately prosperous society in all respects, and at an important stage for accelerating the country's indus-trialization and urbanization. It has onerous tasks to develop the economy and improve the people's livelihood, and thus faces more severe challenges in dealing with climate change than developed countries do . . . Climate change is a common challenge confronting the whole world, and demands the joint efforts of all countries and the entire international community. China will work unremittingly for global sustainable development with other countries and continuously make new contributions to the protection of the climate system.

What is interesting in this statement in terms of the political narrative is the incorporation of the need to 'improve the "people's livelihood"'. 'The People's Livelihood' (*minsheng*) was one of The Three Principles of the People[2] developed by Sun Yatsen as the founding ideology of the Nationalist Party which brought the Qing Dynasty to an end in 1912. Whilst it is perhaps a little tangential to this discussion, it is worthwhile to consider the way Sun Yatsen defined the notion of 'People's Livelihood'. At a lecture on 3 August 1924, Sun (cited in Mackerras 2008, p. 139) asserted:

> No longer can it be said that the material problem is the centre of history. The political, social and economic centres within history all actually boil down to the problem of the people's livelihood (minsheng), so the people's livelihood

is the centre of social history. First we must study the central problem of the people's livelihood clearly, and only then can we find a way of solving problems of society.

In other words, even in regard to the contemporary global challenge of climate change, the continuity and historical fluidity of the political narrative is evident.

This incorporation of 'harmony' into China's international relations and the issue of climate change was highlighted at the 9th annual conference of the China Council for International Cooperation on Environment and Development. At that conference, Premier Wen Jiaobao (Xinhua 14 November 2009) stressed China's commitment to tackling climate change and pledged that China would seek to increase cooperation within the international community on climate change. Further to this, at the World Economic Forum in Davos, Premier Wen (2009a) asserted that 'The world economy is undergoing profound changes and transition. The future and destiny of all countries are more closely interconnected than at any time in history' and proposed that 'to promote world harmony and prosperity', there are a number of areas that require greater international cooperation asserting 'First, tackle climate change. Climate change is a common challenge confronting the entire mankind.' Have nominated the status of climate change as the first priority for international cooperation and action, Wen added that 'China takes this issue very seriously . . . Stronger international cooperation is crucial for addressing climate change.'

However, along with this call for greater cooperation on climate change, Wen (2009a) added:

> We should take into full account the basic national conditions, stage of development, historical responsibility and per capita emissions of different countries in carrying out such cooperation and uphold the framework of sustainable development and the principle of 'common but differentiated responsibilities'.

This distinction between developed and developing countries was further pursued by Wen (2009b) at the United Nations Climate Change Conference in Copenhagen in December 2009 where he reasserted the notion of 'common but differentiated responsibilities' as 'the core and bedrock of international cooperation on climate change'. Wen (2009b) once again pointed to the relatively high level of per capita emissions among developed countries which he said were largely 'attributed to consumption', in stark contrast to developing countries emissions which he argued were 'primarily survival emissions'.

This issue of per capita emissions along with the 'common but differentiated responsibilities' Wen emphasised will undoubtedly continue to be part of the developed versus developing countries debate in regard to emissions and broader issues of climate change. This of course is just one of the challenges surrounding negotiations between states on the implementation of both national and supranational measures to address climate change.

Whilst such state and supra-state negotiations will continue to gain much of the media attention, civil society has a vital role to play in facilitating political responses to climate change within the PRC, at all levels of government. Consequently, civil society actors at all levels who wish to deal with the PRC government or within the PRC with other sub-state actors will need to understand the political context that they must operate within.

8.6 DEALING WITH CHINA

It is quite simply the case that civil society players have an unprecedented opportunity to create positive policy outcomes in the PRC. To take advantage of this opportunity, though, NGOs and other groups that wish to work constructively with the PRC need to understand the nature and relevance of this explicit 'quest for harmony' and the way it shapes China's political process. By having an understanding of the concept of 'harmonious society' and the way that is woven through the political narrative, concerned actors will be better equipped to deal with the PRC government on specific issues such as climate change.

8.6.1 Symbiotic Relationship Between Civil Society and Democracy

This narrative of 'harmony' and the theme of 'listening to the people' fits neatly with the process of grassroots democratisation and the development of a vibrant civil society. Furthermore, there is a symbiotic relationship that exists between democratisation and civil society's development. Alagappa (2004, p. 36) has asserted:

> Just as civil society organizations may influence the distribution of power, norms, and policies of institutions in the other realms, the structure of civil society and the purposes and interaction of its constituent units are shaped by many elements: the normative and material structures at large; the divisions, inequality, and struggles that characterize society; . . . the structure, vitality and policies of state institutions; the vibrancy of political society; and the distribution of intellectual and material resources, which in good part relate to the structure and function of the economy.

Alagappa (2004, pp. 36–7) notes that the relationship between civil society and the state is 'critical'. Civil society must work within 'the political, legal, bureaucratic, and tax framework' the state creates. However, Alagappa (2004, p. 39) also notes that those who ascribe to the 'liberal-democratic school' may conceive civil society as 'protecting the public sphere from the intrusive state, influencing state policy, or altering the regime type'.

Furthermore, the extent to which mechanisms of control tie social organisations to the state serves to highlight the need for NGOs operating within China or even simply negotiating with the PRC authorities to be aware of the political narrative. Mary Gallagher (2004, p. 424) argues that formal social organisations in China are tied to the state via a number of formal mechanisms including legal and administrative guidelines, financial autonomy and political dependence, double-posting of personnel and ideology and interest representation.[3] At the same time, though, Keith et al. (2003, p. 41) in their study of the development of a domestic violence NGO have observed that 'rather than the mass-line notion of social control, ideas and principles have spread through society across a more autonomous, horizontal dimension'. Similarly, Bin Wong (2006, p. 102) has noted that professional, cultural and social voluntary organisations have at times expressed opinions that have 'broadened the political discourse'. Wong (2006, p. 102) argues that such organisations may ultimately become 'vehicles for articulating the interests of citizens' but adds that just how and when that might happen is uncertain.

Wong also notes the clear dichotomy between rural and urban areas. In urban areas, voluntary organisations have not involved large enough numbers to meaningfully negotiate their collective interests with government. In rural areas, though, Bin Wong (2006, p. 162) sees the process of village elections as 'democratic activity that contributes to making people into citizens and defines their membership in the nation in terms of their rights'. However, Bin Wong notes that there are historical linkages that may be drawn in terms of the limitations to the transformative power of both associational activity in urban areas and local village elections in rural areas. Village elections, Bin Wong (2006, p. 162) argues, 'conform to similar political constraints similar to those faced by local self-government'. At the same time, associational activity in urban areas was allowed to function and 'occasionally even flourish' as long as they had 'non-political purposes'.

8.6.2   Nascent Environmental Groups in China

In looking at 'Environmental Movements and Social Organizations in Shanghai' Seungho Lee (2007) notes the comparative autonomy of nonregistered environmental NGOs in Shanghai. With respect to such groups, Peter Ho and Richard Edmonds (2007, p. 338) contend that despite their unofficial status, these organisations develop 'expertise in specific areas' and this development of expertise among unofficially recognized organisations can be seen occurring in 'widely divergent organizations' including established NGOs with a specific technical focus such as 'combating agricultural pesticide use' along with 'groups of student volunteers that gather together for bird-watching or tree-planting'.

However, Lee (2007, p. 274) notes that the very fact that such groups are not officially recognised 'causes them to be politically unstable and often treated with suspicion by the government'. Lee (2007, p. 274) also notes their potential is limited due to the fact that they do not have 'a proper organizational structure or regular staff'. In addition, Lee (ibid.) argues that 'funding is diverse, namely micro grants from international NGOs, foundations, and multinational corporations' along with 'small donations from volunteers, and sometimes symbolic help from local communities, such as the free use of computers and office equipment'. Lee (2007, p. 287) notes the relative access to media and power-holders asserting that 'alliances among GONGOs (Government-operated Non-governmental organizations), quasi-governmental groups, NGOs, and international NGOs have become pervasive, which empower them to contribute to environmental policymaking and implementation'.

8.6.3   Increased Prosperity and a Shift in Focus

In terms of the relationship between the state, civil society and the citizenry, another important factor is the level of prosperity within society. There has been a great deal of scholarship on the issue of post-materialism and political participation.

This notion of increased associational activity in the 'postmaterialist' phase was originally raised by Robert Inglehart (1977). Inglehart (1997, p. 132) asserts that his research on 'Materialist/Postmaterialist value change' was 'guided by two key hypotheses'. These are:

1. *A Scarcity Hypothesis.* An individual's priorities reflect the socioeconomic environment: one places the greatest subjective value on those things that are in relatively short supply.
2. *A Socialization Hypothesis.* The relationship between socioeconomic environment and value priorities is not one of immediate adjustment: a substantial time lag is involved, because, to a large extent, one's basic values reflect the conditions that prevailed during one's pre-adult years.

Dalton (2000, p. 282) asserts that the shift to 'postmaterialism' leads to 'increased political participation outside the boundaries of representative democracy'. In consideration of this theme or shift, Mikiko Eto (2007) has noted the correlation between Japanese women's activism and increased prosperity. Along with this shift, though, is also a shift in political participation in civil society. However, Eto (2007, p. 118) notes the complexity of the issue and cites Tarrow (2000) who 'argues that the new civic activism creates "networks of working relations between citizens and their governments even as those same citizens express their dismay"'.

The relevance of this for China is that NGOs or grassroots organisations that are working within the Chinese domestic setting need to consider their position in light of China's socioeconomic progression. It seems reasonable to expect that there will be greater interest, particularly at the grassroots associational level, in various social, environmental and political issues as China becomes more prosperous. Whilst it is possibly over-simplistic, it is sufficient here to simply argue that in the PRC, as people's basic needs are fulfilled, their attention will continue to shift to 'quality of life' issues. With this shift, there will likely be a commensurate shift in their collective desire for participation in civil society with a view to enacting change.

However, following from Inglehart (1977, 1997), there will be a time lag between increased comparative material advantage and this shift in focus toward politically motivated participation civil society. One could argue further that the reform period which began in the late 1970s ushered in the beginning of this shift. Essentially, also following from Inglehart (1977, 1997), those Chinese who were in their 'pre-adult years' in the 1980s and, more so, the 1990s, are now potential drivers of civil society. Interestingly, more recent research by Inglehart and Welzel (2005) considered generational differences in survival/self-expression values. Inglehart and Welzel (2005, pp. 112–13) noted that there were 'substantial intergenerational differences' in 'the three ex-communist societies examined' which were Russia, Hungary and China. Inglehart and Welzel (2005, p. 113) assert that whilst China is ruled by a communist party: 'its economy and culture have been moving away from the communist model since 1978 – to the point where well over half of its output is now produced in the market sector. In this sense, China constitutes another ex-communist country.'

Regardless of whether you agree or disagree with Ingelhart and Welzel's definition of China as 'non-communist', there is no denying the increased level of material wealth with the Chinese population as a whole. However, in terms of material wealth within the PRC population, there is great variance which could be crudely assessed in terms of the rural–urban disparity of wealth, the regional disparity of wealth and, even more so, at the level of the 'haves and the have nots'. Added to this could be any number of other disparities, even in regard to the relative advantage/disadvantage of certain ethnic minorities for example.[4] Then of course, within the different ethnic groups, there could be further disaggregation on the basis of wealth, education and other factors. The point I am making here is that China is diverse and that diversity needs to be understood and acted on by NGOs trying to operate within the PRC.

What is fundamentally different in today's China is the level of economic development and the related integration with the global economy. This is in itself tied to the issue of the parameters of the state's legitimacy, both in terms of the way that state seeks to define its legitimacy and the way that citizens may ultimately define it. In general terms, the growth of civil society may lead to tests of the state's legitimacy, which is perhaps the function most commonly attributed to the development of civil society. Alternatively, though, civil society may act to reinforce the state's legitimacy. This reinforcing of the state's legitimacy may be related to the way in which formal mechanisms of control (as outlined by Gallagher 2004) are used to control civil society.

8.7 CONCLUSION

Whilst the concept of 'harmonious society' has been personalised by Hu Jintao, the use of the concept is integral to the legitimacy of the CCP as the governing party of the PRC. The shift to the relatively inclusive and somewhat broad concept of attaining a 'harmonious society' as a legitimising concept reflects the shift in expectation of the Chinese people. There is now growing expectation among many Chinese that social needs should be met by government. It is an oversimplification to treat the Chinese as a homogenous group with uniform expectations. Great economic disparities exist within the citizenry but, in general, the continued legitimacy of the CCP is increasingly dependent on a much broader range of issues than mere economic performance, as conveyed in the 'five balances'.

The CCP, as the governing party, is well aware of this shift in focus. There is evidence of this growing awareness within the senior leadership of the party when Hu Jintao, in speaking at the 17th National Party Congress in October 2007, gave substantial attention to the need for greater intra-party democracy. More salient, though, was Hu's emphasis on greater intra-party democracy and of a need for the CCP to 'listen to the people'.

It is within this fluid and dynamic sociopolitical landscape that opportunities for environmental NGOs and other civil society actors are greater than they have been since the inception of the PRC. By understanding the importance and function of the concept of 'harmonious society' under Hu Jintao's leadership, civil society organizations will be better equipped to deal with the governmental and non-governmental sectors within the PRC political context.

NOTES

1. The 'five balances' as they were originally adopted by the 16th Central Committee in 2003 are described by Guo et al. (2008, p. 37) as 'balancing urban and rural development, balancing development among regions, balancing economic and social development, balancing the development of man and nature, and balancing domestic development with opening to the outside world.'
2. The Three Principles of the People were 'Nationalism', 'Democracy' and 'People's Livelihood'. A brief but excellent discussion of the Three Principles of the People along with translations of the lectures delivered by Dr Sun Yatsen on the Three Principles may be found in Mackerras (2008, pp. 127–30).
3. For a full explanation of the mechanisms for state control of civil society organisations see Gallagher (2004, pp. 419–54).
4. The PRC has 55 official ethnic minority groups along with the dominant Han ethnic group.

REFERENCES

Alagappa, M. (2004), 'Civil society and political change: an analytical framework', in M. Alagappa (ed.), *Civil Society in Asia: Expanding and Contracting Democratic Space*, Stanford, CA: Stanford University Press, pp. 25–60.

Bin Wong, R. (2006), 'Citizen, state, and nation in China', in R. Boyd and Tak-Wing Ngo (eds), *State Making in Asia*, Oxford, UK: Routledge, pp. 91–105.

Communist Party of China (CPC) (2006), 'Three Represents', available at http://english.cpc.people.com.cn/66739/4521344.html, accessed 6 March 2010.

Dalton, R.J. (2000), 'Value change and democracy', in S.J. Pharr and R.D. Putnam (eds), *Disaffected Democracies: What's Troubling the Trilateral Countries?*, Princeton, NJ: Princeton University Press, pp. 252–69.

Eto, M. (2007), 'Vitalizing democracy at the grassroots: a contribution of post-war women's movements in Japan', *East Asia*, **25** (2): 115–43.

Gallagher, M. (2004), 'China: the limits of civil society in a late Leninist state', in M. Alagappa, *Civil Society in Asia: Expanding and Contracting Democratic Space*, Stanford, CA: Stanford University Press.

Guo, Y., J. Tian and M. Yanrong (2008), *Key Words for Better Understanding China*, Li Yang et al. (trans.), Beijing: Foreign Languages Press.

Herberer, T. and G. Schubert (2006), 'Political reform and regime legitimacy in contemporary China', *ASIEN 99*, April, pp. 9–25.

Ho, P. and R.L. Edmonds (2007), 'Perspectives of time and change: rethinking embedded environmental activism in China', *China Information*, **21** (2): 331–44.

Holbig, H. (2008), 'Ideological reform and political legitimacy in China', in

T. Herber and G. Schubert (eds), *Institutional Change and Legitimacy in Contemporary China*, London: Routledge, pp. 13–34.

Hu J. (2007), 'Full text of Hu Jintao's report at 17th Party Congress', available at http://news.xinhuanet.com/english/2007-10/24/content_6938749_11.htm, accessed 11 March 2010.

Information Office of the State Council of the People's Republic of China (2008), 'China's policies and actions for addressing climate change', available at http://www.ccchina.gov.cn/WebSite/CCChina/UpFile/file419.pdf, accessed 3 August 2009.

Inglehart, R. (1977), *The Silent Revolution: Changing Values and Political Styles*, Princeton, NJ: Princeton University Press.

Inglehart, R. (1997), *Modernization and Postmodernization*, Princeton, NJ: Princeton University Press.

Inglehart, R. and C. Welzel (2005), *Modernization, Cultural Change and Democracy: The Human Development Sequence*, New York, NY: Cambridge University Press.

International Department Central Committee of CPC (IDCPC) (2007), 'Constitution of the Communist Party of China', available at http://www.idcpc.org.cn/english/cpcbrief/constitution.htm, accessed 30 June 2009.

Keith, R.C. (2009), *China from the Inside Out*, New York, NY: Pluto Press.

Keith, R.C., Z. Lin and H. Lie (2003), 'The making of a Chinese NGO: the Research and Intervention Project in Domestic Violence', *Problems of Post-Communism*, **50** (6), November/December: 38–50.

Kohn, T. (2009), 'China believes climate risk tops credit crisis, Hu aide says', Bloomberg, available at http://www.bloomberg.com/apps/news?pid=20601130&sid=abGKPI3.pEh0, accessed 26 May 2009.

Lee, S. (2007), 'Environmental movements and social organizations in Shanghai', *China Information*, **21** (2): 269–97.

Mackerras, C. (2008), *China in Transformation*, 2nd edn, London: Pearson Longman.

National Development and Reform Commission People's Republic of China (2007), 'China's National Climate Change Programme', available at http://www.ccchina.gov.cn/WebSite/CCChina/UpFile/file188.pdf, accessed 30 July 2009.

Tarrow, S. (2000), 'Mad cows and social activists: contentious politics in the trilateral democracies', in S.J. Pharr and R.D. Putnam (eds), *Disaffected Democracies: What's Troubling the Trilateral Countries?*, Princeton, NJ: Princeton University Press, pp. 270–90.

Weatherley, R. (2006), *Politics in China Since 1949: Legitimizing Authoritarian Rule*, Oxford, UK: Routledge.

Wen J. (2009a), 'Speech at the World Economic Forum Annual Meeting of New Champions Dalian, 10 September 2009', available at http://news.xinhuanet.com/english/2009-09/11/content_12032065.htm, accessed 14 November 2009.

Wen J. (2009b), 'Build consensus and strengthen cooperation to advance the historical process of combating climate change', UN Climate Change Conference, Copenhagen, 18 December, available at http://sy.chineseembassy.org/eng/xwfb/t647462.htm, accessed 1 March 2010.

Xinhua News Agency (2009), 'China concludes celebration of navy anniversary with grand fleet review', *People's Daily Online*, available at http://news.xinhuanet.com/english/2009-04/23/content_11245305.htm.

Xinuhua News Agency (2007), 'Hu Jintao advocates "conservation culture" for first time in keynote political document', *People's Daily Online*, available at http://english.peopledaily.com.cn/90002/92169/92187/6283133.html, accessed 20 June 2009.

Xinuhua News Agency (2009), 'China committed to fully tackling climate change: Premier', *People's Daily Online*, available at http://english.people.com.cn/90001/90776/90883/6813047.html, accessed 14 November 2009.

PART III

Climate change and challenges

9. Managing businesses in uncertain times: sustainable development and an ensemble leadership repertoire

Vikram Murthy

9.1 INTRODUCTION: THE EVIDENCED REALITY OF THE PLANET'S BURGEONING PROBLEMS

The challenges of climate change and sustainable development highlight three complementary hypotheses that form the backdrop to the following discourse. The first of these is that governments will not solve climate change without business at the table as an engaged and involved partner. This is a bold assertion, especially in light of the fact that business was assigned no role to play in Copenhagen (Stigson 2009). Its omission is unfortunate because the second hypothesis is that societal perceptions of the role of business have shifted markedly and it is increasingly being looked to for solutions to global problems (WBCSD 2009). The third and final hypothesis is taking shape even as business continues to jostle for voice and vote at the table of global agendas. Ban Ki-moon, the present Secretary-General of the UN, describes it best when he calls on business to 'give practical meaning and reach to the values and principles that connect cultures and people everywhere' (UNGC 2008, p. 4). This quantum leap in the raison d'être of business is in sharp relief to the prevailing wisdom of thought-leaders as recently as a few decades ago. Today's call for business to 'move from value to values, from shareholders to stakeholders, and from balance sheets to balanced development' (Annan, cited in EFMD 2005, p. 6), for example, is in stark contrast to the unequivocal damning of 'drives for social responsibility in business' (Friedman 1970; cited in Rae and Wong 2004, p. 131).

9.2   CONSENSUS ON THE IMPORTANCE AND URGENCY OF THE SUSTAINABLE DEVELOPMENT CHALLENGE

There is broad agreement amongst all the actors – politicians, practitioners, scholars and the popular press – on the ubiquity of the challenge of sustainable development and the urgency for finding systemic and enduring solutions. Notwithstanding the robust debates around first-cause, prioritisation of the driving forces, effective and equitable remediation strategies, and the timings of and accountabilities for possible actions, there is a common lexicon around this issue both in the lead-up to the global financial crisis (GFC) and in the aftermath of the Copenhagen summit in 2009 on climate change.

There are presidential, prime ministerial and scholarly pronouncements that signpost the ongoing development of such a common worldview. For example, in a post-9/11 but pre-GFC scenario, the three dangers to common humanity in an interconnected world were highlighted as being its profound inequality, instability and unsustainability (Clinton 2007). At the onset of the GFC these three dangers were further amplified as four problems resulting from the globalisation of new economies: firstly, a restructuring of industries and services with the negative collateral of social dislocations; secondly, the severe resources gap as the BRIC countries (Brazil, Russia, India and China) came on stream; thirdly, the increasingly visible divergences in the consumption patterns, and quality of life between rich and poor countries; and, finally, a financial system with global flows of capital and global financial arrangements without an attendant global governance system to solve problems when they arise (Brown 2008).

Even as the first green shoots of recovery from the GFC were being observed, scholarly triangulation to the discussion was provided by Professor Jeffrey Sachs, the Director of the Earth Institute at Columbia University, when he underscored the essentially unpredictable nature of critical uncertainties and the outcomes of their interconnectedness:

> For a long time it had seemed relatively straightforward for the world to achieve 4 or even 5 percent per annum global growth, and no doubt the exuberant equity markets were pricing in such optimistic expectations. Then we were reminded that conventional energy supplies and even food supplies are more precarious than we had assumed . . . Food production is also struggling to keep up with rising populations and rising staples intake per person as the demand for meat rises with incomes (raising the demands for feed grains). The implications of marking down the estimated long-term global growth rate from say 4.5 percent to 3.0 percent per annum can be enough to cut worldwide equity market capitalization very sharply. (Sachs 2009a, pp. 6–7)

Notwithstanding its nuanced taxonomy, the search by governments for global solutions to the issue of sustainable development has been under-whelming. In the lead-up to the *COP15 Copenhagen* (UNFCCC 2009), the UN Climate Chief, de Boer, listed just four modest expectations he had from a successful international agreement in Copenhagen: firstly, how much the industrialised countries are willing to reduce their emissions of greenhouse gases; secondly, how much the major developing countries such as China and India are willing to do to limit the growth of their emissions; thirdly, how the help needed by developing countries to engage in reducing their emissions and adapting to the impacts of climate change is going to be financed; and, finally, how that money is going to be managed (de Boer, United Nations Climate Change Conference, cited in von Bulow 2009).

In retrospect, this bid to rein in expectations was self-fulfilling. As the UK's Secretary of State for Energy and Climate Change admitted, the equivocal outcomes of the conference at best highlight 'the scale of the challenge we face' and at worst underline the 'chaotic process dogged by procedural games' that nations played (Miliband 2009). The world did not get an agreement on 50 per cent reductions in global emissions by 2050 or an 80 per cent reduction by developed countries and even the countries signing the accord merely endorsed the science that says we must prevent warming of more than 2°C, nothing more.

Meanwhile humanity marches inexorably towards massive anthropogenic transgressions of planetary boundaries. Rockström's (2009) apocalyptic warning that 'we have reached the planetary stage of sustainability, where we are fiddling with hard-wired processes at the global earth-system scale', is well supported by his emerging data, see Table 9.1, where for the first time, safe operating boundaries referenced to pre-industrial (pre the period from 1786–93) levels for supporting human development have been estimated. His prognosis is hopeful but cautionary, because while it accepts that reversal is possible as evidenced by the successful restoration of the ozone layer, it stresses that it would be much more difficult and complex given the scale and scope of the problem (Rockström, cited in Biello 2009). While the exact boundary values themselves are a matter of contention, see for example Ehsaan Masood's criticism that they are based not on any new research, but rather on existing data sets (Masood 2009), it is still an urgent call to action for policy makers.

These prevailing conditions have foregrounded radically new and dramatically different strategic challenges around sustainable development for management and leadership in business. What were already regarded as difficult interdisciplinary challenges for leadership leading up to the millennium are clearly compounded today into even more complex business

Table 9.1   The nine planetary boundaries

Earth system	Threshold measure	Boundary	Current level	Preindustrial
Climate change	CO_2 concentration	350 ppm	387 ppm	280 ppm
Biodiversity loss	Extinction rate	10 pm[a]	>100 pm	0.1–1 pm
Nitrogen cycle	N_2 tonnage	35 mmt[b]	121 mmt	0
Phosphorous cycle	Level in ocean	11 mmt	8.5–9.5 mmt	0
Ozone layer	O_3 concentration	276 DU[c]	283 DU	290 DU
Ocean acidification	Aragonite[e] levels	2.75	2.9	3.44
Freshwater usage	Consumption	4000 km^{3}[d]	2600 km^3	415 km^3
Land use change	Cropland conversion	15 km^3	1.7 km^3	Low
Aerosols	Soot concentration	TBD[f]	TBD	TBD
Chemical pollution	TBD	TBD	TBD	TBD

Notes:
[a]   pm = per million
[b]   mmt = millions of metric tons
[c]   DU = Dobson unit
[d] km^3 = cubic kilometres
[e]   Aragonite is a form of calcium carbonate. Measurement is in global mean saturation state.
[f]   TBD = to be determined

Source: Scientific American, 23 September 2009.

imponderables (Murthy and McKie 2009, p. 4). It is against this background of a vocal intelligentsia that makes a pressing case for the escalating pressures on planetary survival (see Sachs 2009b), and the emergence of a genuinely global mobilisation of effort, albeit rambunctious and arguably uncoordinated at times, that this chapter approaches the subject of sustainable development and leadership for uncertain times.

The search for an augmented repertoire of leadership practices to fit the context evolved from a piece of original research involving senior leaders of successful Australian-based local, regional and multinational businesses. Their participation in theorising existing and future challenges facing contemporary Australian businesses resulted in the Ensemble Leadership Repertoire,[1] a description of the elements of an emerging set of leadership practices that could help meet these contemporary challenges. This chapter first discusses the genesis and characteristics of the challenge of sustainable development and thereafter describes the efficacy of the Ensemble Leadership Repertoire for the current business context.

9.3 BUSINESS AND THE CHALLENGE OF SUSTAINABLE DEVELOPMENT

In acknowledging the incomplete nature of its information, but nevertheless urging attention to its findings, *The Limits to Growth: A Report for the Club of Rome's Project on the Predicament of Mankind*, first published in the early 1970s (cited in Meadows and Meadows 2007, p. 196), stressed that:

> There is no reliable and complete information about the degree to which the earth's physical environment can absorb and meet the needs of further growth in population and capital. There is a great deal of partial information, which optimists read optimistically and pessimists read pessimistically. Continuing 'business as usual' policies through the next few decades will not lead to a desirable future, or even to meeting basic human needs. It will result in an increasing gap between the rich and the poor, problems with resource availability and environmental destruction, and worsening economic conditions for most people.

Fifteen years later, the *Report of the World Commission on Environment and Development: Our Future* (Brundtland 1987), in underlining what it perceived as the three vectors of the sustainable development debate, triangulated those with the cornerstones of: economic growth; the needs of the poor; and environmental limits (see Figure 9.1). In its oft-cited definition, Brundtland (1987, p. 54) only served to reinforce the trade-off mindset, even if it did stretch it generationally:

> Sustainable development is development that meets the needs of the present without compromising the ability of future generations to meet their own needs. It contains within it two key concepts: the concept of needs, in particular the essential needs of the world's poor, to which overriding priority should be given; and the idea of limitations imposed by the state of technology and social organisation on the environment's ability to meet present and future needs.

The United Nation's *World Summit on Sustainable Development and its Critical Trends Report* (United Nations 2002) highlighted another, and

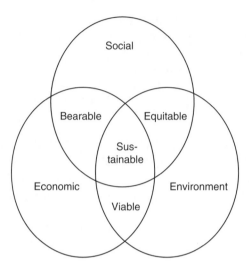

*Figure 9.1   Sustainable development (adapted from the Brundtland Report
1987)*

more telling, dimension to the prevailing trade-off paradigm. This was
that, notwithstanding the globally compounding social and environmental problems, business did not even merit a mention in its report. Perhaps
business was not seen by any of the stakeholders, nor arguably considered
itself, as any part of the solution. The following citation from this report
underscores this argument because, while it lists all the key global challenges, it refrains from any mention of business as forming part of any
concerted response:

> The world will have to support an additional five billion people and a high pro-
> portion of these are in developing countries; poverty and economic inequality
> continues in Latin America and Africa; food consumption is increasing and
> potential to expand crop production is limited; industrial water use increases
> because of development and services provided by fresh water ecosystems
> are threatened; nearly half the world's people will experience water shortage
> by 2025; world's forest area continues to decline; consumption of all types
> of energy is growing; biomass energy is a health threat to billions in poor
> countries; fossil fuel consumption and CO_2 emissions on the rise in developed
> countries; many signs of climate change; over one billion people lack access
> to safe drinking water; malaria is increasing in Africa. (United Nations 2002,
> pp. 4–21)

9.4 THE 'LIMITS' LENS AND THE STRATEGY OF TRADE-OFFS

As stressed above, the traditional view of business has been that economic success and sustainable development are mutually exclusive. This dominant worldview has meant that the discussion on sustainable development has been extremely cautionary and has repeatedly stressed the trade-off between economic development and environmental security (Hargroves and Smith 2005). Business' limits lens thus temporally preceded the more recent 'abundance' lens. The philosophical origins of the limits lens predate even the discussion chronicled above. In fact it harks back to the Enlightenment and Malthus's (2004) compelling if unpopular arguments at the time, that unfettered improvement in the human condition would be ultimately thwarted by the strong and constantly operating check of subsistence. Bourne (2009) provides stark validation of this 'Malthusian collapse' (p. 39) from the green revolution started in the mid-1960s in Punjab, India. Norman Borlaug's irrigation-intensive, synthetic fertiliser and pesticides-based, monoculture farming was heralded as the antithesis to Malthus' law. Four decades later, yields are flat, water tables have dropped precipitously, the land is leached, and people stricken with life-threatening illnesses from the pesticides-contaminated water (p. 46). Trade-off is endemic.

It is this same paradigm of zero-sum trade-offs that has pervaded industry and influenced leadership's mind-set and mental models till very recently. It has resulted in businesses viewing a firm's objective of being financially successful as adversarial to any desire on its part to be socially accountable as well. Further, it has shaped the micro-economic definition of a firm's success with concepts like structure–conduct–performance and sustainable competitive advantage (Porter 1980) which argue in favour of, for example, externalising the negative implications of a firm's operations if that increases profits. Such a limiting definition of a firm's strategic performance tacitly and explicitly encourages business practices (not all of them necessarily ethical) that contrive to bring down the costs of the factors of production. Exploiting lax, nascent or non-existent regulatory regimes in the developing world to compete on cost in the developed world is a common ploy birthed from this exclusive focus on firm success as commercial profitability alone.

It also suggests to businesses that to 'do the right thing' (Porter and Kramer 2006, p. 81), is a self-determinable option to be exercised entirely separately to doing business day-to-day. In the sustainable development arena, it thus provides leadership with an escape clause on the basis that 'no company can jump on every opportunity and sometimes the costs of going green are just too high' (Esty and Winston 2009, pp. 252–3).

The limits lens and the trade-off paradigm have another significant drawback. The lack of a coherent framework to rigorously rate responsible versus irresponsible businesses abets self-serving corporate behaviour. 'The existing cacophony of self-appointed score-keepers' (Porter and Kramer 2006, p. 81) does not permit uniform add-back of the costs of negative externalities to companies' reports and it therefore makes accurate corporate and/or government performance impossible to judge. McGregor and Harvey (2006, cited in Grant 2007, p. 13) provide this interesting disinformation from the Chinese Academy of Science:

> Matters have reached the point that the Deputy Director of the Institute of Sociology of the Chinese Academy of Science has estimated that much of the nominal growth in their country's economy in the last 20 years has come at the expense of the environment; that is, their calculations suggest that it is possible that between 30–100 per cent of the nominal GDP growth in China's economy has been offset by factors traditionally considered to be externalities.

The limits lens is still firmly situated in both literature and practice. A fast-developing conceptual trail, however, is leading to the discovery and use of a second lens of abundance and a strategy of hope that holds great promise for sustainable development provided it supplants the first lens in times to come.

9.5　THE 'ABUNDANCE' LENS AND THE STRATEGY OF HOPE

It was only 5 years into the millennium after the United Nations (UN) declaration in January 2005 – of the start of a Decade of Education for Sustainable Development – that a turning point was reached in the sustainable development discussions. It was at this time that the hitherto entrenched view of sustainable futures as a trade-off can be seen to be losing traction and, more importantly, business was positioned not just as a net contributor to the human-made component of environmental and social equity problems, but as a key and hopeful part of its solution.

This chapter positions the post-2005 discussion as having arrived at a series of cascading conclusions that are significant both for the discourse on sustainable development and for research on emerging leadership practices. For a start, there is now considerable consensus among the scientific community, official government reports and most social stakeholders on climate change. The Australian government's Garnaut Report (Garnaut 2008) offers a concise and useful summary:

On the balance of probabilities and not as a matter of belief, the majority opinion of the Australian and international scientific communities is that human activities resulted in substantial global warming from the mid 20th century, and that continued growth in greenhouse gas concentrations caused by human-induced emissions would generate high risks of dangerous climate change.

This consensus has been paralleled by increasing expert assertions that, rather than being a trade-off, sustainable development is beneficial to society, environment, and business. As the Stern Report on climate change expressed: 'the world does not need to choose between averting climate change and promoting growth and development' (Stern 2006, p. 3). The economic confirmation of the end of trade-off thinking has even been accompanied by a Prime Ministerial acknowledgement that 'business leadership is needed in adopting efficiency measures, mobilizing capital, creating new markets, developing new technologies, driving innovation, deepening our skills base and developing partnerships across the whole community' (Rudd 2008).

Such an explicitly positive outlook has fostered a second lens of abundance and a strategy of hope. This worldview is corner-stoned on the premise that a safe, healthy and just world, which is economically, equitably and ecologically sound is merely an intelligent design problem whose solution already exists. It is predicated on human artifice being considered a living thing with its design incorporating the three essential requirements of vitality, namely: growth, free energy and open metabolism (McDonough and Braungart 2000). Hawken et al.'s (1999) book *Natural Capitalism: Creating the Next Industrial Revolution* anchors this philosophy in the prevailing globalisation debate. In it, the authors assert that the ideology of globalised trade as it currently exists is fundamentally flawed because, while it focuses on financial and manufacturing capital, it does not enhance human and natural capital. Their remedy is to adhere to four principles of natural capitalism, namely: radical resource productivity, biomimicry (Benyus 1997), reconceptualising business as the flow of value and service rather than goods, and reinvestment of firm's profits in natural capital.

Their arguments resonate strongly with certain sections of the business community, which subscribe to the view that taking the lead in integrating a natural capitalism worldview into their operations demonstrates strategic foresight. For example, there are now building architects and town and city planners using the principles of cradle-to-cradle manufacture to ensure sustainable design and eco-effectiveness (McDonough 2009). Similarly, traditionally wasteful materials manufacturers such as floor carpet producers are consciously studying nature and understanding the concepts of biomimicry to find environmentally friendly solutions to customers' needs (Benyus 2005). An increasing number of such organisations in a variety of sectors in the United States, Europe and China provide growing empirical evidence that the principles of natural capitalism do translate to robust design principles that actually deliver quantifiable results (see, for example, RMI 2009). They are further validated by the view of senior scientists, as cited above, that even a redoubtable challenge like climate change is actually a harbinger of many new opportunities (Stern 2006). Perhaps the strongest endorsement of the abundance lens and the strategy of hope is that an erstwhile advocate of business strategy as choosing what not to do and overall low cost as a preeminent generic sustainable competitive advantage (Porter 1980, 1996), should now write about the 'competitive advantage of corporate philanthropy' (Porter and Kramer 2002, p. 57) and strategic corporate social responsibility as transformation of 'value chain activities to benefit society' (Porter and Kramer 2006, p. 89).

From the above discussion it will be clear that sustainable development is a strategic inflection point not just in the lives of nations and their governments, but in the forward trajectories of industries and individual businesses. How leadership and management in business apprehend and process this challenge, and the far-sightedness they demonstrate in seeking solutions that leverage, mitigate and adapt to it will benefit business and the societies it operates in equally (Friedman 2010). The quality of business leadership's responses, however, depends on the myths and realities that abound in the operating environment, and the augmented set of leadership practices in use. The following sections discuss these in turn.

9.6 FOUR MYTHS AND THEIR CONNECTED REALITIES

It is accepted organisational wisdom that the future is everyone's business and must remain a central preoccupation at all levels. In practice, it is viewed as the 'domain of leaders' (Kouzes and Posner 2002, p. xxviii), not least because of its promise of possibilities albeit predicated on the quality of leadership's strategic thinking. Not surprisingly, therefore, there is empirical evidence to suggest mindful contemplation across industry sectors in Australia on current and emerging leadership practices needed to address productive sustainability in the face of these contemporary challenges. Such reflection highlights four prevailing myths that colour organisational world views and leadership responses, and merit more detailed discussion and deconstruction.

Table 9.2   *Eras with significant commonalities and the correlated business strategic and leadership responses*

Era	1940–60	1961–80	1981–95	1996–2001	2005–present
Common strategic environment	Delineable and stable	Stable and mature	Fluid and dynamic	Punctuated and discontinuous	High velocity and complex
Leadership process	Dominant and judgemental	Responsive to analysis	Responsive to learning	Purposeful search for meaning	Change agent
Strategy	Prescriptive (design/plan)	Prescriptive (position)	Learning and emergent	Configuration	
Leadership response	Rigid	Reactive	Reactive Adaptive	Adaptive Generative	Generative
Leadership approaches	Transactional --➤				
		Transformational -----------------------------➤			
				New-new -------------➤	
				Ensemble -----------➤	

Source: Adapted from Mintzberg et al. (1998, pp. 358–9).

The first of these myths is the oxymoron that, in business, change is the only constant. This myth is not new and counts many management practitioners and thinkers amongst its protagonists. One of the most influential and constant of these has been Igor H. Ansoff who in the 1960s labelled strategic change 'so rapid that firms must continually survey the product-market environment' (1965, p. 125), in the 1970s urged attention to the strategic problem of 'new conditions of turbulence' (1979, p. 5), in the 1980s stressed that the 'level of turbulence has progressively escalated' (1984, p. 57), and in the 1990s advocated organisational flexibility for turbulent times (Ansoff 1990). Leading forecasters and strategic thinkers strongly dispute this prevailing meme of endemic turbulence (for example, Makridakis 1990; Mintzberg 1994), with Murthy and McKie (2009) providing a convincing counterpoint to Ansoff when they argue that there are actually eras of significant commonalties and differences in strategic environments, and in each era organisational circumstances correlate with its particular responses, as seen in Table 9.2.

The second myth is that the more things change, the more they remain the same. Labelling such a viewpoint as a myth may, at first glance, appear contradictory to the preceding argument that there are clearly identifiable patterns to leadership and strategy processes and responses in different eras. This is not so because the second myth, and the argument against it, is focussed not on events within an identified era, but rather on the transition *between* eras. It points to the global financial crisis as marking such a temporally sharp transition between eras, using Miller's (1976) and Miller and Friesen's (1980) theory of archetypes that states that transitioning *between* eras is a quantum leap rather than an incremental change. The quotation that the 'more things change, the more they remain the same', is actually an English translation of Jean-Baptiste Alphonse Karr's (1849) famous French quotation in *Les Guêpes.* At its core, it is a tacit, but erroneous, belief widely held by many managers and leaders in organisations that most organisational challenges have a sense of déjà vu. This view, in turn, encourages them to access historical 'master programs for dealing with difficult situations' (Argyris 1998, p. 217) that actually prevents them from 'getting the kind of deep information, insightful behaviour, and productive change they need to cope with much more complex problems' (pp. 213–14) in their prevailing and future business context. It hollows their risk management and weakens their effective response to high-velocity change. This is because, 'fresh thinking and new learning are needed if we are to avoid responding to today's problems with yesterday's solutions, while tomorrow's challenges engulf us' (Dilworth 1998, p. 28).

This view has been robustly ratified by Ian Davis, the Managing Director of global management consultancy, McKinsey and Company. Writing during the depths of the global financial crisis, Davis (2009) predicted the emergence of a 'new normal' (p. 1) for organisations and warned that: 'It is increasingly clear that the current downturn is fundamentally different from recessions of recent decades. We are experiencing not merely another turn of the business cycle, but a restructuring of the economic order' (p. 2).

Leadership can take heart however from the same article's summary assertion that, for those who are able to see beyond this myth of constancy, 'tomorrow's environment will be different, but no less rich in possibilities' (p. 1).

The third myth is that history is the best guide to present and future practice; a notion that is philosophically related to the two myths that have preceded it. In common with them, it could also have deleterious consequences for companies if left uncorrected. This myth refers to the popular practitioner and academic practice of using historical business exemplars to define the drivers of high-performance for future organisational practice. Methodologies are used that are hard-data rich and statistically intensive to retrospectively investigate the target exemplar's management principles, business models and strategies to yield clues to its iconic status and endurance. Such management frameworks are then transferred inter-company, cross-sector, context-imperviously and end up being misleading guides with little validity for effective forward-looking practice for the recipient organisation.

Nowhere is the folly of such an agenda better illustrated than in the subsequent performances of many of the exemplar companies themselves. Fannie Mae, for example, lauded by *Good to Great* (Collins 2001) as being the 'best in the world at capital markets in anything that pertains to mortgages' (p. 101), was placed into the conservatorship of the Federal Housing Finance Agency (FHFA) on 7 September 2008, after it had engineered the single most significant global financial meltdown in seven decades by triggering the subprime mortgage crisis because of systemic failures in its operations, management and leadership. This has led to the most sweeping government interventions in private financial markets in decades and the effects of this incursion continue to resound around the world even into 2010. Fannie Mae stock, bought around the time that the book was published, would have lost over 80 per cent of its initial value by October 2008. Its tag line of excellence reads singularly disingenuously in hindsight.

This failure raises serious issues about the universal application of discrete messages. Simultaneously, it argues that in times of high velocity changes and massive uncertainties, future practice can no longer be based on the retrospective (and even more so, the *restricted* statistics-based retrospective) evidence of management exemplars and models. Instead of looking back for prescriptive guides to future performance, it proposes that research draws more from existing practice and emerging trends to develop better anticipation and more conscious ways of looking ahead. Leadership must rely less on gaining guidance from the past and more on learning for the future from the present.

The fourth and final myth is the belief stated so unequivocally in Friedman's (2002) *Capitalism and Freedom*, that 'there is one and only one social responsibility of business – to use its resources and engage in activities designed to increase its profits so long as it stays within the rules of the game, which is to say, engages in open and free competition without deception or fraud' (p. 133). The fit-for-purpose assumption implicit in Friedman's assertion has already been critiqued. For Friedman, as stated earlier, the trade-off between economic objectives and social obligations is real and present and the business of business is to do business.

Underpinning the rationale that counters this myth is the pressing weight of empirical evidence that demonstrates that the 'most effective method of addressing many of the world's pressing problems is often to mobilize the corporate sector' and that in the long run, 'social and economic goals are . . . integrally connected' (Porter and Kramer 2002, p. 59). The precept that businesses cannot succeed in societies that fail, argues in favour of a strategic approach to corporate involvement in society (Porter and Kramer 2006, p. 89).

9.7   ENSEMBLE LEADERSHIP REPERTOIRE

The preceding sections have highlighted that there is vibrant debate around first cause, final outcomes and adaptive and mitigating responses to anthropogenic climate change because of the incomplete and inconclusive nature of the currently available information. It has, however, stressed that both on the balance of probabilities and in view of the available evidence climate change is arguably an issue of global proportions. Businesses face hitherto unknown challenges as a consequence. These include the significant strategic paradoxes of choosing between a limits and/or an abundance paradigm, as well as resetting a number of operational myths with regards to businesses' raison d'être. On the premise that responding to this redefinition of organisational strategic performance requires businesses and their leadership to learn and deploy an augmented repertoire of leadership practices, this section summarises the findings from a neo-classical grounded theory research study (referred to in the Introduction, Section 9.1). That study examined two related research questions: 'What existing and likely future challenges face contemporary Australian businesses?' and 'What current and emerging practices are leaders using to address productive sustainability?' to arrive at a substantive theory on leadership practices and their successful enactments for complex environments, called the Ensemble Leadership Repertoire (see Figure 9.2). It comprises three practices taken together and working in harmony: firstly, sharing fates and interdependence; secondly, exploring deeper meaning; and, finally, the emerging practice of 'Zeitgeist' (that is, integrating cognition, conscience and collective spirit). As the name 'Ensemble' suggests, these three practices are not manifested individually in exclusion to each other, and/or as a paradigmatic shift from one practice to the other. Rather, successful leadership demonstrates all three practices as appropriate, as an Ensemble Repertoire in the pursuit of sustainable organisational productivity.

The third category of Zeitgeist which is integrating cognition, conscience and collective spirit generates five new enactments which are particularly germane to emerging challenges in the current and future environment. These enactments are: being creative; being present; being in touch; being good; and being a global citizen. Each of these in turn can be much more nuanced and more sharply delineated (see Table 9.3).

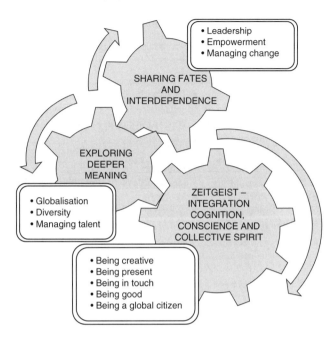

Source: Murthy and McKie (2009, p. 124).

Figure 9.2   The ensemble leadership repertoire

9.8   CONCLUSIONS

The present challenges of climate change and sustainable development require businesses to re-imagine their purpose. This is because for the first time business is being viewed as a responsible and significant actor in the search for systemic and enduring solutions. The traditional view of business has been that economic success and sustainable development are mutually exclusive. This dominant worldview has meant that the discussion on sustainable development has repeatedly stressed the trade-off between economic development and environmental security. It is only as recently as 5 years ago that such a zero-sum paradigm has begun to be supplanted by a second lens of abundance and a strategy of hope that suggests that businesses can grow and develop without abrogating their social responsibility by embracing concepts of natural capitalism. This requires the reconfiguration of dominant organisational wisdom around such fundamental issues like: the nature of change; the recognition of the emergence of a new world economic order; the need to rely more on

Table 9.3   Emerging leadership practice – Zeitgeist

Being creative	Being present	Being in touch	Being good	Being a global citizen
• Under-standing and accepting change • Fresh approach, new ideas • Willingness to experiment • Cross-fertilisation of ideas • Outsider perspective and insider knowledge • Changing organisational context-culture	• Respecting expertise • Being interested and involved • Seeing the world in a new way • Examining and learning from mistakes • Awareness and appreciation of context	• Enriched sense of community • Dialogue with multiple stakeholders • Working together for organis-ational effectiveness • Under-standing diverse perspectives • Formal and informal processes to craft strategy and design	• Positive emotions • Sense of service • Individuals working together for common good • Instilling trust	• Caring for the planet • Showing environ-mental responsi-bility • Doing ethical business • Developing solutions for under-privileged people • Creating global sustainable enterprise models • Playing a part in an inter-connected world

Source: Murthy and McKie (2009, p. 124).

learning for the future from the present; and the fundamental tenet that businesses cannot succeed in societies that fail. Such a redefinition of organisational strategic performance will require businesses to learn and deploy an augmented repertoire of leadership practices. The Ensemble Leadership Repertoire comprised three practices taken together and working in harmony: firstly, sharing fates and interdependence; secondly, exploring deeper meaning; and finally, the emerging practice of 'Zeitgeist' (that is, integrating cognition, conscience and collective spirit) is one such augmented set of practices that has been theorised from researching Australian companies. These have been summarised very briefly in the preceding section and are offered as one example of the gestalt expression of an organisation's reason, emotion and inclusive spirit. This chapter concludes by stressing that in the light of the clear, present and interdependent challenges of climate change, poverty, inequity, pollution, resource depletion, globalisation and demographic shifts (WBCSD 2007, p. 2), businesses' leadership priorities needs such re-imagination.

NOTE

1. Brief excerpts from the author's book, *Please Don't Stop the Music: An Ensemble Leadership Repertoire, Productive Sustainability, and Strategic Innovation for Uncertain Times*, published in 2009, have been used at different times in this chapter.

REFERENCES

Ansoff, H.I. (1965), *Corporate Strategy*, New York, NY: McGraw-Hill.

Ansoff, H.I. (1979), *Strategic Management*, London: Macmillan.

Ansoff H.I. (1984), *Implanting Strategic Management*, Upper Saddle River, NJ: Prentice-Hall.

Ansoff, H.I. (1990), *Implanting Strategic Management*, 2nd edn, Upper Saddle River, NJ: Prentice Hall.

Argyris, C. (1998), 'Good communication that blocks learning', in D. Ulrich (ed.), *Delivering Results*, Boston, MA: Harvard Business School Press, pp. 213–27.

Benyus, J.M. (1997), *Biomimicry: Innovation Inspired by Nature*, New York, NY: HarperCollins.

Benyus, J. (2005), 'Janine Benyus shares nature's designs', available at http://www.ted.com/talks/lang/eng/janine_benyus_shares_nature_s_designs.html, accessed 10 January 2010.

Biello, D. (2009), 'Grappling with the Anthropocene: scientists identify safe limits for human impacts on planet', available at http://www.scientificamerican.com/article.cfm?id=scientists-identify-safe-limits-for-human-impacts, accessed 10 January 2010.

Brown, G. (2008), 'Meeting the new global challenges', available at http://www.cfr.org/publication/17765/meeting_the_new_global_challenges_video.html, accessed 8 January 2010.

Brundtland, G. (ed.) (1987), *Report of the World Commission on Environment and Development: Our Future*, Oxford, UK: Oxford University Press.

Bourne Jr, J.K. (2009), 'The end of plenty', *National Geographic*, **215** (6): 26–59.

Bulow, M. von (2009), 'The essentials in Copenhagen', available at http://en.cop15.dk/news/view+news?newsid=876, accessed 10 January 2010.

Clinton, W.J. (2007), 'Bill Clinton on building Rwanda', available at http://www.ted.com/talks/bill_clinton_on_rebuilding_rwanda.html, accessed 8 January 2010.

Collins, J. (2001), *Good to Great: Why Some Companies Make the Leap and Others Don't*, New York, NY: HarperCollins Publishers.

Dilworth, R.L. (1998), 'Action learning in a nutshell', *Performance Improvement Quarterly*, **11** (1): 28–43.

Davis, I. (2009), 'The new normal', available at https://www.mckinseyquarterly.com/ghost.aspx?ID=/The_new_normal_2326, accessed 8 January 2010.

Esty, D.C. and A.S. Winston, (2006), *Green to Gold: How Smart Companies Use Environmental Strategy to Innovate, Create Value, and Build Competitive Value*, London: Yale University Press.

European Foundation for Management Development (EFMD) (2005), 'Globally responsible leadership: a call for engagement', available at http://www.efmd.org/attachments/tmpl_3_art_060614xvqa_att_060614trmw.pdf, accessed 28 September 2008.

Friedman, M. (2002), *Capitalism and Freedom*, Chicago, IL: The University of Chicago Press.

Friedman, T.A. (2010), 'Who's sleeping now?', available at http://www.nytimes.com/2010/01/10/opinion/10friedman.html, accessed 11 January 2010.

Garnaut, R. (2008), 'The Garnaut Climate Change Review Final Report', available at http://www.garnautreview.org.au/domino/web_notes/Garnaut/garnaut-web.nsf, accessed 30 September 2008.

Grant, J.H. (2007), 'Advances and challenges in strategic management', *International Journal of Business*, **12** (1): 11–29.

Hargroves, K.J. and M.H. Smith (2005), 'Natural advantage of nations', in K.J. Hargroves and M.H. Smith (eds), *The Natural Advantage of Nations: Business Opportunities, Innovation, and Governance in the 21st Century*, London: Bath Press, pp. 7–33.

Hawken, P., A. Lovins and L.H. Lovins (1999), *Natural Capitalism: Creating the Next Industrial Revolution*, New York, NY: Back Bay.

Karr, J.A. (1849), 'Plus ça change, plus c'est la même chose', available at http://en.wikipedia.org/wiki/Alphonse_Karr, accessed 8 January 2010.

Kouzes, J.M. and B.J. Posner (2002), *The Leadership Challenge*, 3rd edn, San Francisco, CA: John Wiley and Sons.

McDonough, W. and M. Braungart (2000), 'A world of abundance', *Interfaces*, **30** (3): 55–65.

McDonough, W. (2009), 'Key note address: business as an agent of world benefit', available at http://www.youtube.com/watch?v=DogArXwGWlI, accessed 10 January 2010.

Makridakis, S. (1990), *Forecasting, Planning, and Strategy for the 21st Century*, New York, NY: Free Press.

Malthus, T.R. (1798 [2004]), *An Essay on the Principle of Population*, Oxford, UK: Oxford University Press.

Masood, E. (2009), 'Nature podcast', available at http://www.nature.com/nature/podcast/v461/n7263/nature-2009-09-24.html, accessed 12 April 2010.

Meadows, D.H. and D. Meadows (2007), 'The history and conclusions of *The Limits to Growth*', *System Dynamics Review*, **23** (2/3): 191–7.

Miliband, E. (2009), 'The road from Copenhagen', available at http://www.guardian.co.uk/commentisfree/2009/dec/20/copenhagen-climate-change-accord, accessed 10 January 2010.

Miller, D. (1976), 'Strategy making in context: ten empirical archetypes', unpublished PhD thesis, Faculty of Management, McGill University, Montreal.

Miller, D. and P.H. Friesen (1980), 'Archetypes of organisational transition', *Administrative Science Quarterly*, **25**: 268–99.

Mintzberg, H. (1994), *The Rise and Fall of Strategic Planning*, Hemel Hempstead, UK: Prentice Hall.

Mintzberg, H., B. Ahlstrand and J. Lampel (1998), *Strategy Safari: A Guided Tour Through the Wilds of Strategic Management*, New York, NY: The Free Press.

Murthy, V. and D. McKie (2009), *Please Don't Stop the Music: An Ensemble Leadership Repertoire, Productive Sustainability, and Strategic Innovation for Uncertain Times*, London: Inderscience.

Porter, M.E. (1980), *Competitive Strategy: Techniques for Analyzing Industries and Competitors*, New York, NY: The Free Press.

Porter, M.E. (1996), 'What is strategy?', *Harvard Business Review*, **74** (6): 61–78.

Porter, M.E. and M.R. Kramer (2002), 'The competitive advantage of corporate philanthropy', *Harvard Business Review*, **80** (12): 57–68.

Porter, M.E. and M.R. Kramer (2006), 'Strategy and society: the link between competitive advantage and corporate social responsibility', *Harvard Business Review*, **84** (12): 78–92.

Rae, S.B. and K.L. Wong (2004), *Beyond Integrity: A Judeo-Christian Approach to Business Ethics*, 2nd edn, Grand Rapids, MI: Zondervan.

Rocky Mountain Institute (RMI) (2009), 'Natural capitalism and transformational design', available at http://www.youtube.com/user/RockyMtnInstitute#p/a/736C335DA44C4782/1/leuEW-vBpOQ, accessed 11 January 2010.

Rudd, K. (2008), 'Leadership for long term sustainability: the roles of government, business and the international community', Address to the National Business Leaders Forum on Sustainable Development, Australia.

Sachs, J. (2009a), 'Achieving global cooperation on economic recovery and long-term sustainable development', *Asian Development Review*, **26** (1): 3–15.

Sachs, J.D. (2009b), *Common Wealth: Economics for a Crowded Planet*, New York, NY: Penguin Press.

Stern, N. (2006), 'Stern Review: the economics of climate change summary of conclusions', available at http://www.hm-treasury.gov.uk/media/9/9/CLOSED_SHORT_executive_summary.pdf, accessed 23 September, 2008.

Stigson, B. (2009), 'Governments cannot deliver without business', available at http://www.wbcsd.org/Plugins/DocSearch/details.asp?DocTypeId=251&ObjectId=MzY5NTc, accessed 11 January 2010.

United Nations (2002), 'Report of the World Summit on Sustainable Development', Johannesburg, South Africa, 26 August–4 September, Geneva: United Nations.

United Nations Framework Convention on Climate Change (UNFCCC) (2009), 'Copenhagen Accord', available at http://unfccc.int/files/meetings/cop_15/application/pdf/cop15_cph_auv.pdf, accessed 8 January 2010.

United Nations Global Compact (UNGF) (2008), 'Corporate citizenship in the world economy', available at http://www.unglobalcompact.org, accessed 5 November 2008.

World Business Council for Sustainable Development (WBCSD) (2007), 'Business for development: the new role of corporate leadership in global development', available at http://www.wbcsd.ch/DocRoot/9cJReM0SYOSeVahE1usM/Bizwithworld_LR.pdf, accessed 24 September 2008.

World Business Council for Sustainable Development (WBCSD) (2009), 'Business role', available at http://www.wbcsd.org/templates/TemplateWBCSD5/layout.asp?type=p&MenuId=MTEzOA&doOpen=1&ClickMenu=LeftMenu, accessed 11 January 2010.

10. Climate change and human security issues in the Asia–Pacific region

Malcolm McIntosh and Tapan Sarker

The impacts of climate change are not evenly distributed – the poorest countries and people will suffer the earliest and most. And if and when the damages appear it will be too late to reverse the process . . . Such temperature changes would take us into territory unknown to human experience and involve radical changes in the world around us . . . The analysis of climate change requires, by its nature, that we look out over 50, 100, 200 years and more.

Stern Review on *The Economics of Climate Change*

10.1 INTRODUCTION

Global climate change is one of the biggest threats over the coming century (van Lieshout et al. 2004). According to the United Nations (UN), the world's population will have increased by one-third – to 9 billion – by 2050. More than 90 per cent of this growth will take place in developing countries (Werz and Manlove 2009). It is also estimated that, due to the effects of global warming, approximately 200 million people will be newly mobilised as climate migrants by 2050. This increased migration will very likely affect human security in the developing countries, particularly in the vulnerable Asia–Pacific region (Woodward 1998; CSIRO 2006). The Asia–Pacific region already encounters a number of challenges to human security. How might the future effects of climate change interact with these human security challenges? Compared with other parts of the world, the Asia–Pacific region experiences a comparatively high number of ethno-political and armed conflicts (Reilly 2002). This can be attributed to a number of factors specific to that region, such as the lack of a stable supply of food and water, natural disasters and progressive degradation of ecosystem goods and services. These factors also work together to undermine human security and threaten the health and sustainability of communities in the Asia–Pacific region (DuPont and Pearman 2006).

The impacts of climate change on human security in particular are of serious concern, and are an important focus of the policy debate surrounding human security, climate change and environmentally induced migration (Edwards 1999; Dokos 2008).

This chapter describes an assessment of the effects of climate change on human security and socioeconomic development with a particular focus on the Asia–Pacific region, using a sustainable enterprise economy perspective. It also examines the recent move towards a low carbon sustainable enterprise economy in the Asia–Pacific region that can meet the challenges to climate change and human security across a range of geopolitical scales (McIntosh 2009).

10.2   THE HUMAN SECURITY PERSPECTIVES

Human security is defined in many ways by various scholars and agencies (Figure 10.1).

'Human security' as a phrase was first used by the UN in a 1994 Development Report. However, the concept found its origins in the upheaval of the Second World War, as part of pre-post-industrial reckoning in democratic societies on both sides of the Atlantic. The importance of the concept of human security can be seen in the creation of the 1948 United Nations Universal Declaration of Human Rights in the United States, and the creation of the National Health Service in the United Kingdom. On 6 January 1941, US President Franklin D. Roosevelt made a speech in which he talked about the 'Four Freedoms': freedom of speech or expression, freedom of religion, freedom from want and freedom from fear. His wife Eleanor used the ideas and some of the language of this speech in the preamble to the 1948 UN Declaration of Human Rights when she said that these four freedoms were the 'highest aspirations of the common people' (*United Nations Declaration of Human Rights* General Assembly Resolution 217A 1948).

The importance of human security has not diminished over the years. In 2007, the United Nations Security Council held its first-ever debate on the impact of climate change on human security. In that debate it was argued that climate change was about 'our collective security in a fragile and increasingly interdependent world, and that it could not only have serious environmental, social and economic implications, but implications for peace and security' (United Nations Security Council 2007). These implications for human security are especially grave in the vulnerable Asia–Pacific region, where different population groups face multiple stresses such as conflicts, poverty, unequal access to resources, weak institutions, food insecurity and spreading of diseases.

The notion of human security itself embraces three main ideas: the 'survival, dignity and livelihood, freedom from fear . . . freedom from want . . .'

'a new security framework that centers directly on people . . . human security focuses on shielding people from critical and pervasive threats and empowering them to take charge of their lives . . . the consensus on the meaning of security is eroding . . . existing institutions and policies unable to cope with weakening multilateralism and global responsibilities . . . the state has the primary responsibility for security, but the security challenge is complex and various new actors attempt to play a role . . . so we need a shift in paradigm'.

'Protecting people in violent conflict; protecting and empowering people on the move; protecting and empowering people in post-conflict situations; economic insecurity – choices in a world of opportunity; health for human security; knowledge, skills and values – for human security; and linking the many initiatives'.

'The Report introduces a new concept of human security, which equates security with people rather than territories, with development rather than arms. It examines both the national and the global concerns of human security. The Report seeks to deal with these concerns through a new paradigm of sustainable human development, capturing the potential peace dividend, a new form of development co-operation and a restructured system of global institutions. For too long, the concept of security has been shaped by the potential for conflict between states. For too long, security has been equated with the threats to a country's borders. For too long, nations have sought arms to protect their security.'

Human Security Now
UN Commission on Human Security (2003)
chaired by Sadako Ogata and Amartya Sen
www.humansecurity-chs.org

'A humane world where people can live in security and dignity, free from poverty and despair, is still a dream for many and should be enjoyed by all. In such a world, every individual would be guaranteed freedom from fear and freedom from want, with an equal opportunity to fully develop their human potential. Building human security is essential to achieving this goal. In essence, human security means freedom from pervasive threats to people's rights, their safety or even their lives.'

New dimensions of human security
UNDP Human Development Report (1994)

'Human security has become both a new measure of global security and a new agenda for global action. Safety is the hallmark of freedom from fear, while well-being is the target of freedom from want. Human security and human development are thus two sides of the same coin, mutually reinforcing and leading to a conducive environment for each other.'

A perspective on human security
Chairman's Summary
1st Ministerial Meeting of the Human Security Network,
Lysøen, Norway, 20 May 1999

Figure 10.1   Defining human security

sanctity of the individual, the relationship of the individual to the community and the preservation of people and communities in the face of national, international and global intervention.

However, there is 'a consensus that the meaning of [human] security is eroding; existing institutions and policies (are) unable to cope with weakening multilateralism and global responsibilities. The state has the primary responsibility for security, but the security challenge is complex and various new actors attempt to play a role.' This requires a paradigm shift.

In 2003, the UN Commission on Human Security, chaired by Sadako Ogata and Amartya Sen, reported that the world needed 'a new security framework that centers directly on people'. 'Human security', they argued, 'focuses on shielding people from critical and pervasive threats and empowering them to take charge of their lives'. Accordingly, the Commission sought to develop a global framework focussed on 'survival, dignity and livelihood; freedom from fear, and freedom from want'. The Commission was particularly concerned with the most vulnerable individuals who need protection from violent conflict, those people who are on the move and those people who are economically insecure due to the global economic system having failed to enrich them or whose lives have been destabilised by forces far beyond their control. By contrast, more traditional approaches to human security issues tend to focus on military security and territorial issues. 'The concept of security has until now tended to be shaped by the potential for conflict between states and this has often meant that threats to human security have been equated with threats to a country's borders. As a result, for too long, nations have sought arms to protect their security.'

However, the effects of economic globalisation and open global social networks mean that the professional worlds of humanitarianism, development, human rights, conflict and business must find space to meet and integrate. As the 1994 UNDP Report said: 'For most people today a feeling of insecurity arises more from worries about daily life than the dread of a cataclysmic world event. Job security, income security, health security, environmental security, and security from crime – these are emerging concerns of human security all over the world'. As a result, the paradigm shift required to achieve a fuller understanding of human security requires all stakeholders (for example, business, government, civil society and individuals) to develop a new framework of human security, encompassing a new low carbon sustainable enterprise economy.

10.3 THE NEW SUSTAINABLE ENTERPRISE ECONOMY

A sustainable enterprise economy (SEE) is 'an economy that sees no conflict between self-interest and obligation to community, where any enterprise – corporate, social, public, state-owned or individual – aims to have as little impact on the environment as possible *and* is mindful of its social impact' (McIntosh 2008). This approach can be compared to a typical enterprise economy, where the spirit of the community is geared to risk taking, innovation, creativity, problem solving, entrepreneurialism and enthusiasm for life, while recognising that mobility, exchange and trade are part of what it means to be human. By contrast, a *sustainable* enterprise economy uses these human characteristics to create wealth and nurture wellbeing within a framework of peace and social justice. This framework may include initiatives such as income distribution, the provision of fundamental public goods like health and education, the observance of the rule of law and the upholding of human rights. Accordingly, the SEE preserves natural capital, while at the same time creating social and human capital. Unlike the typical enterprise economy, it allows for the management of the trade-off and the space between financial capitals, manufactured capital, natural capital, social capital and human capital (the five capitals model) (Porritt 2006). The SEE builds on the concept of natural capital (Hawken et al. 1999) and the five capitals model to create a new, more complex and sophisticated model of economics.

The five capitals model comes with some qualifications and caveats. For instance, in using this model it is necessary to acknowledge that the concept of 'capital' is useful and that while traditionally these capitals have been land, labour and capital (financial), in the new model these capitals are both tangible and *in*tangible, some hard and some soft, some to be used and spent, and some to be preserved, cherished and left untouched as totems of our learned wisdom about the state of the world.

The idea of sustainable enterprise is a progression from largely voluntary corporate social responsibility and corporate citizenship ideas and practices that have developed over the last few decades in response to the loosely regulated market economy. This has created a more inclusive model of the economy that recognises that the old separations of business, government and civil society are not necessarily as valid or useful as they once were, and hence should not be applied too rigidly. SEE is a model that acknowledges the growth over the last few years of stakeholder engagement, new social partnerships and strategic alliances, and recognises that many of our largest economic institutions and multinational corporations are state-owned institutions.

This new modelling of the economy also recognises that many of the gains in accountability, responsibility, transparency and sustainability (ARTS) are a precursor to a new economy which delivers both private wealth *and* public goods. As such, the first step toward developing a sustainable enterprise economy is to recognise that economic growth is not an end in itself but is merely a means to achieving 'the enjoyments and realities of life' (Keynes 1936).

The Christian Bible refers to the Four Horsemen of the Apocalypse as pestilence, war, famine and death. For almost one-third of the world's population, these Four Horsemen of the Apocalypse reflect the day-to-day realities of life. However, they will become the realities of life for all of us if we do not take urgent action to deal with five main issues: better local and global governance of people, planet and wellbeing; climate change adaptation; energy conservation, production and use; water management and use; and population control. These five issues – governance, climate change, energy, water and population – are the priorities for humanity today, not just in the Asia–Pacific region, but worldwide.

The sustainable enterprise economy requires a better understanding of complex dynamics and systems (particularly fragile earth ecosystems), and also a better understanding of an increasingly continuously connected and boundaryless social world, which both transcend traditional territorial boundaries and established institutional social mechanisms. This requires a paradigm shift away from traditional approaches, toward a more holistic and integrated framework. Two examples serve to illustrate this recent phenomenon.

In April 2009, during a meeting of the G20 group of the 20 largest economies in London, a man died after being hit several times by the police. He was not part of the good-tempered anti-globalisation and anti-banking demonstrations that were taking place across London during the week. The subsequent enquiry elicited numerous still photographs of the police action and many minutes of video footage. It is easy to forget that the surveillance society watches you and I, but also watches agents of the state. It is even easier to forget that this evidence can be made available worldwide instantaneously – to those who have electricity and the electronic means. The same week Facebook announced that it had 200 million users worldwide (which has risen to nearly 600 million in January 2011), which led the *New York Times* to describe it as 'the Web's dominant social ecosystem and an essential personal and business networking tool in much of the wired world'.[1] Both of these instances illustrate the challenges faced in relating to local and global environmental and social issues in an increasingly interconnected world.

The new economy is no longer just for businesses. Instead, it is inclusive of all enterprises and organisations. The challenge now for all institutions is to change the way they relate to local and global environmental and social issues to align themselves with the reality of the interconnectedness of the modern world. This will require a massive paradigm shift, where government departments will have to rethink the way they work, community organisations and local government reorganising themselves, global corporations aligning their mission, purpose and practices with the realities of climate change and sustainable development, and individuals making this happen by actively participating in the changes.

The problem is real and immediate. Recently conferring with a colleague, who is a reviewer for the Intergovernmental Panel on Climate Change (IPCC), we agreed that the question we are asked most often, both of us having been talking about these subjects for some 20 years, is: 'are you optimistic or pessimistic about our chances of surviving?' We agreed that we have developed nuanced answers to this question. First, as individuals we are all going to die anyway. Second, many people in the world currently live marginalised, uncomfortable lives and for them and succeeding generations this revolution is an answer. Third, the human race has been fantastically successful – we have bred like rabbits, most of us live longer than previous generations and modern medicine, housing, healthcare and nutrition has made us the over-dominant species on planet earth. So now is the time to accept that and take the next step. Fourth, in terms of the history of the universe our life on earth has been a wondrous miracle of perfect conditions, but a mere flash in time. Fifth, my scientific colleague and I *are* pessimistic about our future on earth because of our rapacious and greedy capacities, which are the legacy of having to survive under difficult conditions in the swamp, on the land and as a minority. This means that the only real question left for humanity to answer is: now that we have found ourselves, and the limits of our home, what shall we do next?

10.4   THE GLOBAL FINANCIAL CRISIS

The global financial crisis (GFC), or credit crunch as it is known in some countries, was partially caused by the West's access to cheap cash from Asia. This access to cheap borrowed funds also led to greater mass consumption of goods mostly made in Asia. The corollary of this increased consumption was a significant increase in the greenhouse gas emissions (GHG) by Asian manufacturing countries. China is often reproached by Western nations for being one of the largest emitters of GHGs. China's response to these comments is that the developed world exported its toxic wastes and GHGs to developing countries because they had lower unit costs and higher productivity. India has faced a similar scenario. This means that both China and India have massive economic inequality to deal with and both have significant human rights and human security issues in terms of dominant ethnic groups, social cohesion and social mobility, even though one is a centrally planned economy and one a democracy.

In the Asia–Pacific region, there are clear links between the GFC, and climate change policy. The Asia–Pacific region has seen more innovation and investment in clean technology than any other part of the world, particularly by China and South Korea. China's investment in the US economy is huge, amounting by the end of 2009 to about US$1.61bn (Ferguson and Schularick 2009). 'Chimerica', as Niall Ferguson has called the union between China and the United States, accounted for about one-third of the world's economic output and two-thirds of economic growth from 1998 to 2007. Asian savings, from China, Japan and other countries in the region, have been invested in the United States and European economies because those Western economies were led both by rapid consumption models, a saving deficit and property ownership. Western capitalism rests on the ability of profit takers to retain those profits and often invest them in property.

In many Asian countries, especially China, earned income is difficult to invest in property since all land and property is owned by the state. This created an incentive for those in Asian countries to invest their surplus savings in overseas property. As Andro Linklater has pointed out if the growing affluent middle classes in China had been able to invest in property they would not have invested their savings in the United States and Europe (Linklater 2010). These factors led to a ready availability of borrowed funds invested in sub-prime mortgages in the United States and Europe, which ultimately caused the collapse of the global financial system.

The Stern Report on the Economics of Climate Change (2010) remarked that climate change presented 'a unique challenge for economics' because 'it is the greatest and widest-ranging market failure ever seen'. Although challenging many of the core assumptions of economics, this conclusion has already been widely recognised. Even those who financially benefit from the market economy readily acknowledge that free markets do not necessarily produce socially or environmentally optimal outcomes.

However, this market failure should not be attributed to capitalism itself, but rather to the regulatory frameworks that operate to manage investment, risk taking, entrepreneurism and profit taking. In other words, the solution is to rebuild the foundations of capitalism, but this time taking into account all the capitals involved (not solely financial), and implementing adequate regulatory controls to prevent undesirable behaviour occurring. Accordingly, we need locally built sustainable enterprise economies everywhere that are founded on the principles of people, planet and wellbeing, and can knit together globally. In this day and age, the most important topic that can be tackled by a new academic research and teaching centre is that of local and global governance of people, planet and wellbeing. However, this requires reaching an understanding of the other, related factors, such as climate change adaptation, energy conservation production and use, water management and use and population control.

10.5   THE RISE OF THE BRIC COUNTRIES

Despite the global economic downturn, the BRIC countries (Brazil, Russia, India and China) are experiencing rates of economic growth of between 5–10 per cent. This means that their populations' per capita carbon footprints are increasing dramatically, and will soon be near those of the most polluting countries (such as Australia and the United States), which is in the region of 20 tonnes per person per annum. By contrast, the poorest third of the world have per capita emissions of between 1–5 tonnes per annum, and the comparable figure for Europe is approximately 10 tonnes per annum. The Asia–Pacific region is characterised by per capita emissions which range from 1 to 20 tonnes.

There is much discussion on the role of China this century and the close relationship of China and the United States. China's economic growth, which has seen some 400 million people lifted out of absolute poverty, has been based on exports, the same model as led Japan and Germany out of destitution at the end of the Second World War. However, since China's growth has been based on the industrial revolution of the West, it has fuelled global overconsumption and massive natural resource use. As such, China is an increasing cause of global warming through their emission of GHGs.

China plays an important role in almost every part of our lives, whether it be through contact with the smallest of manufactured goods, or through their recycling of cash into the global banking system. Japan, China and the United States account for some 15 per cent of the world's land surface, a quarter of the world's population, and about 50 per cent of global economic output. This means that, as major producers and consumers, these three countries also determine any negotiations and outcomes on climate change. However, while Japan, China and the United States acknowledge that international cooperation is absolutely vital, there is recognition of local politics and states of development which impact the way these three countries approach the problem of climate change.

For example, Japan has a remarkably egalitarian society with recognised wealth distribution across a densely populated citizenship. The story in the United States is radically different with significant differences in income between rich and poor, while for China the discrepancy is even more pronounced as China's rapid economic growth has created vast income disparities. About one-third of the 1.4 billion Chinese citizens still live on less than US$1000 a year, and about 15 per cent live on salaries comparable with an average European wage. This means that it is likely that China will continue to concentrate on economic growth (to improve the living standards of all its citizens) at the expense of the environment. Perhaps it is true that the most significant event in the twentieth century was Deng Shao Ping's market reforms in China, which turned it from an agrarian economy to an industrial giant in a matter of decades, and, because of its sheer size, allowed it to dominate global economic activity and, increasingly, manufacturing.

At the end of the first decade of the twenty-first century about 30 per cent of global economic activity was engaged in by the United States. While this percentage will diminish as the Chinese economy grows, most people will continue to live Americentric lives as that country spends more than 50 per cent of all defence spending annually and maintains over 500 overseas forward projection bases across Europe and the Pacific. By contrast, given China's focus on lifting its citizens out of poverty, it is unlikely to invest as heavily in overseas military projections in the near future. By controlling the world's seas, air and space, the policy of the United States is one of pre-emption and disruption, going to war rather than peace-building, except when the target country can become a forward security base and when part of US economic trade interests – as in the case of Japan and Germany's post-war development.

10.6 HOW WE GOT TO THE CROSSROADS: ASIA–PACIFIC REGIONALIZATION AND THE GLOBAL ECONOMY

It is conventional wisdom to say that we are entering a multipolar world again as power slips from the United States and Europe towards the Asia–Pacific region. It is true that this is the Pacific century with G2, China and the United States, the most powerful marriage on the planet and the Asia–Pacific region holding most of the world's largest economies – Japan and India as well as China and the United States. It is also true that the politics of change, compassion, collectivism *and* exceptionalism are in the air. Both China and the United States think of themselves as exceptional, as special, as representing governance models that are identifiably different.

But the birth of G2 has also witnessed the birth of G20, led by countries such as Australia, and the re-emergence of a powerful G77. G20 is a significant step in the direction of new global governance because it relegates G8's role and promotes a greater dialogue between industrialised, developed, emerging and other countries and recognises the way the world has changed since the end of the Second World War, the establishment of the Bretton Woods Institutions and the birth of the UN.

We have *re*-learnt recently that people are not always rational, that markets do not necessarily self-correct, and that risk is often pushed on to those who can least afford to carry it. We have also *re*-learnt that there are some people who can always find the gap between our collective good intentions and making money, and that these people use their greedy exploitative natures to defraud the many in the pursuit of their own ends. Some of them work in perfectly legitimate areas of business and in fully incorporated business. J.K. Galbraith called this 'innocent' fraud (Galbraith 2004).

So what solutions can be put forward to the problems posed above?

First, the authors suggest that new ways of knowing, learning and sharing perception are necessary to find solutions to the humanitarian and ecological situations that face us all and the planet.

The world that we want to investigate requires knowledge creation that sees hard and soft edges, that can sense the tangible and the intangible, that is left and right brained, that is founded on what is known but also reaches into the energy of chaos for new ideas. We live in an age of reconfiguration, of decay and resurgence, a state where new value clusters are being created through the realignment of social networks and public–private–civil partnerships. Enterprise, innovation, creativity and action are creating a new economy that is at once local and global founded on a greater understanding of organisations as living social systems nested within living organic ecosystems.

Second, there are some imperatives. While understanding the past is essential, there *is now* something to learn about, something to come terms with. The planet on which humans depend for survival is in need of more loving care and attention than humans have given it thus far.

This neglect has primarily been championed by those who insist on maintaining the myth that there is an incompatibility between green growth and comfort, or between economic wealth creation and sustainability. This has led to significant steps being taken to incentivise change to what is loosely termed 'the green economy'. Interestingly, in the most enlightened cases, economic recovery per se is linked to taking steps to create a low carbon sustainable enterprise economy. Some of the best research is being carried out by the global institutions that are most affected by the current financial crisis. Amongst these are one of the world's largest banks, HSBC, and one that has not been carrying toxic debts to any substantial degree. Their team, led by Nick Robins, looked at 20 national economic recovery plans in February 2009 and identified 18 common investment themes that can be summarised in 'stabilising and then cutting global emissions of greenhouse gases'. This action represented 15 per cent of the US$2.8trn in fiscal measures to restart national economies with leaders being the United States and China (Robins 2009).

10.7 BUSINESS CONFUSION AND UNCERTAINTY

If the world was hoping for a clearer outcome from COP15 at Copenhagen, then business expectations were even more specific. The emerging low carbon sustainable enterprise economy requires that carbon and other GHGs are priced. Although price is crucial to both business and government planning, it seems that the world will have to wait a year or so for a definite price, even though there are already numerous price signals through existing trading regimes. Setting legally binding carbon emission targets would have provided a greater indication of the distance that has to be travelled over the next few decades towards combating climate change. Australia has committed to cutting GHG emissions by 60 per cent from 2000 levels by 2050, Japan by 50 per cent by 2050, the UK is legally committed to cuts of 80 per cent by 2050 and the European Union (EU) is committed to targets of between 20–30 per cent by 2020. All countries' targets should have been clarified by the end of January 2010 under the Copenhagen Agreement.

There has been significant leadership and initiative in the business–civil society nexus on issues of environmental management and corporate social responsibility since the 1970s, some of which has been led or followed by increased regulation by individual governments. Generally those countries that have led by legislation in the areas of environmental management and corporate responsibility have tended to see significant gains in exports of clean technology and associated trade, as well as a clear link between innovation in public policy and community cohesion and social resilience. Similarly, countries with tight banking controls were more resilient in the face of the 2008/9 GFC as they were less exposed to toxic assets such as sub-prime mortgages. This is the reason for Australia's resilience in the face of the GFC.

A useful example of this combination of public policy and the new economy comes from research conducted by the Global Climate Network in the UK, United States, China, India, Germany, Brazil, Australia and

South Africa. This research demonstrated that bold public policy incentivising rapid climate-friendly innovations creates new jobs and a low carbon economy. While calling for concerted and coordinated investment in low carbon technology across the G20 countries, the research showed that China stood to gain 40m jobs and lose 10m by 2020, the UK 70 000 jobs in the offshore wind industry (Global Climate Network 2010).

However, making the link between public policy, fiscal incentives and the new economy has been easier for some governments than others. After the 2008/9 GFC, many governments invested heavily in their economies to provide liquidity for business to continue. Other, more forward-looking governments made strategic investments into the new economy. China led this change by targeting 40 per cent of its fiscal incentive of US$576bn to low carbon innovations. By comparison, the United States targeted just 12 per cent of their US$775bn investment. Similarly, some Asian economies have signalled significant cuts in emissions levels led by South Korea with 30 per cent and Japan with 25 per cent by 2020. It is worth noting that these economies will find it much harder to make these cuts than, for instance, the United States and Australia, because South Korea and Japan are already relatively efficient while the United States and Australia will benefit from these cuts as they are extremely inefficient economies which have relied on cheap and plentiful energy sources during their development. China and Australia both rely for their wealth on coal, the former's economic growth being based on using 'the black stuff' and the latter's economy significantly based on selling it and other extractive products to China.

Supporting the idea that domestic policy and regulation can increase a country's competitiveness, there is clear evidence that California, Germany and Japan have led in clean technology because of proactive environmental management regulations which raised the bar in those areas. In the twenty-first century that advantage has been taken by China, which now has the majority of production in wind turbines, solar and PVC production as well as the world's largest electric car factory.

From environmental management in the 1970s and the first corporate social accounting in California in the same period, to the introduction of what John Elkington termed 'triple bottom line' reporting in the 1980s and 1990s, which involved a matrix of reporting against financial, environmental and social criteria, innovative work is still ongoing and has taxed the minds of many in business, not least chief financial officers for whom quantifying soft issues such as human capital and human rights against the apparently hard numbers of finance has proved difficult. Today, it is the combination of environmental, social and governance (ESG) issues that are the subject of discussion in enlightened boardrooms and in the international public policy debate.

The measurement and understanding of the relationship between economic performance and social progress has been at the heart of the corporate social responsibility movement for the last 30 years and is central to the new economy. If we cannot find a way to live within the earth's limits and to know human wellbeing when it is met, then we will continue to base our economic system on greed, exploitation, consumption and waste. In 2009, a Commission, headed by Professors Sen and Stiglitz and established by French President Nicolas Sarkozy, reported that 'it has long been clear that GDP is an inadequate metric to gauge well-being over time particularly in its economic, environmental, and social dimensions, some aspects of which are often referred to as *sustainability*'.[2]

This means that the moves in the business world to engage with a range of stakeholders beyond shareholders, employees and customers on issues of accountability, transparency and reporting are mirrored in the field of public policy. There is much work to be done on the links between the two. It could be argued that the private development of numerous voluntary codes, initiatives and management systems around ESG and TBL issues contains lessons for public policy development, and vice versa.

10.8 LEARNING, UNLEARNING, NETWORK AND ACTION

This is what Rajendra Pachauri, Chairman of the IPCC and winner of the Nobel Peace Prize 2007, had to say in March 2009 about the link between the possibility of sustainable enterprise economics and wellbeing:

> The beauty of (the) desirable changes lies in the fact that they would produce a huge range of so called co-benefits which if anything will enhance the welfare of human society such as through higher energy security, lower levels of pollution at the local level, stable agricultural yields and additional employment. I wonder why we are dragging our feet in the face of such overwhelming logic? (Pachauri 2009)

The answer to Pachauri's own question lies in the lack of real leadership amongst politicians and business leaders. As he says:

> The answer lies in forward looking policies on the part of governments, which of course, will cause some discomfort in certain sectors and to certain actors. A complete reorientation of thinking among the leadership of the corporate sector and a significant change in lifestyles of people across the globe, most importantly in the rich countries, is now overdue. If a perceptible shift in all these three respects can be initiated adequately and soon perhaps Copenhagen

December 2009 will be a success, for which future generations would have reason to thank those that bring about such a movement. (Pachauri 2009)

Pachauri has a six-point plan of action:

- Invest heavily in energy conservation, eco-efficiency and sustainable design;
- Introduce comprehensive carbon pricing;
- Dramatically improve water efficiency;
- Induce lifestyle and behavioural changes;
- Adapt to climate change now; and
- In doing so, leave no one behind.[3]

If humanity is tenuously embarking on the fourth revolution, as has been argued in this chapter, then it is also a period of great learning. Indeed it might be apposite to say that the fourth revolution is as much concerned with learning as it is with sustainability because sustainability is a continuous process of learning, unlearning, networks and action. At the heart of this process is a set of characteristics that will be dominant in the transition, or rather, the great transformation.

They are:

- A love of innovation and experimentation. This involves understanding that, while we should not make too many mistakes, mistakes are often the best way to learn. Since discontinuity is at the heart of any paradigm shift, that tolerance and learning by failing is important;
- The ability to embrace unpredictability, since this will be a key characteristic of climate change effects;
- Reworking the balance between free markets and collective action in order to produce sustainable social democracies; and
- New employment patterns containing an emphasis on enterprise and innovation, on reuse, rethink, reduce, recycle, return and longevity. This means not just up skilling but also sideways skilling in order to adapt existing skills to the new economy.

10.9   CONCLUSIONS

This chapter is written in the immediate aftermath of COP15: the Copenhagen Summit (December 2009). We will have to wait and see what transpires, but there are many who regard that conference as a missed opportunity, as a disastrous outcome and as having failed to deliver the outcomes that are so needed if humanity is survive on earth. But, it is also possible to survey the wreckage and find hope and positive signals. If the conference failed to deliver targets of GHGs it did succeed in forcing the major players into the open, and, in the middle of night, tired and emotionally spent, to say what they really meant. Second, the conference saw the limitations of trying to negotiate with 192 countries with equal UN voting rights. The world also saw that the US President is severely limited in action because of the US Constitution. Here, we saw US exceptionalism to the fore. Here too, we saw China unable to manoeuvre on the world stage trying to be a member of G2, G20 and G77. Is China an emerging economy or a dominant global player? The truth is that it is both.

This chapter has addressed the nexus between climate change, sustainable enterprise and change with specific reference to the Asia–Pacific region. Climate change is already causing significant disruption to many communities across the world as random severe weather events force people from their homes, create energy and food security problems and highlight the fragility of many poor people's lives – those that will be affected by climate change the most and the earliest.

The rise of the BRIC countries and, in particular, China and India mean that manufacturing costs and output will be determined by those countries' policies and growth trajectories. Almost everything that we use on a daily basis is in some way connected to China. This means that population growth must be halted and reversed as this action would see one of the greatest improvements in wellbeing for the vast majority of the world's poorest people, as well as significantly reducing carbon emissions. This policy would not just have application to people in developing countries but to cities in every country in the world. If we are to focus on resilience and community cohesion, this is an issue that political leaders must not shy from.

The GFC has led to some countries virtually bankrupting themselves as private debt has become public liability and yet the systems are not being reformed. This will lead to severe political instability and cuts to the very public services that keep the poorest communities alive. The United States will continue to dominate the planet economically and militarily, but will have to be gentler in its relations with other countries as they jostle for voice in a crowded world.

However, to survive in business or government this century, the astute leader has to be totally conversant on climate change science, international economics, Chinese politics, population control and conflict resolution. These are the issues that are determining the challenges and opportunities as the new economy – the low carbon sustainable enterprise economy – develops.

NOTES

1. *The New York Times* in association with *The Observer*.
2. http://www.stiglitz-sen-fitoussi.fr/en/index.htm.
3. Dr Rajendra Pachauri speaking at the UN Global Compact Leaders Summit in Geneva 9 July 2007.

REFERENCES

Copenhagen 2009 (2009), http://www.erantis.com/events/denmark/copenhagen/climate-conference-2009/index.htm, 24 March 2010.
CSIRO (2006), 'Climate change in the Asia/Pacific region', *CSIRO Marine and Atmospheric Research*, pp. 48–51.
Dokos, T. et al. (2008), 'Climate change: addressing the impact on human security', Hellenic Foundation for Defence and Foreign Policy, ELIAMEP Policy Paper, p. 91.
DuPont, A. and G. Pearman (2006), *Heating up the Planet: Climate Change and Security*, Hong Kong: Lowy Institute, http://www.asiastudies.
Edwards, M. (1999), 'Security implications of a worst-case scenario of climate change in the south-west Pacific, *Australian Geographer*, **30**: 311–30.
Ferguson, N. and M. Schularick (2009), 'The Great Wallop', *The New York Times*, 16 November.
Galbraith, J.K. (2004), *The Economics of Innocent Fraud*, Penguin: London
Global Climate Network (2010), available at http://www.globalclimatenetwork.info/researchprojects/, accessed 30 March 2010.
Hawken, P., A.B. Lovins and L.H. Lovins (1999), *Natural Capitalism*, London: Little, Brown and Company.
Human Security Network (1999), 'A perspective on human security', Chairman's Summary, 1st Ministerial Meeting of the Human Security Network, Lysøen, Norway, 20 May 1999.
Keynes, J.M. (1936), 'The general theory of employment, interest and money', cited in J.G. Speth (2009), *The Bridge at the Edge of the World: Capitalism, the Environment, and Crossing from Crisis to Sustainability*, New Haven, CT: Yale University Press, p. 108.
Lieshout, M. van et al. (2004), 'Climate change and malaria: analysis of the SRES climate and socio-economic scenarios', *Global Environmental Change*, **14**: 87–99.
Linklater, A. (2010), 'A place of one's own', *Prospect*, January: 59–62.
McIntosh, M. (2008), 'Editorial', *The Journal of Corporate Citizenship*, **30**: 3–9.
McIntosh, M. (2009), 'What is a sustainable enterprise economy?', APCSE Thinking Aloud, No. 1, May.
The Observer (2009), '200 million and counting', 5 April, London, p. 1.
Pachauri, R. (2009), 'Why Copenhagen is important for the future of human civilization', available at http://blog.rkpachauri.org/blog/13/Why-Copenhagen-is-important-for-the-future-of-human-civilization.htm, accessed 1 April 2010.
Porritt, J. (2006), *Capitalism as if the World Matters*, London: Earthscan, pp. 111–94.
Reilly, B. (2002), 'Internal conflict and regional security in Asia and the Pacific', *Pacifica Review*, **14**: 8.

Robins, N. et al. (2009), 'A climate for recovery: the colour of stimulus goes green', HSBC Climate Change, available at www.research.hsbc.com, 25 February.

Stern Review (2010), 'The economics of climate change', available at http://site resources.worldbank.org/INTINDONESIA/Resources/226271-1170911056314/3428109-1174614780539/SternReviewEng.pdf, accessed 21 March 2010.

Stern Review Report (2010), available at http://www.hm-treasury.gov.uk/stern_review_report.htm, accessed 19 March 2010.

United Nations Commission on Human Security (2003), 'Human Security Now', available at http://humansecurity-chs.org.

United Nations Declaration of Human Rights General Assembly Resolution 217A (1948).

United Nations Development Programme (UNDP) (1994), 'Human Development Report', Geneva: United Nations.

United Nations Security Council (2007), available at http://www.un.org/News/Press/docs/2007/sc9000.doc.htm, accessed 19 March 2010.

Werz, M. and K. Manlove (2009), 'Climate change on the move: climate change will affect the world's security', Centre for American Progress, *Energy and Environment*, December.

Woodward, A. et al. (1998), 'Climate change and human health in the Asia Pacific region: who will be most vulnerable?', *Climate Research*, **11**: 31–8.

11. Media framing of public discourse on climate change and sea-level rise: social amplification of global warming versus climate justice for global warming impacts

Harun Rashid

11.1 INTRODUCTION

The recent explosion of public discourse on climate change and sea-level rise and its coverage in the news media may be attributed to the rebirth of environmentalism, which has acted as a catalyst for a host of overlapping environmental agendas, such as the carbon cycle, carbon footprints, greenhouse gas (GHG) emissions, global warming, melting of polar icecaps and sea-level rise (Hart and Victor 1993). Because of the failure of the international community to reach meaningful agreements to curb emissions of GHGs, the calls for alternative measures to mitigate global warming impacts have gained prominence in public discourse. The concept of climate justice, perhaps derived from a more specific context of environmental justice or social justice (Hannigan 1995; Kasperson and Kasperson 2005), is a socially constructed frame which lays out a set of claims concerning the physical and socioeconomic impacts of global warming and sea-level rise. More specifically, it demands that those who contributed most to the adverse consequences of global warming and climate change should take the responsibility of mitigating these adverse impacts (Adams and Luchsinger 2009). By the same token, countries that have contributed the least amounts of pollution-causing GHG emission, but are more vulnerable to their impacts, should receive the aid they need to counter the effects of climate change (Jimenez-David 2009).

The 2007 Nobel Peace Prize for Al Gore and the Intergovernmental Panel on Climate Change (IPCC) for their leadership on critical global warming issues has provided legitimacy for climate justice issues in public discourse. Despite this recognition, public discourse and the media reports on climate change and its impacts have been characterised by two competing paradigms which tend to divert attention from the central issues and their mitigation. One of these characteristics is that often some of the coverage on climate change is replete with exaggerations, conforming to a paradigm that the news media tend to amplify environmental risks by employing different types of symbols (Kasperson et al. 1988), without paying adequate attention to the broader contexts of the underlying issues. The public discourse on climate justice, in particular, has attracted a variety of symbolic expressions, catchphrases and metaphors. In an attempt to interpret such symbolic expressions in social, institutional and cultural contexts, Kasperson et al. (1988) have further postulated that whenever individuals cannot deal with the full complexity of risks, often they use simplifying mechanisms, such as symbolic connotations, to evaluate risks and to shape responses. In this context, Wilkins (2000) has proposed an alternate paradigm on the role of symbolic connotations in hazard mitigation. The main goal of this chapter is to delineate the major themes of global warming and sea-level rise in public discourse, as these are presented in newspaper reports, incorporating elements of these two competing paradigms. Using content analysis of a selected number of the US and international newspaper reports, the specific objectives of this study are, thus, two-fold: first, to differentiate between the objective scientific elements and interpretive claims on global warming and its impacts and, second, to demonstrate that the symbolic connotations associated with the call for climate justice are not only an outcome of social amplification of global warming but also a search for social justice for mitigating inequity in global warming impacts.

11.2   RESEARCH METHODS

11.2.1   Theoretical Framework

The theoretical framework for the content analysis was based on a social constructionist perspective, according to which the public discourse on global warming and sea-level rise may incorporate one or more of the following angles of news:

1. Verifiable objective facts, that is, assembling scientific information;
2. Contesting claims on the extent and impacts of global warming;
3. Competing policy options for promoting alternative mitigation measures (Hannigan 1995); and
4. Symbolic production of news (Wilkins 2000; Lorimer and Gasher 2001).

Data obtained from the content analysis of newspaper reports were reviewed to assess how each category of news conformed to the above classification scheme and to one or more of the following research paradigms.

First, to a large extent, de-contextualisation of environmental news results from production constraint of most of the news organisations, which use angles or framing on a routine basis for moulding particular contents (Tuchman 1973; Hannigan 1995). This allows journalists to transform an environmental issue into a manageable problem by focussing on the immediate issue rather than on the underlying causes and mitigation strategies (Wilkins 1996). To what extent did the selected reports conform to this news media paradigm? Second, mitigation of global warming impacts includes a variety of measures designed to minimise GHG emissions as well as to promote long-term sustainable initiatives, such as adaptation to sea-level rise. By their very nature, often these ameliorative measures involve competing policy options. How did the newspaper reports frame these competing issues? Third, the literature on social amplification of risk suggests that the news media tend to amplify environmental risks by employing different types of symbolic connotations (Kasperson et al. 1988). What were the types of symbolic connotations in public discourse on climate change and in the call for climate justice in search for lasting mitigation of global warming impacts?

11.2.2 Nature of the Content Analysis

The *Newspaper Source Plus* (*EBSCOhost*), an electronic retrieval system was used as the primary tool for retrieving relevant web-based versions of newspaper reports on climate change/global warming, and sea-level rise. The terms climate change and global warming are used interchangeably throughout the media reports and are therefore used in the similar manner in this chapter. Because of the vast and varied population sizes of web-based newspaper reports on climate change and related topics, a purposive sampling technique was used for retrieving three categories of reports:

1. Those on the general topics of climate change/global warming;
2. Reports with an emphasis on sea-level rise; and
3. Reports covering the 2009 Copenhagen Summit.

Using climate change/global warming as the search key words, reports published in 2009 were retrieved from each of the following newspapers: *New York Times, USA Today, Washington Post, Wall Street Journal* and *Chicago Tribune* (Table 11.1). These newspapers were selected because

Table 11.1   Content analysis of reports on climate change/global warming

Newspaper*	Scientific element (%)	Physical impacts (%)	Socio-economic impacts (%)	Mitigation policies (%)	Risk amplification (%)
New York Times (N = 5) Words: 4351	9	10		69	12
Washington Post (N = 5) Words: 4224	12	4	29	38	17
Wall Street Journal (N = 5) Words: 5860	14	5	14	38	29
Chicago Tribune (N = 5) Words: 3563	33	22	5	23	17
USA Today (N =5) Words: 2835	27	17	19	34	3
Total number of reports: 25					
Total number of words: 20 883	18	10	13	42	17

Notes:
* Dates of publication: January to October 2009
N indicates the number of reports
% indicates the per cent of total number of words in a report.

they published more reports on these topics than other US newspapers. Specific reports on sea-level rise due to global warming are less numerous than those on global warming itself. Therefore, the search was extended beyond the US newspapers to several international newspapers and the dates of publication were extended up to 2006 (prior to 2006, there were very few reports on sea-level rise) (see Table 11.2).

A hermeneutic approach was adopted for the content analysis in which the total content of each newspaper report – counted as the total numbers of words in a report – was classified into different segments of news, each belonging to one of the five concepts listed in Tables 11.1 and 11.2. Prior to classification, each report was saved as a Microsoft Word document, which permitted rapid classification of a report by using its word count function. In all, 65 reports were used as the database. The texts of reports on climate change/global warming (25) and sea-level rise (15) were classified formally, whereas the reports on the Copenhagen Summit (25) were reviewed mainly in the context of climate justice without formal classification of the text.

Table 11.2   Content analysis of reports on sea-level rise

Newspaper*	Scientific element (%)	Physical impacts (%)	Socio-economic impacts (%)	Mitigation policies (%)	Risk amplification (%)
New York Times (N = 1) Words: 975	15	53		17	14
Washington Post (N = 1) Words: 1351	1	2	44	45	8
Sacramento Bee (N = 1) Words: 548		16		73	11
Toronto Star (N = 1) Words: 299		23		37	40
Winnipeg Free Press (N =1) Words: 364	31	36			33
Irish Times (N = 2) Words: 1273	59	4		19	18
The Age, Melbourne (N = 2) Words: 1706				51	49
New Castle Herald (N =2) Words: 252		26		74	
Adelaide Sunday Mail (N = 1) Words: 501	38	36		20	6
New Zealand Herald (N = 1) Words: 521				80	20
Western Morning News, Plymouth, UK (N = 1) Words: 363		9		62	29
Hindustan Times (N = 1) Words: 564		22	24	23	31
Total number of reports: 15					
Total number of words: 8717	14	15	8	40	23

Notes: * Dates of publication: March 2006 to July 2009, except *Toronto Star* (22 June 2002).

11.3   CONTEXTS OF GLOBAL WARMING AND SEA-LEVEL RISE

11.3.1   Natural Versus Anthropogenic Greenhouse Effect

Global warming is related to the greenhouse effect, which is an analogy for the basic heating mechanism of the atmosphere. The greenhouse analogy applies to the atmosphere because the principal gases of the atmosphere, that is, nitrogen and oxygen, are relatively transparent to incoming solar radiation. Like the glass roofs and windows of a greenhouse, the atmosphere lets in incoming solar radiation relatively easily, but it absorbs large quantities of outgoing thermal radiation from the earth's surface by a number of greenhouse gases, notably water vapour, carbon dioxide and methane. The bulk of the atmospheric heating is accomplished by its absorption of thermal radiation from the earth's surface (Walker and King 2008). Thus, the greenhouse effect is a natural process (Spencer 2008). Without it, the earth's average temperature would be at least 20°C cooler than its current temperature (Houghton 2004).

The natural greenhouse effect of the earth's atmosphere is attributable primarily to water vapour (Barry and Chorley 2003). Not only is water vapour more abundant than other GHGs, it absorbs parts of both incoming shortwave solar radiation and outgoing longwave infrared thermal radiation. Like water vapour, carbon dioxide is also a naturally occurring GHG, which absorbs certain bands of both solar radiation and infrared thermal radiation. However, it differs from water vapour in its ability to accumulate in the atmosphere. Since the amount of water vapour in the atmosphere is controlled by the hydrologic cycle, specifically by the negative feedback of evaporation leading to condensation and rainfall (Archer 2007), human activities cannot contribute significantly to the concentration of water vapour in the atmosphere; whereas burning of fossil fuels and other human activities have been increasing the atmospheric concentration of carbon dioxide steadily for at least the last two centuries. It then follows that any increase in the atmospheric concentration of carbon dioxide would lead to an increase in the absorption of both solar radiation and thermal radiation from the earth's surface, leading to an increase in atmospheric temperature. This process has been termed variously as enhanced or human-induced or anthropogenic greenhouse effect (Barry and Chorley 2003; Archer 2007).

Methane is another powerful natural and anthropogenic GHG that is enhanced significantly by human activities, such as mining, natural gas, petroleum industry, rice paddies enteric fermentation, landfills and so forth (Houghton 2004). Although its atmospheric concentration is significantly lower than that of carbon dioxide (380 ppm for carbon dioxide versus 1400 ppb for methane), the level of methane has doubled during the last 200 years, from about 700 ppb to 1400 ppb (Oldfield 2005). Further, the global warming potential of methane is at least 20 to 23 times higher than that of carbon dioxide for a 100 year time horizon (Houghton 2004; Archer 2007).

Ozone plays much more complex roles than either carbon dioxide or methane in heating the atmosphere. It is mainly a naturally occurring gas with maximum concentration in the mid-stratosphere (about 25 km over the tropics and 15 km over polar latitudes). In the stratosphere, it is a beneficial gas because it absorbs harmful ultraviolet radiation, protecting us from sunburn and skin cancer. By absorbing radiation at high altitudes, it has a negative effect on global warming in the lower atmosphere (troposphere). However, this beneficial effect is cancelled out near the ground where ozone is produced in surface smog by reaction of gases from industrial activity, mostly automobile exhaust (Archer 2007). Such anthropogenic ozone acts as a GHG in the lower atmosphere by absorbing a narrow band of thermal radiation, but its overall role in global warming is minor. Ozone also reacts adversely with chloroflurocarbons (CFCs) in the stratosphere, resulting in its severe depletion in the form of the ozone hole. The CFCs are entirely anthropogenic and absorb thermal radiation in a narrow band. Their global warming potential has been reduced significantly following the signing of the Montreal Protocol in 1987, phasing out any further production of this harmful GHG (Archer 2007). Nitrous oxide, also known as laughing gas, is a minor natural and anthropogenic GHG. Yet, its global warming potential is a concern because of its steady increase in atmospheric concentration from natural and agricultural ecosystems, biomass burning and the chemical industry (Houghton 2004).

The current public discourse on global warming is dominated by an assumption that it is entirely or largely the result of anthropogenic GHGs. Since the earth's past climates had several ice ages with intervening warmer periods due to natural factors, global warming may be defined more objectively as 'a natural or human-induced increase in the average global temperature of the atmosphere near the earth's surface' (Botkin and Keller 1995). Among other natural factors, volcanic eruptions and variations in solar output (that is, sunspot activity) have been linked to changes in global average temperatures (Oliver and Hidore 2002; Houghton 2004; IPCC 2007). More significant changes in global temperatures, associated with the rhythms of ice ages and interglacial warmer periods, have been attributed to variations in the earth's orbit around the sun (Archer 2007), but the long geologic time cycles (thousands to hundreds of thousand years) within which these operate are not comparable to the relatively short historical time horizons within which the current global warming trend has been occurring.

11.3.2 Sea-level Rise

The television pictures of ocean waves breaking directly on the streets of Funafuti, the capital of the Pacific island nation of Tuvalu, are the visible signs of rising sea levels due to global warming. One of the drives for seeking climate justice seems to be the risk of extensive inundation of low-lying coastal areas of many developing nations, notably Bangladesh (the Ganges–Brahmaputra delta), Egypt (the Nile delta), the Maldives (Indian Ocean) and several Pacific island nations. Notwithstanding the nature of the risk, the contributing factors for sea-level rise are often generalised in public discourse as a simplistic assumption of rising sea levels due to melting glaciers. There are at least four interrelated factors which have implications for sea-level rise at a specific coast. First, about 50–60 per cent of the sea-level rise is expected to occur due to thermal expansion of sea water, since oceans absorb large quantities of heat from the atmosphere (Houghton 2004; Archer 2007). Second, the remaining 40–50 per cent may be attributed to melting of land glaciers, but floating sea ice and ice shelves do not have any effect on sea levels because the melt-water fills out the void created by the floating ice. Further, the rates of sea-level rise are minimised by isostatic adjustments, that is, rebounding of lands which were depressed by the overburden of thick glaciers. Third, whereas the isostatic rebound raises lands upward, sedimentation in deltaic environments results in subsidence, accelerating the rates of sea-level rise. Fourth, there are geographical variations in the rates of sea-level rise in different parts of the oceans. Using reliable tide gauge records and satellite altimetry, recent studies by a number of Australian scientists indicate that sea levels have risen in the eastern Pacific and the eastern Indian Ocean, but the western Pacific and the western Indian Ocean have recorded minor decline (Church et al. 2004; Church and White 2006). This decline does not include the Maldives, contrary to the findings of an earlier study by Morner et al. (2004).

Among all of the low-lying nations, Bangladesh is particularly vulnerable to sea-level rise because of the compounding effects of global warming and land subsidence due to removal of groundwater and the weight of accumulation of huge quantities of river sediments in the Ganges–Brahmaputra delta (Houghton 2004). The most recent projections by the IPCC estimate global sea-level rises within the range of 0.18–0.59 m (IPCC 2007). These estimates are considerably lower than that of the first IPCC Assessment in 1990 (70 cm by 2100), but are more consistent with recent findings by Church and White (2006) and Church et al. (2004, 2006a, 2006b). Much more catastrophic projections (exceeding a rise of 1 m by the end of 2100) by a group of non-IPCC scientists are based on computer simulations of accelerations of glacier melting (Munro 2006). Even with a conservative estimate of 70 cm of sea-level rise (the maximum projection of the first IPCC assessment), Bangladesh is likely to experience a sea-level rise of up to 1.9 m by 2100, largely because of the remaining contribution by land subsidence (Houghton 2004). Since the 2007 IPCC assessment projects about 10 per cent lower sea levels than in its first assessment, thus prorated, Bangladesh is still expected to experience a sea-level rise of about 1.7 m. This amounts to a rate of 1.7 cm of rise per year. Expressed in this manner, this may not sound alarming, but in a low-lying coastal environment with extremely gentle slopes, large areas are at risk of inundation. Estimates by the United Nations Environmental Programme (UNEP) indicate that about one-fifth of the land area of Bangladesh would be inundated by the end of this century, displacing at least 15 million people (Houghton 2004).

11.4   DISCOURSE ANALYSIS AND INTERPRETATIONS

The discourse analysis and the related interpretations of the classified text are based on the theoretical framework postulated in Section 11.2.1. Among the five categories of news listed in Tables 11.1 and 11.2, *scientific elements* of global warming, climate change and sea-level rise and some of their *physical impacts* belonged to the verifiable objective facts. Because of inadequate scientific contexts in the public discourse, some of the physical impacts might appear as contested claims, whereas most of the *socioeconomic impacts* were subject to interpretations with elements of contested claims. More clearly, *mitigation policies* belonged to the contested claims since these involved competing policy options. *Risk amplification* in global warming news, on the other hand, may be attributed not only to the symbolic production of news by the media but more importantly to a broader process of social amplification of risk.

11.4.1   Scientific Elements of Global Warming and Sea-level Rise

As data in Table 11.1 indicate, 18 per cent of the analysed text on global warming/climate change covered scientific information on these topics. With only 14 per cent of the coverage, scientific information on sea-level rise was more limited (Table 11.2). Although these may appear to be relatively small proportions of the media discourse on such critical issues, the data provide evidence of the role of newspapers in communicating critical scientific information to the lay public in relatively non-technical language (Reckelhoff-Dangel and Petersen 2007). In conveying scientific concepts to the public, Mileti et al. (2004) have emphasised the need for explaining complicated phenomena in non-technical terms. Experts generally cannot accomplish this. Newspaper reports by journalists seem to do a better job. An example of this is a report in *Chicago Tribune* about two peer-reviewed articles in *Nature*, dealing with the polar freeze/thaw cycle (Mullen 2009). The *Tribune* report explains that the research reported in *Nature* was based on sediment core samples extracted from the Antarctic Ocean floor in 2006 as part of one of the largest scientific undertakings ever for the continent. By examining millions of years' worth of sediments, researchers found that the ice in West Antarctica collapsed and melted about every 40 000 years during the Pliocene epoch 3 to 5 million years ago – a time when there were warm spells, similar to those projected to occur over the next century. Natural polar freeze/thaw cycles occur due to a periodic shift in the tilt of the earth's axis, known as the Milankovitch Cycle. However, the current rise in carbon dioxide levels – driven largely by human activity over the last 200 years, mostly by the burning of fossil fuels – is causing unprecedented global warming and putting West Antarctica on the fast track to melting. Although the complete melt-off of the West Antarctic ice might take several thousand years, according to these articles, even a partial melt-off raising sea levels by 4 feet would put at risk an estimated half a billion people who live along shorelines (Mullen 2009).

Another example of a similar newspaper report, which is rich in scientific content, is a *Reuters* article on sea-level rise, which appeared in the *Irish Times* (Doyle 2007). This article summarises the main findings of the IPCC 2007 draft report on its *Fourth Assessment of Climate Change*. Although the title of the *Reuters* article may initially appear to be somewhat alarmist – 'Sea levels to rise for the next 1000 years' – the details of projected increases in atmospheric temperatures and rise in sea levels merely confirm the long-term projections of the IPCC scientific panel. Further, the draft report projects more droughts, rains, shrinking Arctic ice and glaciers, and rising sea levels throughout this century, but the projections are more optimistic for both temperature increases (within the range of 2–4.5°C) and sea-level rises (within the range of 28–43 cm) than in its *Third Assessment* in 2001 (temperature increases within the range of 1.4–5.8°C and sea-level rises within the range of 9–88 cm). The IPCC report explains that the sea levels will continue to rise for more than 1000 years because of the long lag period required for removing the existing carbon dioxide from the atmosphere.

From a social constructionist perspective, these two reports were rich in contexts and would, thus, seem to contradict the first research paradigm, that is, newspaper de-contextualization of environmental news (postulated in Section 11.2.1). However, not all newspaper reports were rich in contexts. Out of the 25 reports on global warming and climate change (Table 11.1), only 14 had some scientific content. Among them, 12 reports were rich in contexts on global warming. There were significant variations among the newspapers in the quality of scientific contents and contexts. Only one report in the *Wall Street Journal* and two each in the *New York Times*, *Washington Post* and *USA Today* had adequate context, whereas all of the five reports in *Chicago Tribune* were rich in context on global warming. Out of the 15 reports on sea-level rise, only seven had some scientific content (Table 11.2). Among them, only three had rich context and three had inadequate scientific elements. In general, contexts were rich when newspaper reports summarised findings from scientific articles in peer-reviewed journals. Other reports, representing opinions by a commentator or by a representative of an activist organisation, generally lacked scientific context. Between these two extremes, some of the reports were rich in scientific content but were inadequate in context. These were normally reports on computer simulations, which did not necessarily explain global warming context adequately. An example is a report in the *Winnipeg Free Press* summarising the results of a powerful computer simulation (operated by the US National Center for Atmospheric Research) by two scientists – one from the University of Arizona and another from the University of Calgary (WFP 2006). According to their simulation, if the current trend of GHG emissions and atmospheric temperatures continue to climb, by 2100 Arctic summers could be as balmy as they were 130 000 years ago (due to slight changes in earth's orbit), when heat waves triggered glacial melting. The model predicts that by the end of this century the sea-level rise would exceed the IPCC forecast by a significant margin and the maximum rise would amount to 4–6 m over several centuries beyond 2100. Low-lying areas of North America, such as Florida, coasts of British Columbia (Canada), the Maritimes (Canada) and the Arctic would be inundated; so would countries such as Bangladesh and the Netherlands. The report does not emphasise the time horizon beyond 2100 when most of the postulated impacts are plausible, thus lacking an important part of the context.

11.4.2   Global Warming Impacts

11.4.2.1   Uncertainties of feedbacks
The greenhouse effect is a scientifically verifiable objective process. In laboratory experiments, it is possible to measure how much infrared

radiation is absorbed by carbon dioxide and to compute how much surface warming would occur due to such absorption (Spencer 2008, p. 67). Based on this process, the public discourse is dominated by a simplistic assumption that an increase in anthropogenic GHG emissions would result in a corresponding increase in the average global temperature. In understanding the global warming forecast, however, the feedbacks are everything (Archer 2007 p.4). In particular, the uncertainty with the water vapour and cloud feedbacks has generated considerable amounts of contesting claims about the global warming forecasts and their impacts (Spencer 2008). A *New York Times* report emphasises the pitfalls of such contesting claims in the climate change debate (Revkin 2009). The report points out exaggeration in Al Gore's public statement in which he made an unsubstantiated claim that a sharp spike in fires, floods and other calamities around the world was due to global warming. At the other extreme, George Will, a *Washington Post* columnist, chided climate scientists for predicting an ice age three decades ago and asserted erroneously that a pause in warming in recent years and the recent expansion of polar sea ice undermined visions of calamity ahead. Contrary to this assertion, the study by a scientific group found that the polar sea ice has been shrinking in size and not expanding, as Will has claimed citing the same source (Revkin 2009).

11.4.2.2 Physical impacts
At least one in two reports on global warming had some references to its potential physical impacts (Table 11.1). The leading reported impacts included the following:

1. Impact of burning brown coal on carbon dioxide emissions;
2. Negative effect of replacing forests by biofuel crops on the levels of atmospheric carbon dioxide;
3. Adverse effects of excessively high temperatures on crop productivity;
4. Effects of drying out Canada's forest lands, leading to fire hazards and insect infestation;
5. Potential effects of carbon sequestration on groundwater and earth tremors.

Similarly, one in two reports listed in Table 11.2 had some references to the effect of sea-level rise on inundation of low-lying coastal areas, such as Florida, the Netherlands, coastal Bangladesh, the Maldives, Tuvalu, Kiribati and other smaller Pacific islands.

11.4.2.3 Socioeconomic impacts

Reports on socioeconomic impacts of global warming were much more limited than those on physical impacts, but two major issues were covered at some length in several reports. First, the cost–benefit analysis of cutting GHG emissions and improving energy efficiency appeared in the *Washington Post* (Eilperin 2009b) and the *Wall Street Journal* (Lomborg 2009). The public discourse on this issue was influenced by ideology. For example, the proponents of the US Senate climate change bill claimed that the economic incentives in the bill for the green energy sector would lead to significant employment opportunities in this emerging sector, whereas the opponents predicted massive job losses in the conventional energy sector from the proposed cap-and-trade system of controlling greenhouse gas emissions (Eilperin 2009b). Analyses by independent research groups indicated that both of these estimates were exaggerated, but the majority of the economic models predict that at the current rates of unconstrained global warming the GDP of both rich and poor countries would shrink by unequal amounts of 2 per cent and 5 per cent, respectively (Lomborg 2009). Second, population displacement due to sea-level rise has emerged as a major concern in public discourse on global warming, because of its potential for widespread socioeconomic disruption. A report in the *Washington Post* framed this issue in the general context of migration due to environmental calamities, including the drought of the 1930s (Dust Bowl) in the US Midwest (Vedantam 2009). The report then quotes the President of Kiribati, a Pacific nation of low-lying islands, as saying that he is exploring ways to move all of its 100 000 citizens to a new homeland because of fears of sea-level rise. A more comprehensive report on this issue was published in the Indian daily *Hindustan Times* drawing from a study by a researcher from an Indian Institute of Technology (Nag 2008). This study predicts that climate change impact would be immediately felt by almost 125 million people in India, Bangladesh and Pakistan who live in the low elevation coastal zone of less than 10 m above the average sea level. The study further postulates that about 75 million people from Bangladesh would migrate to India as climate change, sea-level rise, drought, shrinking water supplies and monsoon variability would take a toll on coastal Bangladesh. In addition, about 50 million from densely populated coastal regions of India could become homeless seeking new homes on higher grounds in inland states. Mumbai (Bombay), Chennai (Madras) and Kolkata (Calcutta) – situated at average elevations of 2–10 m – are particularly vulnerable (Nag 2008).

11.4.3   Mitigation of Global Warming

The newspaper reports on global warming and sea-level rise were dominated by discourse on mitigation of global warming. At least 40 per cent of the analysed texts were devoted to mitigation (Tables 11.1 and 11.2). With the exception of some minor references to alternative energy initiatives, mitigation measures reported in the analysed discourse can be classified into two broad categories, namely geo-engineering and emission reductions.

11.4.3.1   Geo-engineering
Geo-engineering projects can be further classified into two categories:

1. Temperature management, which moderates heat by blocking or reflecting a small portion of the sunlight hitting the earth; and
2. Carbon management, which gradually removes large amounts of carbon from the atmosphere.

One of the solar radiation interception schemes proposes placing reflectors in the stratosphere or in the orbit between the earth and the sun, diminishing the amount of solar radiation incident on the earth (Govindasamy and Caldeira 2000). Another geo-engineering experiment for controlling atmospheric temperature, proposed by a Nobel laureate atmospheric chemist, would involve injecting sulphur dioxide particles in the stratosphere to induce reflection of parts of the incoming solar radiation back into space (Dyer 2008, p. 196). A similar project, featured in a *Wall Street Journal* commentary by Lomborg (2009), would involve spraying seawater droplets from boats into clouds, to enhance reflection of sunlight back into space, augmenting the natural process of reflection by water vapour and clouds. Perhaps, the most radical geo-engineering proposal is a call by the IPCC for the scientists and engineers to investigate how the North and the South Poles could be cooled to end sea-level rise (McDonald 2009).

In contrast to the proposed schemes for climate modification, considerable progress has been made in carbon management experiments, particularly in carbon sequestration projects. In *geo-sequestration* projects, carbon is extracted from industrial emissions and then buried in deep underground rock reservoirs by pumping it through drilled holes in the bedrock. An excellent contextual report on a geo-sequestration project (the Mountaineer Power Plant in New Haven, Mason County, West Virginia) was published in the *New York Times* (Wald 2009). In *coal gasification* experiments carbon dioxide is converted into gasoline and other transport fuels. Besides the *New York Times*, the so-called carbon science projects have also been reported in the *Chicago Tribune* (Secter 2009) and *USA Today* (Davidson 2009). The problems with coal gasification and geo-sequestration projects are that these are energy-intensive and there are many technical challenges of sequestering the carbon (Secter 2009). In biosequestration projects, the goal is to remove carbon from the atmosphere by using different experiments, such as releasing microscopic iron particles in ocean water – a process called *iron fertilization* – to induce accelerated growth of plankton, leading to an increase in carbon removal from the atmosphere by the planktons' intake.

11.4.3.2 Emission reductions

Whereas the general goal of all global climate conventions – from the Kyoto Protocol to the COP15 in Copenhagen – was to reach an agreement on curbing GHG emissions, public discourse on the related issues had many conflicting messages, some dealing with technical limitations of emission reductions and others with the uncertain prospects of a global agreement. The *New York Times*, for example, covered the main findings of a study published in *Science*, according to which the Kyoto Protocol's cap-and-trade scheme has been underestimating GHG emissions from burning biofuels, because it does not take into account the source of the fuel. Thus, if a forest is cleared in Indonesia and the biofuel produced on the cleared land ends up in Europe, Indonesia does not count the loss of forest as equivalent land-use emissions and Europe does not report the tailpipe emissions (Sindya 2009). Besides such accounting problems with emission rates, very few newspapers reported data on emission rates. Among them, an article by an activist organisation, published in *The Age* (Melbourne), criticised the Australian Government's carbon pollution reduction scheme legislation, which proposed a cut by only 5 per cent by 2020, instead of 25 per cent recommended by some groups aligned with the government (Rose 2009). According to a *Washington Post* report, even much steeper cuts in emission rates by the United States and the European Union (EU) (73–80 per cent, respectively, by 2050) were considered by a research group to be insufficient for reducing global average temperature (Eilperin 2009a).

News media tend to accord disproportionate coverage to dramatic events and uncertainties (Kasperson et al. 1988). Many reports leading to the COP15 in Copenhagen, thus, focussed on disagreements among leading polluting nations in curbing GHG emissions. For example, refusal by both India and China to reduce GHG emissions under any international protocol was featured in many newspapers, such as in a 4 August 2009 report in the *Wall Street Journal*. Another report in the *Washington Post* framed similar disagreements as follows: leaders of the world's major economies formally embraced limiting the rise in earth's temperature, but declined to set numerical targets for reducing GHG emissions (Fletcher and Fahrenthold 2009). Perhaps, because of such disagreements, the United States and other leading GHG-emitting countries have concluded that it was more useful to take incremental but important steps toward a global agreement rather than to try to jam through a treaty that was either too weak to address the problem or too onerous to the ratified endorsement (Broder 2009).

11.4.4   Social Amplification of Global Warming

It appears from the preceding analysis that the public discourse on global warming has been characterised by significant amounts of contesting claims and disagreements on the extent of global warming, its impacts and mitigation measures. To assess if some of these claims constituted social amplification of global warming, initially an attempt was made to delineate parts of the newspaper discourse which seemed to have certain elements of risk amplification. It should be emphasised, however, that the data obtained in this manner (17 and 23 per cent, respectively, in Tables 11.1 and 11.2) are somewhat incomplete because risk amplification was construed largely based on the media presentation of a storyline, using symbolic statements, catchphrases and metaphors. According to the theory of social amplification of risk, the original message may be amplified (or attenuated) both at the source and at various 'amplification stations' (Kasperson et al. 1988). On further analysis of the data, beyond and including those in Tables 11.1 and 11.2, the following sources of amplification (the so-called amplification stations) for the public discourse on global warming and sea-level rise have been identified.

11.4.4.1   Nature of the global warming science

The science of global warming is in the midst of rapid development with many new assumptions, new data and hypothesis testing. It is largely an empirical science and consequently some of its data are subject to interpretation. Upon further discovery and availability of new data, some of the earlier assumptions may either be confirmed or rejected. A case in point is a 2006 projection of catastrophic sea-level rise exceeding 1 m by the end of this century, which was the result of including computer simulations of accelerations of glacier melting. Drawing from a peer-reviewed article in *Science*, this projection was featured in a *Winnipeg Free Press* report (Munro 2006). The projection may appear as an exaggeration compared to the IPCC's fourth assessment, which emphasises that its forecast does not include glacier-melt acceleration because of the lack of availability of natural data on this process at the time of its assessment (IPCC 2007). Another study, sponsored by the UNEP, predicts that the global average temperature may increase by a staggering 6.3°F by the end of this century. This projection may again appear to be an exaggeration compared to the IPCC's projection of 3.6°F, but the UNEP study postulates runaway greenhouse warming based on new (2008) evidence of expanding ice-free passage through Canada's Arctic islands and accelerating rates of ice-loss from the ice sheets in Greenland and Antarctica (UNEP 2009). Notwithstanding the scientific verifiability of new data, public discourse on such topics is a potential source of confusions in readers' minds, leading to misrepresentations about global warming.

11.4.4.2 Leaders' opinion

Institutional leaders with a mandate to promote public policies on environmental and ethical issues may influence the global warming debate. A commentary by a futurist at the San Francisco-based Institute for Ethics and Engineering Technologies was featured in the *Wall Street Journal* with a sensational heading: 'It's time to cool the planet: Cutting greenhouse gases is no longer enough to deal with global warming' (Cascio 2009). This commentary is a classic example of amplification of issues of global warming mitigation in public discourse, both in its style of presentation as well as in its substance. In its style, the commentary uses an advocacy approach with many catchphrases and symbolic statements. Admittedly, the commentary reviews potential risks and adverse environmental impacts of two related geo-engineering projects, namely injection of sulfate particles in the stratosphere and brightening of clouds in the troposphere by spraying mists of sea water into the clouds from ship-based stations (as cited earlier). Yet, the main problem with the commentary lies in its emphasis as if the earth's temperature could be managed by geo-engineering with adequate attention to these projects. Judging from the past record of limited success with much simpler cloud seeding experiments (Barry and Chorley 2003), the prospects for cooling the planet by geo-engineering projects appear to be an exaggerated claim.

11.4.4.3 Media amplification of global warming

The news media constitute perhaps the most powerful transmitter of the original message. As a key amplification (attenuation) step, the media transmission process transforms the original message by 'filtering of signals'; for example, only a fraction of all incoming information is actually processed (Kasperson et al. 1988). Filtering of the original message is a part of media framing designed to maximise the effectiveness of the message. Frames, like news angles, are organising devices that help both the journalist and the public make sense of issues and events and thereby inject them with meaning (Hannigan 1995, p. 61). Framing devices used routinely by the media include metaphors, examples, catchphrases, depiction and visual images (Gamson and Modigliani 1989). One of the outcomes of framing environmental issues with symbolic statements and catchphrases is that the news process consistently fails to address the deeper issues, such as the underlying causes and solutions of the problems, thus removing the contexts in which the problems occur (Altheide 1976). Besides contexts, news sources play an important role in shaping the story content, providing credibility to the report (Hannigan 1995, p. 60).

The data on risk amplification in Tables 11.1 and 11.2 mostly represent elements of sensational statements, exaggerated claims, catchphrases and metaphors. Samples from five US newspapers are reproduced below:

New York Times (25 February 2009): Unsubstantiated claims

- A sharp spike in fires, floods and other calamities
- Spreading famine and storms that are growing stronger with each passing hurricane season

New York Times (22 September 2009): Use of metaphors

- Coal is the drug of choice
- Methadone cure of addiction

Washington Post (28 October 2009): Sensational statements and metaphors

- For 30 cents a day we will protect our kids from dangerous pollution
- The CBO [Congressional Budget Office] view of the world is a green eyeshade, rear-view mirror that cannot factor in the technological revolution in our country

Wall Street Journal (28 August 2009): Use of metaphors

- Brilliance of our rhetoric
- Stop promising the moon

Chicago Tribune (12 June 2009): Sensational statements and metaphors

- Virtual carbon bomb
- Earth's lungs have come down with emphysema

USA Today (8 January 2009): Sensational statements

- Disastrous food shortage for billions of people
- Human consequences of climate change could be enormous

In addition to the nature of framing, the news sources of each story were reviewed, although no numerical data are presented here. Reliable news sources for global warming and climate change included articles by scientists, technical reports (especially, the IPCC assessment reports) or reports on scientific conferences. These news sources implied indirect contexts because scientists and experts considered the underlying issues; therefore, even in the absence of adequate explanations of the underlying issues, any claims on global warming and/or its impacts based on these sources were not considered as exaggerations. With the exception of only a limited number of reports, the majority of them had reliable news sources, thus minimising apparent media amplification reported in the tables.

11.4.5   Climate Justice

11.4.5.1   Origin of climate justice

According to the theory of social amplification of risk, one of the key amplification steps consists of 'attaching social values to the information in order to draw implications for management and policy' (Kasperson et al. 1988). Applied to the public discourse on global warming and sea-level rise, social values have been attached heavily to the scientific elements of climate change for justifying demands for certain management actions. Concerns for the future generations, who would inherit the projected warmer climate and its impacts, and for the plight of the global warming-impacted impoverished nations are examples of social values that have driven political demands for mitigation of global warming. Along with a global network of youth movement for climate action, such as the US-based *StepItUp2007.org* and the Australian Youth Climate Coalition (McKibben 2007; Rose 2009), a rapidly growing number of social movements and civil society organisations across the world who are mobilising around the climate justice agenda seem to be what Kasperson et al. (1988) have hypothesised as 'a secondary impact of social amplification of risk'.

As implied in the introduction, the climate justice movement is a corollary of the concept of social justice (Kasperson and Kasperson 2005) or environmental justice, which is normally associated with the claims for compensation from those who have suffered from pollution by a hazardous waste disposal site (Hannigan 1995, p. 126). Residents adjacent to such sites may typically be liable to environmental injustice. More specifically, an environmental injustice occurs when members of certain disadvantaged social groups suffer disproportionately at the local, regional or national levels from environmental risks or hazards. As a corollary to this proposition, disproportionately adverse impacts of global warming on some of the impoverished nations, who had very little contribution to global warming, constitute global climate injustice.

11.4.5.2 Symbolic value of climate justice

Not only does the term 'climate justice' (or 'climate injustice') evoke symbolic images of global climatic calamities, there are implications of carbon footprints of the industrial societies responsible for the bulk of the problem. Because of the symbolic nature of the term, public discourse on climate justice has spawned many symbolic expressions and metaphors. A commentary by an Australian Youth Climate Coalition coordinator, published in *The Age*, a Melbourne newspaper, provides examples of such symbolic expressions (Rose 2009):

- It is clear to me that not taking the necessary action on climate change is a violation of the rights of today's young people, whether they be Bangladeshi children scared of rising seas or young Victorians already scarred by bushfires.
- When recent climate science suggests Australia should make greenhouse pollution cuts of at least 50 per cent by 2020 to protect our future, the Government's target is only 5 per cent. How I wish it was just a typo and they accidentally left off the zero! But no, it's not a typo – just a betrayal of our generation.
- And a power shift is what we are demanding. A power shift away from fossil fuels to renewable energy, green jobs and strong greenhouse gas reduction targets that will help secure a global deal to reduce emissions.

Even other less passionate reports have used such symbolic terms as *ecomigrants* and *climate refugees* (Vedantam 2009; Nag 2008). Ecomigrants are ecologically displaced population due to a variety of environmental degradations, including desertification, drought, deforestation, riverbank erosions and sea-level rise. Although such symbolic phrases are parts of social amplification of global warming, Wilkins (2000) has postulated the role of symbolic connotations in hazard mitigation. In her comparative study of two catastrophic floods in the Mississippi and the Red Rivers, respectively, she postulated that the media coverage of flood disasters would continue to focus on the immediate flood events and on the symbolic discussion of flood-control failure in the basins until the emergence of a successful flood alleviation measure as a 'symbol for the success of mitigation' (Wilkins 2000, p. 86; Rashid 2011). For global warming, climate justice seems to be a search for such symbolic mitigation of inequity in global warming impacts. Realistically, a satisfactory climate justice may never be achieved and, therefore, the movement will perhaps continue and the media reports on global warming will be dominated by contesting claims on global warming impacts and symbolic discussion of failure of the international community to reach an agreement for curbing GHG emissions.

11.4.5.3   Call for climate justice during the COP15

Conforming to the preceding assumption, public discourse during the Copenhagen Summit and the media discourse on it were, indeed, dominated by reports on the failure of the Summit, the impending danger of rising sea level and a spike in the call for climate justice. Out of 25 randomly/arbitrarily selected web-based international media reports on the Summit (published between 9 and 21 December 2009 and retrieved by using the key words 'Copenhagen Summit' and 'climate justice'), nine were on the failure of the Summit, nine on sea-level rise, five on climate justice and the remaining two had references to climate adaptation. The failure of the Summit to reach an effective agreement for curbing greenhouse gas emissions was featured in a *Washington Post* report with a pointed headline: 'Climate deal falls short of key goals'. The report summarised this failure succinctly as: 'Climate deal provides for monitoring emission cuts by each country but sets no global targets for cutting greenhouse gases, and no deadline for reaching a formal international climate treaty' (Eilperin and Faiola 2009). Perhaps to draw attention to the perils of not reaching an agreement, many newspapers (for example, the 17 December issues of the Canadian newspapers *Guelph Mercury* and *Winnipeg Free Press*; and the Australian daily *Sydney Morning Herald*) highlighted a revised forecast for higher sea levels, based on a new study published in *Nature*. The new study predicts that an additional 2°C of warming by the end of this century would lead to an accelerated melting of the Greenland and the Antarctic ice sheets, leading to a sea-level rise of up to or greater than 6 m. Compared to the IPCC projections, this is an alarming prediction. Much of Bangladesh and the Netherlands would be submerged. There were several reports on sinking smaller Pacific islands, such as the Solomon Islands, Kiribati and Tuvalu (*USA Today*, 9 December; *The Guardian*, 16 December; *Illawarra Mercury*, 16 December) and on the 'life and death of the Maldives' (*The Guardian*, 14 December).

In the wake of the failure of the Copenhagen Summit, a British ethicist declared that 'We are all eco-warriors'. In a commentary published in *The Guardian* (21 December), he wondered 'if civil disobedience was warranted

*Table 11.3   Call for climate justice during the COP15 Summit in
              Copenhagen*

Media (date)	Headline
The Telegraph, UK (15 December 2009)	Copenhagen Climate Summit: Desmond Tutu calls for climate justice
Canada Climate Justice Website (16 December 2009)	Climate justice activists occupy Harper's Constituency Office
An Phoblacht (Sinn Fein Weekly) (17 December 2009)	Massive protest demands climate justice at Copenhagen
Tri-State Defender Online (18 December 2009)	Will there be Climate Justice?
The Guardian, UK (21 December 2009)	We are all eco-warriors

to stop past injustices, isn't it warranted right now to stop what is probably the greatest amount of harm any group of human beings ever inflicted on any other?' (Garvey 2009). The Sinn Fein weekly, *An Phoblacht* featured a prominent headline: 'Massive protest demands climate justice in Copenhagen'. The report claimed that 100 000 people from around the world took over the Danish capital to demand immediate action on reducing carbon emissions and climate justice for the developing world. A sharp increase in the call for climate justice during the COP15 Summit is evident from at least five such demands within a short period of less than one week (Table 11.3). In a seminar held at the Liu Institute for Global Issues, University of British Columbia, Vancouver, Canada, the Society for Bangladesh Climate Justice reminded about the global responsibility for climate change impacts on Bangladesh (SBCJ 2009).

11.4.5.4   Climate justice for Bangladesh
In a speech at the Copenhagen Summit, the Prime Minister of Bangladesh demanded that Bangladesh and other 'most vulnerable countries' (MVCs) must be provided with compensatory grants and easily accessible adequate funds to meet the full cost of adaptation to climate change (*The Daily Star*, Bangladesh, 17 December 2009). Earlier the Government of Bangladesh demanded that it should receive 15 per cent of the fund pledged to help poor nations fight climate change (*The Canadian Press*, 9 December 2009). Considering the fact that Bangladesh is the most populous nation among the MVCs, this seems to be a justified claim, especially because this demand has been made in the context of climate adaptation. As the flood-plain residents of Bangladesh have been 'living with floods' for generations

by using different types of indigenous flood adaptation measures (Rasid 2000), climate adaptation has a similar potential to become a symbol of climate justice for global warming impacts on Bangladesh. However, it appears from the earlier analysis of public discourse on mitigation of global warming (Section 11.4.3) that very little attention has been given to this potential. Out of the 40 reports analysed (Tables 11.1 and 11.2), only four dealt with different methods of adaptation to rising sea levels, but they provided valuable insights for climate adaptation.

Coastal defence infrastructure   In a report published in the *New York Times* (22 October 2009), architects proposed building soft infrastructure to combat storm surges with rising sea levels. These included a network of piers, artificial islands, wetlands and oyster beds (Ouroussoff 2009). It may not be feasible or necessary to build such structures along the coasts of Bangladesh, but there is already a network of cyclone shelters and coastal polders (enclosed embankment systems for agriculture and shrimp cultivation). Both of these structures have proven to be effective in saving lives during cyclone storm surges (Paul et al. 2010). Thus, expanding the network of cyclone shelters and elevating the polder embankments have potentials for providing protection against rising sea levels in Bangladesh for an interim period.

Elevated building foundations   On 6 May 2008, *The New Castle Herald* (Australia) reported on the proposed building code of a small Australian city to raise floors of all new buildings by a minimum of 49 cm in addition to the existing requirement of 50 cm above the 100-year flood level. The plan is based on an assumption of 91 cm of sea-level rise by 2100. The new policy will result in a building life of 50 years above the rising sea level. The floodplain residents of Bangladesh are familiar with the indigenous methods of raising homesteads above flood levels by borrowing excavated earth from the surrounding common property (Rasid 2000). The existing indigenous method could be reinforced by building homes on raised platforms on bamboo poles or wooden piers, following the architectural design of the Mekong delta. If this method is adopted formally as a part of the climate adaptation projects, it has a potential for transforming the architectural designs of rural homes in coastal Bangladesh.

Natural coastal buffer   The main recommendation of a *Biodiversity and Climate Change Adaptation Seminar* in Exeter, UK, was to abandon the coastlines back to natural habitats for combating climate change and sea-level rise (*Western Morning News*, Plymouth, UK, 24 October 2008). In Bangladesh, the natural coastal buffer in the form of mangrove forest has been severely depleted by deforestation. Coastal tree plantations, reinforcing the mangrove vegetation, may go a long way to retard storm surges during tropical cyclones, irrespective of the rising sea levels (Paul et al. 2010).

Raising land levels by river silt   On 20 March 2009, the *New York Times* reported on an accidental discovery of an indigenous method of raising land levels in Bangladesh by diverting river silt into floodplain depressions (Sengupta 2009). The major rivers of Bangladesh, particularly the Ganges, the Brahmaputra (locally called the Jamuna) and the Meghna, carry huge amounts of sediments into the Bay of Bengal. With the rise in sea levels, the lower reaches of these rivers would experience decreased velocities due to progressive backwater effect, resulting in accelerated sedimentation rates. As the report suggests, diverting some of these sediments into the floodplains, either by indigenous methods or by major engineering interventions, holds some promise for raising local land levels and thus living with rising sea levels for an interim period.

Resettlement   There were many reports on resettlement of the entire population of the Maldives (Indian Ocean), Tuvalu, Kiribati and several other smaller Pacific islands. Because of their relatively small population size, resettlement may be a feasible option for them. In the case of Bangladesh, resettlement poses a major problem because of the displacement of huge numbers of people – at least 15 million people due to loss of one-fifth of its land and perhaps much more, according to some of the more recent projections. Loss of productive agricultural land would undermine recent gains in food security. Lack of land for resettling climate refugees is an even greater challenge. The previous experience with resettlement of the displaced population due to riverbank erosion, cyclones, floods and general rural poverty has been entirely unplanned, as most of the displaced poor have squatted in major urban slums, especially in Dhaka, the capital of the country (Rashid et al. 2007). A master plan is needed to redistribute the displaced population in all of the major urban centres of the country. Such a plan can benefit from the significant amounts of research that have already been conducted on the problems of resettlement of the displaced population due to riverbank erosion (Zaman 1991, 1996).

11.5   MANAGEMENT IMPLICATIONS AND CONCLUSIONS

Despite the dire predictions of global warming impacts on coastal Bangladesh, time is of the essence for managing the postulated impacts.

The predicted changes would perhaps occur gradually over periods of decades and there is a large amount of uncertainty about how these changes would unfold. Whenever a management situation involves a large amount of uncertainty, an adaptive management approach can provide valuable insights for handling such uncertainty. The term adaptive means 'response to change'. Thus, adaptive management can be defined as 'an approach that develops policies and practices to deal with the uncertain, the unexpected, and the unknown' (Dearden and Mitchell 1998, p. 537). Essentially, adaptive management is an experimental approach from which we can learn by trial and error. With the major exception of the time horizon, the adaptive management model is somewhat similar to the real-time reservoir management model, in which the amount of water released from a reservoir (dam) is adjusted based on the stochastic or uncertain variables of precipitation, evaporation and inflow from the drainage basin (Rasid and Can 1986). Whereas a real-time reservoir management model uses a short time horizon of hours or days, an adaptive management approach can be applied throughout a longer period of time, perhaps years and decades. As the projected coastal inundation in Bangladesh would evolve gradually, most of the preceding adaptations, such as coastal infrastructures and housing architecture, could be adjusted accordingly. Eventually, when all of these measures would fail due to continuing inundation, resettlement would be the main option available for coping with rising water levels. Thus, an early start with the resettlement project is a move for achieving sustainable mitigation of global warming for Bangladesh. In this context, the demand for adequate funds from the industrial societies seems to be the search for climate justice for Bangladesh, because it would require the necessary funds for achieving this goal.

Using discourse analysis of newspaper reports, this study has demonstrated that global warming and climate change pose a major challenge to the industrial society 'accustomed to mastering of its environment through technology' (Smith 1992). The challenge arises mainly out of its failure to manipulate climate change effectively by employing various types of geo-engineering projects. In the absence of realistic geo-engineering solutions, the main focus of the international community has been on efforts to reduce GHG emissions. The failure of the Copenhagen Summit to reach a meaningful agreement for curbing emissions has underlined the difficulties of reaching a consensus on extremely complex and interrelated issues. Social amplification of global warming has been an outcome of the continuing lack of resolutions of these issues. The call for climate justice may be a form of social amplification of global warming, but it is a justified search for a symbolic mitigation of inequity in global warming impacts.

ACKNOWLEDGEMENTS

The University of Wisconsin-La Crosse Murphy Library provided access to its electronic resources for retrieving all newspaper reports analysed in this article. Sincere thanks are due to the co-editors, particularly Dr Moazzem Hossain, and the anonymous referees for their constructive criticisms and helpful suggestions.

REFERENCES

Adams, B. and G. Luchsinger (2009), *Climate Justice for a Changing Planet: A Primer for Policy Makers and NGOs*, Geneva: The United Nations Non-Governmental Liaison Service.

Altheide, D.L. (1976), *Creating Reality: How TV News Distort Events*, Beverly Hills, CA: Sage.

Archer, D. (2007), *Global Warming: Understanding the Forecast*, Malden, MA: Blackwell Publishing.

Barry, R.G. and R.J. Chorley (2003), *Atmosphere, Weather and Climate*, 8th edn, London: Routledge.

Botkin, D. and E. Keller (1995), *Environmental Science: Earth as a Living Planet*, New York: John Wiley & Sons.

Broder, J.M. (2009), 'As time runs short for global climate treaty, nations may settle for interim steps', *New York Times*, 21 October 2009.

Cascio, J. (2009), 'It's time to cool the planet: cutting greenhouse gases is no longer enough to deal with global warming', *Wall Street Journal*, 15 June 2009.

Church, J.A. and N.J. White (2006), 'A 20th century acceleration in global sea-level rise', *Geophysical Research Letters*, **33**, L01602, doi: 10.1029/2005GL024826.

Church, J.A., N.J. White, R. Coleman, K. Lambeck and J.X. Mitrovica (2004), 'Estimates of the regional distribution of sea-level rise over the 1950 to 2000 period', *Journal of Climate*, **17** (13): 2609–25.

Church, J.A., N.J. White and J.R. Hunter (2006a), 'Sea level rise at tropical Pacific and Indian Ocean islands', *Global and Planetary Change*, **53** 155–68.

Church, J.A., J.R. Hunter, K.L. McInnes and N.J. White (2006b), 'Sea level rise around the Australian coastline and the changing frequency of extreme sea levels', *Australian Meteorological Magazine*, **55**: 253–60.

Dearden, P. and B. Mitchell (1998), 'Adaptive management', in *Environmental Change and Challenge: A Canadian Perspective*, Toronto: Oxford University Press, pp. 200–213.

Davidson, P. (2009), 'Greenhouse gas villain rehabbed: companies develop methods to repurpose carbon dioxide', *USA Today*, 25 February 2009.

Doyle, A. (2007), 'Sea levels to rise for the next 1000 years', *Irish Times*, 26 January 2007.

Dyer, G. (2008), *Climate Wars*, Canada: Random House.

Eilperin, J. (2009a), 'New analysis brings dire forecast of 6.3-degree temperature increase', *Washington Post*, 25 September 2009.

Eilperin, J. (2009b), 'Economics of climate change in forefront: senate panel takes up bill, setting stage for fight over estimates', *Washington Post*, 28 October 2009.

Eilperin, J. and A. Faiola (2009), 'Climate deal falls short of key goals', *Washington Post*, 19 December 2009.

Fletcher, M.A. and D.A. Fahrenthold (2009), 'Nations agree to curb emissions: rift remains between poor, rich countries', *Washington Post*, 10 July 2009.

Gamson, W.A. and A. Modigliani (1989), 'Media discourse and public opinion on nuclear power', *American Journal of Sociology*, **18**: 373–93.

Garvey, J. (2009), 'We are all eco-warriors', *The Guardian*, 21 December 2009.

Govindasamy, B. and K. Caldeira (2000), 'Geoengineering earth's radiation balance to mitigate CO_2-induced climate change', *Geophysical Research Letters*, **27** (14): 2141–4.

Hannigan, J.A. (1995), *Environmental Sociology*, London and New York: Routledge.

Hart, D.M. and D.G. Victor (1993), 'Scientific elites and the making of US policy for climate change research, 1957–1974', *Social Studies of Science*, **23**: 643–80.

Houghton, J. (2004), *Global Warming: The Complete Briefing*, 3rd edn, Cambridge, UK: Cambridge University Press.

Intergovernmental Panel on Climate Change (IPCC) (2007), 'Climate Change 2007: Synthesis Report', contributions of Working Group I, II and III to the *Fourth Assessment Report of the Intergovernmental Panel on Climate Change*, Core Writing Team, R.K. Pachauri and A. Reisinger (eds), Geneva: IPCC.

Jimenez-David, R. (2009), 'At large climate justice', *Philippine Daily Inquirer*, 22 December 2009.

Kasperson, R.E. and J.X. Kasperson (2005), 'Climate change, vulnerability and social justice', in J.X. Kasperson and R. Kasperson (eds), *The Social Contours of Risk Volume I: Publics, Risk Communication and the Social Amplification of Risk*, London and Sterling, VA: Earthscan, pp. 301–21.

Kasperson, R.E., O. Renn, P. Slovic, H.S. Brown, J. Emel, R. Goble, J.X. Kasperson and S. Ratick (1988), 'The social amplification of risk: a conceptual framework', *Risk Analysis*, **8** (2): 177–87.

Lomborg, B. (2009), 'Technology can fight global warming', *Wall Street Journal*, 28 August 2009.

Lorimer, R. and M. Gasher (2001), *Mass Communication in Canada*, 4th edn, Don Mills, ON: Oxford University Press.

McDonald, F. (2009), 'Climate experts urge engineering solutions to "directly cool the planet"', *Irish Times*, 12 March 2009.

McKibben, B. (2007), *Fight Global Warming Now: The Handbook for Taking Action in your Community*, New York, NY: Henry Holt and Company.

Mileti, D., S. Nathe, P. Gori, M. Greene and E. Lemersal (2004), *Public Hazards Communication and Education: The State of the Art*, update of Informer Issue 2: Public Education for Earthquake, Boulder, CO: Natural Hazards Research and Application Information Center, University of Colorado at Boulder.

Morner, N.-A, M. Tooley and G. Possart (2004), 'New perspectives for the future of the Maldives', *Global and Planetary Change*, **40**: 177–82.

Mullen, W. (2009), 'Great polar melt-off feared: global warming, human activity speed Antarctic thaw, experts say', *Chicago Tribune*, 19 March 2009.

Munro, M. (2006), 'Climate change to redraw map', *Winnipeg Free Press*, 24 March 2006.

Nag, S. (2008), '75 million Bangladeshis may inundate India', *Hindustan Times*, 26 March 2008.

Oldfield, F. (2005), *Environmental Change: Key Issues and Alternatives*, Cambridge, UK: Cambridge University Press.

Oliver, J.E. and J.J. Hidore (2003), *Climatology: An Atmospheric Science*, 2nd edn, Upper Saddle River, NJ: Prentice-Hall.

Ouroussoff, N. (2009), 'Future dangers for a maritime city', *New York Times*, 22 October 2009.

Paul, B.K., H. Rashid, M.S. Islam and L.M. Hunt (2010), 'Cyclone evacuation in Bangladesh: tropical cyclones Gorky (1991) vs Sidr (2007)', *Environmental Hazards: Human and Policy Dimensions*, **9**: 89–101.

Rashid, H. (2011), 'Interpreting flood disasters and flood hazard perceptions from newspaper discourse: tale of two floods in the Red River Valley, Manitoba, Canada', *Applied Geography*, **31** (1), 35–45.

Rashid, H., L. Hunt and W. Haider (2007), 'Urban flood problems in Dhaka, Bangladesh: slum residents' choice for relocation in flood-free areas', *Environmental Management*, **40** (1): 95–104.

Rasid, H. (2000), 'Reducing vulnerability to flood disasters in Bangladesh: compatibility of floodplain residents' preferences for flood alleviation measures with indigenous adjustments to floods', in D.J. Parker (ed.), *Floods*, Vol. II, London and New York: Routledge, pp. 46–65.

Rasid, H. and E.K. Can (1986), 'Real-time management models for improving reservoir operation', *The Canadian Geographer*, **30**: 350–57.

Reckelhoff-Dangel, C. and D. Petersen (2007), *Risk Communication in Action: The Risk Communication Workbook*, Cincinnati, OH: EPA Office of Research and Development, National Risk Management Research Laboratory.

Revkin, A.C. (2009), 'In debate on climate change, exaggeration is a common pitfall', *New York Times*, 25 February 2009.

Rose, A. (2009), 'Young people must take the lead in fighting climate change', *The Age* (Melbourne), 16 March 2009.

SBCJ (2009), 'Seminar on climate change impacts on Bangladesh: global responsibilities', held on 9 December 2009 at the Liu Institute for Global Issues, University of British Columbia, Vancouver, British Columbia, Canada.

Secter, B. (2009), 'Experimental coal plant poised to move forward', *Chicago Tribune*, 12 June 2009.

Sengupta, S. (2009), 'In silt, Bangladesh sees potential shield against climate shift', *New York Times*, 20 March 2009.

Sindya, B.N. (2009), 'Calculating emissions is problematic', *New York Times*, 23 October 2009.

Smith, C. (1992), *Media and Apocalypse: News Coverage of the Yellowstone Forest Fires, Exxon Valdez Oil Spill, and Loma Prieta Earthquake*, Westport, CT: Greenwood Press.

Spencer, R.W. (2008), *Climate Confusion: How Global Warming Hysteria Leads to Bad Science, Pandering Politicians and Misguided Policies that Hurt the Poor*, New York: Encounter Books.

Tuchman, G. (1973), 'Making news by doing work: routinization of the unexpected', *American Journal of Sociology*, **79** (1): 110–31.

UNEP (2009), 'Climate change', in *UNEP Year Book: New Science and Development in our Changing Environment*, Nairobi, Kenya: United Nations Development Programme, Ch. 3, pp. 21–30.

Vedantam, S. (2009), 'Climate change fears drive ecomigrants across globe', *Washington Post*, 23 February 2009.

Wald, M. (2009), 'Refitted to bury emissions, plant draws attention', *New York Times*, 22 September 2009.

Walker, G. and King, D. (2008), *The Hot Topic: What we can do about Global Warming?*, Vancouver/Toronto: Douglas & McIntyre.

WFP (Winnipeg Free Press) (2006), 'Climate change to redraw map', *Winnipeg Free Press*, 24 March 2006.

Wilkins, L. (1996), 'Living with the flood: human and governmental responses to real and symbolic risk', in S.A. Changnon (ed.), *The Great Flood of 1993: Causes, Impacts, and Responses*, Boulder, CO: Westview Press, pp. 218–44.

Wilkins, L. (2000), 'Searching for symbolic mitigation: media coverage of two floods', in D.J. Parker (ed.), *Floods*, Vol. II, London and New York: Routledge, pp. 80–87.

Zaman, M.Q. (1991), 'The displaced poor and resettlement policies in Bangladesh', *Disasters*, **15** (2): 117–25.

Zaman, M.Q. (1996), 'Development and displacement: toward a resettlement policy for Bangladesh', *Asian Survey*, **36** (7): 691–703.

Index